THE TIES OF LATER LIFE

Edited by
Jon Hendricks
Oregon State University

Perspectives on Aging and Human Development Series
Jon Hendricks: Series Editor

BAYWOOD PUBLISHING COMPANY, INC.
Amityville, New York

Library of Congress Catalog Number: 94-19532
ISBN: 0-89503-166-3

Library of Congress Cataloging-in-Publication Data

The ties of later life / edited by Jon Hendricks.
     p. cm. - - (Perspectives on aging and human development series)
  Includes bibliographical references.
  ISBN 0-89503-166-3
  1. Aged- -United States- -Family relationships.   2. Aged- -United States- -Psychology. I. Hendricks, Jon, 1943- . II. Series.
HQ1064.U5T54 1995
306.874- -dc20   94-19532
                                     CIP

Table of Contents

Introduction:
KITH, KIN AND KIND IN LATER LIFE
MORE COMPLEXITY THAN
MEETS THE EYE

Jon Hendricks

In light of the fact that the vast majority of us spend so much time in families, it is somewhat surprising that we do not understand them any better than we do. Maybe a large part of the problem has to do with the fact that the ideology of the family overwhelms the reality of family life. What seems to happen is that if our own experience does not measure up, we particularize our personal situation but do not challenge the stereotype. As we get older there is a little more reality orientation but when we get to a concern with old age a sizable proportion of us think the family is and will be there to provide nearly everything that is needed. Throughout the 1980s successive administrations in Washington, D.C. seemed intent on promulgating the notion that it is the family's responsibility to care for the elderly, that such a view is part of "family values" and that since the family is there anyway, no alternatives are needed.

The truth is something else, just what has been a source of strenuous debate. No doubt that family life, being part of a couple, having ties with children or grandchildren are important sources of support and affirmation. They can also be sources of stress. It is easy to make pronouncements about families being responsible for their needy elderly; in reality such a charge falls almost inevitably on the shoulders of the family's female members. So far as science knows, there is not a gene for family care giving. The fact that kin keeping and kin caring fall predominately in one direction is a consequence of a gendered ideology. If the ideology defines it as women's work, so it shall be women's work. Hopefully, we have come to our ideological senses and begun to realize that nothing is anybody's work. There are no divine decrees or genetics that make it so—childbearing not withstanding. Actually, when you get right down to it, the greater musculature of males might dictate that they be the care givers. As Huber [1] noted, the idea of biological explanations for gender differences has finally given way to the recognition that there is a close relationship between our ideas about economic matters and our notions about appropriate gender roles. There is a "triple overlap" between our moral economy [2], our market economy and what is implicitly said about gender and the family [3].

As will be seen in the chapters in Section I of this volume, this is not simply "ivory tower" theorizing. Neither should it be seen as debunking of something sacred. What it is, in fact, is a sound framework for understanding how older women and men view their spousal relationships and how family interaction styles come about. Riley [4] pointed out that the nature of the dynamics among older families is sure to change as a consequence of the demographic revolution. In the past there were fewer issues for older couples to face because there were fewer older couples, death having claimed one or the other, most often the male, before they reached the age where anyone would think of them as older [5]. The changing patterns of mortality that have brought about an aging of the population have also brought new issues to the fore when talking about older families. With longer lives come more extensive kinship networks but also opportunities for elder abuse. With more generations on the scene, more grandchildren know their grandparents while all the while those in the middle try to balance obligations to both generations. With industrialization we have gained labor saving devices, modern technology, and the institutionalization of retirement for those who worked outside the home. The question is, have those who worked inside the home benefitted equally? Have labor saving devices shortened the workweek for them, or the time spent maintaining the home? Have marriages been reformatted or undergone some other kind of change in the course of modernization? One thing that has happened is that marriages are surviving long enough to affirm their importance as sources of satisfaction and well being in later life and long enough to end in divorce.

As Riley [4] pointed out, the prolongation of marriages means one thing for sure: the need for mutual accommodation to the shifting realities brought by the passing years will increase. Part of the accommodations that are necessary will be wrought, in part, by changes in roles assumed outside the family, in part by internal dynamics, and in part by alterations in physical and economic well-being. There is another, sometimes overlooked component of the demands put on families or on the marital couple that derives from membership in various cultural, racial and/or ethnic groups. Diversity in cultural background spells family diversity too [6]. Though thoughtful research is not as plentiful as it should be, what research as is available has suggested that there is a proliferation of family roles and family structures among culturally distinct groups. Even within the same cultural group, socioeconomic factors affect how the family unit actually functions and what it really looks like. What is true of the family as a whole is also true for its members. That is, the impact of widowhood, for example, cannot be said to have the same consequences for a family of Hispanic, African American or Asian origin as for a mainstream white family. Not only will widowhood bring about changes in the pattern of social networks and social participation, but these will also reflect the surviving spouse's health, economic status, gender and ethnicity. Then, too, the types of services, the form they take and the extent to which formal alternatives are considered will each incorporate racial and ethnic memberships [7]. Given what is happening in the workplace and changing patterns of employment, together with the likelihood of having discretionary income, and it becomes apparent that the flow of family resources may even change direction from one racial or ethnic group to another.

There is another facet of family living that has not always been acknowledged. In fact, there is a group of persons which is oftentimes discussed as though they existed outside the bounds of any family. Older gay men and lesbians comprise another family type just as sure as any of the other types. It is one that may be highly relevant within the context of a discussion about aging. To the extent that gay and lesbian relationships endure for periods comparable to many heterosexual marriages, it would be a mistake to dismiss them as outside the realm of concern. Gay men and women affiliate with one another in order to create a sense of family, a situation not totally dissimilar to what increasing numbers of elderly seem to be doing [8].

As a well-known sociologist pointed out many years ago, inside of every marriage are two marriages—her's and his. In reading the chapters in the first section, one pattern that emerges clearly is that older couples are no different from couples of any other age, their views are equally diverse and their problems just as pronounced. Keith and her colleagues underscore the importance of equity between marital partners. The next three chapters look at how spousal characteristics, perceptions of marital satisfaction, and sense of fairness play out among older couples. Whatever factors shape the nature of marital interaction, when special circumstances occur they happen not just to one partner but to both. Health and disability are examples of how the status of one partner has a major impact on the life of the other. Based on research conducted in France, the chapter by Grand and colleagues makes clear how the management of disabilities is closely linked to the sense of cohesion and division of labor negotiated by the partners over the years.

Families come apart for a variety of reasons: death, divorce and sometimes just emotionally—despite the fact that the members may remain together. When death occurs, it is a given that the nature of the survivor's social world will change dramatically. In Section II there are two chapters on widowhood and two on abuse. Both events render the bonds that held the couple together null and void. Obviously they do not mean the same thing, but neither phenomenon can be denied and each is deserving of attention as we attempt to understand the nature of family life in the later years.

There is still another dimension of family interaction deserving of attention—grandparenting. Nearly all the available research suggests interaction between grandparents and grandchildren is a significant source of emotional satisfaction for both generations. Certainly there are instances where conflict and disagreement are frequent, yet these intergenerational relationships are most often felt to be emotionally bonding. If there is variation in every other aspect of family life, there will also be variation in the types of relationships found between grandparents and grandchildren. In an effort to impose some order on the types of patterns they found, Cherlin and Furstenberg [9] developed a typology of styles and strategies of grandparenting. They outlined three distinctive types; detached, passive, and active. For the most part their labels are self-explanatory with interaction styles ranging from remote and virtually uninvolved, to passive but emotionally satisfying, to regular and routine interaction deemed central to the lives of both parties. The Strom and Strom chapter reprinted here is narrowly focused on intervention strategies to improve grandparents' ability to contribute to family well-being. It is an interesting perspective since their point is that with a little help expectations can be made more realistic. Next, Roberto and Stroes ask college-aged grandchildren about their interactions with their grandparents; they found clear gender differences in the way grandparents were perceived. Thomas makes a similar point and applies it more globally. Hodgson writes that adult grandchildren's perceptions of the emotional connection between the two generations is positive, even as the younger group move into adulthood themselves. Hodgson, together with Langer, asserts that the relationship is more than merely symbolic. While additional research is called for, the chapter on Black grandparents is suggestive of the importance of grandparents in African American families. Strom and his coauthors focus on the dimensions of strength that derive from intergenerational interaction among African American families. Finally, in light of the divorce and remarriage rates we see today, it would be negligent to omit any reference to the blended family and the role of stepgrandparents. The final chapter, by Trygstad and Sanders, provides a sound empirical look at both the interaction between stepgrandparents and stepgrandchildren in reconstituted families.

REFERENCES

1. J. Huber, A Theory of Family, Economy, and Gender, in *Gender, Family, and Economy,* R. L. Blumberg (ed.), Sage, Newbury Park, California, 1991.
2. M. Minkler and T. R. Cole, Political and Moral Economy: Not Such Strange Bedfellows, in *Critical Perspectives on Aging: The Political and Moral Economy of Growing Old,* Baywood, Amityville, New York, 1991.
3. R. L. Blumberg, The "Triple Overlap" of Gender Stratification, Economy, and the Family, in *Gender, Family, and Economy,* R. L. Blumberg (ed.), Sage, Newbury Park, California, 1991.

4. M. W. Riley, The Family in an Aging Society: A Matrix of Latent Relationships, *Journal of Family Issues, 4,* pp. 439-454, 1983.
5. G. Hagestad, Demographic Change and the Life Course: Some Emerging Trends in the Family Realm, *Family Relations, 37*, pp. 405-410, 1988.
6. L. Burton, Families and the Aged: Issues of Complexity and Diversity, *Generations, 17*, pp. 5-6, 1992.
7. V. Bengtson, C. Rosenthal, and L. Burton, Families and Aging: Diversity and Heterogeneity, in *Handbook of Aging and the Social Sciences, 3/e*, Academic Press, San Diego, 1990.
8. D. C. Kimmel, The Families of Older Gay Men and Lesbians, *Generations,* pp. 37-38, 1992.
9. A. J. Cherlin and F. F. Furstenberg, Jr., *The New American Grandparent,* Sage, Beverly Hills, 1985.

Section I

Couplehood in Later Life

Chapter 1

OUTCOMES OF EQUITY/INEQUITY AMONG OLDER SPOUSES

Pat M. Keith
Robert B. Schafer
and
Robbyn Wacker

Perceptions of equity/inequity among older couples were studied. The association between perceptions of equity/inequity and dissatisfaction, disagreement between spouses, partners' regard for one another, gender-role attitudes, and their background characteristics was investigated. The degree to which equity/inequity differentially affects husbands and wives was considered.

EQUITY IN RELATIONSHIPS

Origins of propositions central to equity theory are articulated in more detail elsewhere, including documentation of the lack of studies of equity in intimate relationships [1]. Although much of the research has demonstrated principles of equity in more casual relationships, there are some reasons why such premises would guide intimate lives as well.

Equitable relationships are thought to be present when individuals assessing the relationship believe they experience equal gains. Inequity may be observed when a partner believes his/her ratio of inputs to outcomes is unequal to that of the other, either larger or smaller [1]. Individuals who conclude their outcomes are inequitable may be under or overbenefited; it is believed distress may be fostered by either circumstance. The overbenefited, who get more than they think their efforts warrant, may feel guilt at having taken advantage of an intimate whereas the underbenefited, who obtain less than they feel they deserve, may be angry, resentful, or demoralized by having received unfair treatment at the hands of one to whose welfare they have contributed.

There is contention among scholars as to whether long-term intimate relationships involve conceptions of equity on the part of the partners or whether love as an unconditional commitment could possibly entail calculations of fairness [2]. In marital relationships, there is the expectation of reciprocity, although the exchange may be anticipated to occur at an unspecified time and even the nature of the transaction may be determined by the other partner.

In long-term, intimate affiliations the nature of the calculations of fairness may differ from more casual relationships. With intimates, comparisons may be less self-serving, and individuals may take others' welfare into account. Furthermore, permanence in a relationship is conducive to downgrading differences in inputs [3]. Moreover, assessments of equity in long-term associations may be buffered by affection and the possibility that contributions may be renegotiated. Inequity in the present may be less distressing because there is the option that contributions may be negotiated and made equitable in the future.

The relative contribution of equity in specific situations and more general relative deprivation to psychological well-being of couples in one and two-job families has been studied [4]. Inequity between spouses in the provider and housework roles was associated with depressive symptoms of spouses in both one and two-job families and for most persons relative deprivation also was distressing.

EQUITY OVER TIME

What is known about the course of equity in relationships over time? Does equity in marital roles differ for younger and older spouses? The hypothesis is that perceptions of equity will increase as a relationship progresses. Because inequity is troublesome, it is thought that couples will attempt to make the relationship more equitable perhaps by the underbenefited demanding more and the overbenefited taking steps to reduce the disadvantage of their partners.

Research addressing changes in equity over time has yielded somewhat inconsistent findings. Hatfield, et al. concluded most research does not confirm relationships become more equitable over time [1]. Such a conclusion is probably premature because none of the research on which this thinking is based followed persons over a lengthy period of time. One study sampled college students twice within a three to five month period and concluded relationships did not become more equitable over time [5]. Compared with a marriage of several years, three to five months is a very brief time from which to claim that equity does not increase in long-term relationships.

In other research, older women estimated in retrospect how equitable their marriages had been over various stages of their lives (from the time they were dating through age 80). No increase in equity was observed from their youth to later life [6].

An exception to these findings was observed among couples in four life stages ranging from parents with children under age six to older spouses over age sixty with no children in the home [2]. In this research, information was obtained from both husbands and wives. Perceptions of equity in family roles including food preparation, housekeeping, provider, and companion, were greater among couples in the older life stages.

None of the research reviewed on equity over time used comparable samples, designs, or similar periods of time over which equity was assessed. Yet, there are several reasons why we expect to find equity among older spouses. Perceived equity, of course, may not increase with the length of marriage; rather, those in inequitable partnerships may be more likely to leave their marriages. Inequitable relationships have been found to be less stable than those described as equitable. As relationships mature, there is cognizance that favors and services average out over time, and less attention is given to calculations of give and take. Perceptions of equity may increase as spouses adjust and accommodate themselves to the other and act as a partnership rather than as individuals. When their marriages were inequitable, most spouses, however, tended to find them imbalanced in their favor [1]. But inequity tended to be associated with diminished well-being.

CORRELATES OF EQUITY/INEQUITY

In this research an interest was investigating correlates of perceptions of equity/inequity and the implications of the latter for well-being in the marital relationship. Hatfield et al. observed equitable relationships will be compatible relationships, and partners in them should be more content than those who are under or overbenefited [1]. One aspect of contentment in an intimate relationship may be the regard spouses have for one another. We expected to find equitable relationships that were comprised of spouses with high regard for one another, who were contented and satisfied with their family roles, and who were less inclined to disagree over tasks.

Research Questions

Using previous research to inform the investigation, the following questions about equity in older families were addressed:

1. What prompted greater equity in relationships in old age? What were the characteristics of spouses who were prone to judge the efforts of their partners more critically?

2. Did couples with equitable practices in one area maintain them in other areas as well?
3. To what extent did equity correlate with increased disagreement and decreased satisfaction among older spouses? Was inequity in some activities more damaging than in others? Did partners with greater feelings of inequity also have more dissatisfaction, disagreement, and lower regard for one another?

Procedures

Sample

Data were analyzed from a sample of eighty-two couples in which the wife was age sixty or over and no children were living in the home. Both husbands and wives were interviewed as part of a study of nutrition and family life. The couples were selected from a random area sample based upon their population concentration. The population was subsampled using sampling rates that reflected the proportions of couples in this age group in the state of Iowa.

The sampling and screening procedures were designed by the Statistical Laboratory at Iowa State University. A structured interview schedule, which included questions on background, work and family roles, and indices of psychological well-being, was administered by trained interviewers.

The sample was Caucasian. The mean age was seventy-one years for men and sixty-nine for women. Length of marriage ranged from two to sixty-three years with a mean of forty-three years. About 45 percent of the husbands and 30 percent of the wives has less than a high school education. Twenty-seven percent of the men were retired. Twelve percent of the women were employed, 23 percent retired, and the remainder were homemakers.

Measures

Equity/Inequity

To measure perceptions of equity and inequity in the marital relationship, respondents evaluated their own and their spouses' levels of effort in four roles: housekeeping, food preparation, provider, and companion. They first rated their individual performances: "Do you feel you should either increase or decrease your own efforts in the following to make the marriage relationship more fair for both of you?" To assess perceptions of spouses' level of effort, they were asked: "Do you feel your husband/wife should either increase or decrease his/her efforts in the following tasks to make the marriage relationship more fair for both of you?" The five response categories ranged from: decrease effort a great deal (1) to increase effort a great deal (5).

The equity scores for each respondent in each of the four areas were determined by taking the difference in scores of self-evaluation and evaluation of the spouse for each of the four roles. This resulted in a nine point scale, −4 to +4. The negative scores represented inequity that was unfavorable whereas the positive scores indicated inequity that was favorable. This procedure was necessary to obtain the difference between perceived efforts of husbands and wives. Their scores were recoded from one to five with the higher scores indicating greater equity and the lower scores reflecting greater inequity. The recoding procedure was done so that inequity, both favorable and unfavorable, was located at one end of the continuum with equity at the other point.

Global equity was assessed by asking husbands and wives "Considering what you put into and get out of your marriage, compared to what your wife/husband puts into and gets out of it, how does your marriage relationship 'stack up'?" Response categories ranged from "My partner is getting a much better deal" (1) to "We are both getting an equal deal" (4) to "I am getting a much better deal" (7). Responses were recoded with the lowest scores indicating the greatest inequity to equity represented by the highest score. Scores ranged from 1 to 7 ($\overline{X} = 4.13$, $sd = .86$).

DISAGREEMENT AND DISSATISFACTION

Disagreement over family roles was measured by asking spouses how often, if ever, they and their partner disagreed about food preparation, housekeeping, being a provider, and being a companion or friend to their spouse. Five response categories ranged from never (1) to very frequently (5). The score for disagreement was based on the combined responses to the four items with a higher score indicating greater disagreement. Scores ranged from 1 to 4 ($\overline{X} = 1.6$, $sd = .61$, $alpha = .70$).

Dissatisfaction was determined by asking how dissatisfied respondents were with performing each of the four roles listed above. Responses ranged from satisfied (1) to very dissatisfied (4). Higher scores from combined responses to the four items represented greater dissatisfaction. Scores ranged from 1 to 4 ($\overline{X} = 1.67$, $sd = .61$, $alpha = .42$).

GENDER-ROLE ATTITUDES

Gender-role attitudes were assessed by preferences for the division of labor in the family. Respondents indicated whether the husband or wife—"husband always," (1), "wife always" (5)—should have more responsibility for four activities: food preparation, housekeeping (except childcare), provider, and caring for and training children. A higher mean score indicated more traditional preferences. Scores ranged from 2 to 5 ($\overline{X} = 3.89$, $sd = .54$, $alpha = .62$).

REGARD FOR SPOUSE

Respondents' appraisals of their spouse were studied in relation to equity in companionship. Regard for spouse was assessed by responses to seven pairs of adjectives (e.g., likeable/not likeable, incapable/capable; intelligent/unintelligent) in which persons rated their spouse on a seven point scale. Scores were summed across the items with a higher score representing higher regard. Scores ranged from 4 to 7 ($\overline{X} = 6.00$, $sd = .75$, $alpha = .81$).

Demographic characteristics (education, income, length of marriage) were coded so that higher values indicated amounts or a longer period of time. Employment status was coded: employed (0); not employed (1).

Analyses

Paired t-tests were used to assess the difference between husbands and wives on global equity and specific equity in the four areas studied. The Bonferroni test was used to take into account that five comparisons were made. The significance level used for the t-tests was $p < .02$.

Multiple regression analyses of global and specific equity were performed separately for husbands and wives. Multicollinearity was not present among the demographic characteristics used as independent variables. A .05 level of significance was used.

Results

Correlates of Global Equity/Inequity

Partners indicated whether they or their spouses were getting a better or an equal deal in their marriage. A paired t-test conducted to compare views of husbands and wives on equity showed their perceptions of global equity did not differ ($t = 0$, ns).

Did similar circumstances foster perceptions of global equity among older men and women? Multivariate analyses were used to answer questions about the relative importance of background characteristics and the salience of gender-role attitudes for perceptions of global equity. Separate multiple regression analyses were conducted for global equity of husbands and wives. Family income, education, employment status of both spouses, length of marriage, and attitudes toward gender roles were included in the analyses. Significant correlates and the amount of variance explained in perceptions of global equity are noted in the text for each analysis.

Perceptions of Global Equity by Husbands

The employment status of husbands was not associated with either their own or their spouses' assessments of global equity in their marriage. Wives' employment status, however, was correlated slightly with their husbands' perceptions of equity ($r = -.16$, $p < .10$). Husbands whose wives were still in the labor force described greater inequity although wives' employment did not figure significantly in the regression equation for global equity. Husbands who had been married longer believed their relationship was fairer ($r = .20$, $p < .05$). In the multivariate analysis no single factor made a significant contribution to the global equity reported by these older husbands ($R^2 = .08$).

Perceptions of Global Equity by Wives

In the multivariate analysis of global equity including attitudes toward gender roles, education, income, employment status of both spouses, and length of marriage, only perceptions of gender roles were salient in assessments of equity among women ($r = .24$, $p < .05$; $R^2 = .04$). Older wives who held more traditional views of work-family tasks believed their marriages were more equitable.

Correlates of Specific Assessments of Equity/Inequity

Spouses indicated whether they experienced equity or inequity in four roles in the family: food preparation, housekeeping, provider, and companion. Paired t-tests were used to compare spouses' perceptions of equity in the four areas. Equity was coded so a higher value indicated greater equity. These spouses shared views of equity in food preparation ($t = 0$, ns), being a provider ($t = .55$, ns) and companion ($t = .56$, ns). There was a tendency for more wives than husbands to describe equity in housekeeping ($t = 2.28$, $p < .05$) although the inequity experienced by men primarily attributable to their being overbenefited. In general, these older spouses tended to share perceptions of equity in their roles.

In multiple regression analyses fairness in each of the four specific tasks was considered in relation to employment status, education, income, length of marriage, and attitudes toward gender roles for husbands and wives. There were no consistent predictors of equity across the four specific areas for husbands or wives. Significant correlates and the amount of variance explained in perceptions of global equity are noted in the text for each analysis.

Attitudes toward gender roles were predictors of equity in food preparation for both husbands and wives ($r = -.30$, $p < .05$; $R^2 = .06$ and $r = .19$, $p < .05$; $R^2 = .08$, respectively). But the direction of the relationship was opposite with husbands who held traditional gender-role attitudes perceiving greater inequity whereas traditional wives tended to view their situations as more equitable. Traditional men were overbenefited in this area.

Length of marriage was associated with greater equity in housekeeping among women ($r = .24$, $p < .05$; $R^2 = .10$). Wives who had been married longer estimated that their marriages were fairer in the area of housekeeping than those in more recent marriages. None of the variables predicted a significant amount of variance in equity in housekeeping among husbands.

Husbands whose wives were not employed outside the home enjoyed feelings of greater equity in the provider role ($r = .36, p < .01; R^2 = .16$). Older wives with more education $r = .23, p < .05$) and with more modern attitudes toward women as providers ($r = .22, p < .05$) described greater equity in this role ($R^2 = .08$).

The background variables and attitudes toward roles had few linkages with perceptions of equity/inequity in companionship for either spouse. Only education had a significant effect for men so that those who were better educated felt they experienced less equity ($r = -.25, p < .05; R^2 = .12$). Any inequity in companionship described by wives was independent of background characteristics or attitudes toward gender roles.

Equity/Inequity, Dissatisfaction and Disagreement

Was inequity in some activities more damaging to satisfaction and agreement between spouses than others? If inequity is distressing as has been hypothesized in the literature, we would expect to find that functioning in inequitable situations would diminish satisfaction in performing these roles. To the extent an attempt is made to reduce inequity, then conflict may result [1]. Research on dating students found persons involved in equitable relationships were happier and more contented than those whose partnerships were less balanced efforts. That equitable relationships are thought to be compatible relationships led to the expectation partnerships identified as having greater equity would have fewer disagreements over the accomplishment of specific tasks.

First, did perceptions of equity foster relationships with fewer disagreements and more satisfaction? And did the effects of inequity, if any, vary by type of activity? We examined the relationship between perceived equity in a given activity and the satisfaction derived from participating in the activity and the amount of disagreement about it (Table 1).

Generally, there was little support for the hypothesis that contentment would accompany greater equity in household tasks. Of the twelve tests linking dissatisfaction and disagreement with inequity, only three were significant at the .05 level. Inequity in the tasks of food preparation and housekeeping did not tend to limit the satisfaction derived by men or women from their involvement in these activities or contribute to conflict. Thus, inequity in the roles studied was not troublesome for the majority of spouses.

We investigated how views of fairness in companionship might affect the regard spouses had for one another. Equity in companionship was not associated with the esteem in which wives held their husbands ($r = .08$, ns), and there was only a slight tendency for husbands in equitable relationships to have higher regard for their partners ($r = .14, p < .05$). For most then, negative evaluations of their partners' contributions as companions and friends did not result in diminished regard. As reflected in dissatisfaction, disagreement, and regard for one's spouse then, inequity as a whole was not costly for these older couples.

Table 1. Correlations Between Perceptions of Equity
and Distress in the Family

Equity in:	Husbands		Wives	
	Dissatisfaction	Disagreement	Dissatisfaction	Disagreement
Food preparation	.01	.07	−.07	−.06
Housekeeping	−.04	−.13	−.06	−.11
Provider	−.14	−.29**	−.21**	−.01
Companionship	.09	−.22**	−.15*	.03

*$p < .10$
**$p < .05$

Correlations Between Equity in Four Roles

Was there a tendency for households with equitable practices in one area to maintain them in others? For the most part, correlations between assessments of equity in one kind of activity were positively correlated with one another although those of men were somewhat more highly related than those of women (Table 2). Five of the six relationships were significant at the .05 level for men whereas four were for women. Both husbands ($r = .53, p < .001$) and wives ($r = .49, p < .001$) who found their practices in food preparation equitable tended to make similar observations about housekeeping as well. Men who experienced equity as a companion also described a similar situation in their role of provider ($r = 41, p < .001$). In general then, families in which equity was prevalent in one role often enjoyed it in others as well.

Summary and Discussion

Much of what is known about the outcomes of perceptions of inequity has been based on information from younger persons who were often not in long-term intimate relationships. Furthermore, both spouses in older couples rarely have been studied. This research provided an opportunity to address some of these omissions:

1. What have we learned about the factors that fostered global and specific equity among these older spouses? From our analyses, we must conclude social status characteristics were of little importance in setting the context of equity for these older couples. Income and educational levels may be determinants of the amount of effort put forth by men and women in the household at retirement, but they did not consistently influence the observations about specific or global equity of these husbands and wives [7].

Multivariate analyses indicated retirement, either their own or their spouses, did not figure prominently in the perceptions of equity among husbands or wives. In

Table 2. Correlations Between Equity Across Family Roles[a]

Equity in:	Food Preparation	Housekeeping	Provider	Companion
Food preparation	—	.53*	00	.29*
Housekeeping	.49*	—	.30*	.30*
Provider	.19*	.11	—	.41*
Companionship	.24*	.17*	.07	—

[a]Correlations for husbands are above the diagonal and those for wives are below. A high score indicated greater equity.

*$p < .05$

general, irrespective of reallocations of household tasks occurring at retirement that might reshape observations about fairness in the relationship, among these spouses thoughts about equity were largely independent of employment or retirement status.

In the current generation of middle-aged and older men and women, there was probably little in their gender-role socialization to prompt significant reallocations of tasks between spouses in later life or to reshape their calculations of fairness. Indeed, on the global measure wives with more traditional views of gender roles also felt their relationships were fairer. It may be tempting to overanticipate the effects of retirement on patterns as entrenched as those that are the products of lifelong gender-role socialization.

2. Did families with equitable practices in one area maintain them in others? In general, partners who were favored with equity in one area of their lives sustained it in others as well. Indeed, among these older spouses the best predictor of equity in most of the specific areas was fairness in other aspects of life.

3. Was inequity in some activities more damaging to well-being than others? Was equity correlated with fewer disagreements and greater satisfaction? For the most part, this research did not support the thinking [1] that equity in relationships will prompt contentment and compatibility between partners. In general, discontentment reflected in dissatisfaction and disagreement between spouses was independent of equity/inequity in the roles studied. When inequity influenced disagreement or dissatisfaction, it tended to be in the provider and companion roles, not in the more conventional domestic activities.

The theory linking inequity to incompatibility or discontent may be less applicable to older relationships. Inequity may be less troublesome and have less sting in a relationship of give and take and negotiation over a sustained period. In such relationships comparisons used to calculate fairness may be less self-serving, individual contributions to the partnership may be downgraded, and assessments may be buffered by affect for the spouse [3]. Or for other couples, long-term inequity may be expected as a cost of remaining together, accepted, and fail to foster dissatisfaction and disagreement.

Finally, the findings of this research should be regarded as exploratory. Larger, more representative samples may reveal different relationships between assessments of work-family roles and perceptions of fairness in later life. In the future, better measures of equity/inequity in older families need to be developed to measure perceptions of fairness more accurately.

REFERENCES

1. E. Hatfield, J. Traupmann, S. Sprecher, M. Utne, and J. Hay, Equity and Intimate Relations: Recent Research, in *Compatible and Incompatible Relationships,* E. Ickes (ed.), Springer-Verlag, New York, 1985.
2. P. Keith and R. Schafer, *Relationships and Well-Being Over the Life Stages*, Praeger, New York, 1991.
3. W. Austin, Equity Theory and Social Comparison Process, in *Social Comparison Processes*, J. Suls and R. Miller (eds.), Hemisphere, Washington, D.C., pp. 279-305, 1977.
4. P. Keith and R. Schafer, Relative Deprivation, Equity/Inequity, and Psychological Well-Being, *Journal of Family Issues, 8*, pp. 199-211, 1987.
5. E. Hatfield, G. Walster, and J. Traupmann, Equity and Premarital Sex, *Journal of Personality and Social Psychology, 37*, pp. 82-91, 1978.
6. J. Traupmann and E. Hatfield, How Important is Marital Fairness Over the Lifespan? *International Journal of Aging and Human Development, 17*, pp. 89-101, 1983.
7. M. Szinovacz, Retirement, Couples, and Housework Work, in *Aging and the Family*, S. Bahr and E. Peterson (eds.), Lexington Books, Lexington, Massachusetts, 1989.

Chapter 2

SPOUSAL CHARACTERISTICS AS PREDICTORS OF WELL-BEING IN OLDER COUPLES

Cécile Quirouette
and
Dolores Pushkar Gold

Research has demonstrated that although both married men and women tend to have better mental health than do never-married, widowed, and divorced men and women, the positive association between marriage and mental health is more salient for men than for women [1-3]. Married men are in better mental health than married women and unmarried men are in poorer mental health than unmarried women. Research further revealed that marital happiness, rather than marital status itself, is the important factor in global well-being, with marital happiness being the best predictor of mental health and global happiness for both married men and women [4, 5]. In addition, studies found that men tend to be more satisfied than women with their marriage [6-8] and that marital satisfaction is a stronger predictor of mental health for women than for men [5].

In order to explain the processes within marriage that promote unequal levels of well-being for men and women, several authors [9-11] have proposed that compared to male roles, the traditional female roles are more demanding and put women at greater risk for psychological distress. The core roles of wife and mother, compared to the role of financial provider, are believed to entail greater emotional reactivity to both positive and negative family events.

In older cohorts in particular, women were expected, by virtue of their family caregiving role, to be attentive to their husbands' well-being and satisfaction and to respond physically and emotionally to their needs throughout marriage. Indeed, research data on conjugal social support indicate that older men tend to engage in and rely on supportive exchanges primarily with their wives who, in contrast, rely on children and friends in addition to their spouses [6]. Compared to men, older women tend to receive less affective support (confiding and reassurance) within marriage and this sex difference appears to remain constant with age [7]. Thus, a lifetime of traditional sex roles seems to carry over into post-retirement years and to promote in wives, more than in husbands, high levels of emotional responsiveness to the psychological and physical well-being of their spouse.

Recently, the importance of spousal variables as correlates of psychological well-being has begun to be examined. Studies have shown that spousal illness has a detrimental effect on both wives' and husbands' psychological well-being. For wives, the negative effect is mediated by their husbands' morale [12], by strain on the financial situation of the couple and/or by strain in the marital relation [13]. The reasons why an ill spouse is a source of distress for older men have not been established, as there appear to be no indirect effects mediating the negative effects on husbands of illness of the spouse. Similarly, with regard to mental illness, research indicates that the presence of psychiatric symptoms in one spouse tends to result in psychopathology in the marital partner, with greater effect for women [11].

Although personality characteristics are important determinants of both one's own mood states [14] and the stability and quality of the marital relationship, spousal personality variables have not been studied as predictors of psychological well-being. In a longitudinal study of marital compatibility, Kelly and Conley [15] found that low impulse control on the part of husbands high in neuroticism typically lead to divorce, while low social extroversion in the same type of men lead to stable but unsatisfied marriages. The authors concluded that although neuroticism in husbands or wives results in marital disturbance, the husband's personality characteristics seem to play a greater role in creating and maintaining an unsatisfying marriage or in bringing marriage to an end.

Other longitudinal studies indicated that couples become more similar over marriage and when changes in intellectual abilities occur over time, the wives' abilities tend to be predicted by those of their husbands. The results of the Intergenerational Studies revealed that living with a spouse whose IQ was markedly different (higher or lower) influenced the study member's IQ change between adolescence and middle age, with a stronger effect for females [16]. Consistent findings were reported by Gruber-Baldini and Schaie who investigated changes in couple similarity over a twenty-one year period [17]. Comparisons of performance on measures of cognitive abilities and three dimensions of personality-flexibility revealed that in all significant correlations, husband's performance predicted wives' subsequent performance. No research has examined the relations between spousal education or intelligence and married people's psychological well-being.

To summarize, research data indicate that while marriage and marital satisfaction are significant predictors of mental health for both men and women, married men are generally in better mental health than are married women, and women are more affected than men by marriage quality. Sex-role theory and research further suggest that traditional sex-roles within marriage put women at risk for psychological distress. Finally, despite the paucity of empirical studies on the specific relations between spousal characteristics and the psychological well-being of married people, the literature reviewed consistently suggests women have a greater sensitivity to a variety of spousal variables. This study was designed to test the hypothesis of differential emotional responsiveness of husbands and wives to spousal variables. It was predicted that husbands' characteristics would account for more variance in wives' global psychological well-being than wives' characteristics in relation to husbands' psychological well-being.

METHOD

Participants

The participants were drawn from a larger investigation examining cognitive and social function in elderly people, aged more than fifty years, living in the community, who were recruited with a variety of local community agencies, e.g., community newspapers. Volunteers asked to participate in the present study were those who were married for at least ten years and whose spouse was available to participate. The sample consisted of 120 men and women in longstanding marriages (mean length = 39.13 years, SD = 8.12) with a mean age of 68.35 (SD = 4.21) for men and 65.90 (SD = 4.21) for women. With a mean rating of 50.44 (SD = 13.52), the sample was of working class socio-economic background according to the Blishen scale of occupational prestige [18]. Eighty-one percent of the male subjects were retired and the major occupation of 80 percent of the wives during their married lives had been that of homemaker. The majority of the participants had at least some high school education, the mean number of years of education being 10.78 (SD = 4.27) for men and 10.58 (SD = 3.89) for women. Most of the subjects reported few serious symptoms or illnesses and those who used prescribed medication used them mostly for problems related to hypertension and other physical ailments rather than for psychiatric or psychological disorders.

Measures

A short structured interview gathered demographic data relative to the participants' occupational, marital, and academic backgrounds. The Locke and

Wallace short-form Marital-Adjustment Test assessed the current accommodation of husband and wife to each other [19]. The scale has a high internal reliability coefficient of .90 and has been found to differentiate between individuals known to be maladjusted and those known to be exceptionally well-adjusted in marriage. The Jemail and LoPiccolo Marital Defensiveness Scale, assessed defensiveness about disclosing the nature of the marital relationship [20]. The internal reliability of the male and female versions of the scale has been established at .88 and .90, respectively. The Marital Defensiveness Scale, a content specific scale, has been found to be more sensitive than a global measure of social desirability in tapping defensiveness associated with marital adjustment. The Memorial University of Newfoundland Scale of Happiness [21], designed to measure psychological well-being in nonclinical samples of older adults, was used to assess current mood and general psychological well-being. The scale has been designed to sample four aspects of well-being, i.e., positive and negative affect and positive and negative experience, which are usually combined to give three scores, positive dimension, negative dimension and overall well-being scores, which are regarded as necessary for a complete examination of well-being [22]. The MUNSH has a test-retest reliability of .70 for an interval of six to twelve months and has been found to predict avowed happiness significantly more accurately than other measures of well being [23]. The Eysenck Personality Inventory measured two independent personality dimensions, introversion-extraversion and neuroticism-stability [24]. The test-retest reliability coefficients of this scale range between .84 and .94 and the validity of the orthogonal, two-dimensional conceptual scheme has received empirical support. The vocabulary subtest of the Revised Examination "M" (M-Test) was used as a measure of verbal intelligence. The M-Test is a measure of intelligence developed for the Canadian Army during World War II [25]. Scores on the M-test have been found to correlate ($r = .80$) with scores on the American Army Alpha Test. A shortened version of the Seriousness of Illness Rating Scale [26] assessed the subjects' health status. The criterion validity of this scale has been indicated by high levels of agreement, $r = .95$, between medical and non-medical health evaluations. Respondents were asked to check off the symptoms and diseases they had experienced in the past two years. The participants also listed the names of any prescribed drugs they were taking.

Procedure

All subjects were tested in one session, usually at their homes, less frequently at the university, according to their preference. Each spouse was tested separately and consecutively, so that wives and husbands could not confer. Both spouses were interviewed by the same interviewer and two interviewers, both female, collected the data. Administration of the measures took approximately one hour per spouse. The couples received $10.00 and a summary of the general results of the study upon completion.

Results

Husbands and wives generally obtained high scores on the positive dimension ($M = 9.75$ and $M = 9.48$, respectively) and low scores on the negative dimension ($M = 1.35$ and $M = 2.28$) respectively; results which are typical of older community-based respondents [27]. Relative to the means reported by Locke and Wallace [19], both husbands and wives appeared to experience average degrees of marital adjustment, with mean scores of 117 ($SD = 22.37$) and 108 ($SD = 27.82$) respectively. Compared to the means reported by Jemail and LoPiccolo [20], subjects expressed high marital defensiveness, with mean scores of 11.67 ($SD = 5.06$) for men and 12.02 ($SD = 4.61$) for women.

Based on the results of the correlation matrices of husbands' and wives' variables (see Tables 1 and 2), the number of variables to be used in subsequent multivariate analyses was reduced, thus obtaining more acceptable participant/variable ratios for multivariate analyses. Age and vocabulary were omitted from further analyses since they did not appear to be relevant to the well-being scores criterion. Only one significant relationship existed between age and vocabulary and well-being scores. Consequently, the eight variables retained for the multivariate analyses included education, illness, extroversion, neuroticism, the positive and negative dimensions of well-being, marital adjustment, and marital defensiveness. The results of the evaluations of the assumptions of normality, linearity, and homogeneity of variance indicated that the assumptions were not significantly violated.

A multivariate analyses of covariance (MANCOVA), adjusted for the covariate marital defensiveness, compared wives and husbands on age, education, illness, extroversion, neuroticism, positive and negative dimensions. The covariate of marital defensiveness had a significant effect on the scores of the dependent variables, ($F(9,116) = 7.39, p < .0001$). Despite the effects of the covariate, there was a significant multivariate difference between husbands and wives ($F(7,111) = 3.70, p = .001$). As reported in previous research, husbands reported better marital adjustment ($F(1,117) = 7.19, p < .01$) and had lower negative dimension scores ($F(1,117) = 6.11, p < .01$) than did wives. Husbands and wives did not differ on extroversion but husbands had lower scores on neuroticism ($F(1,117) = 9.67, p < .01$). No differences were found between spouses on measures of positive dimension of well-being and physical health, although husbands were older ($F(1,117) = 8.66, p < .01$) than wives.

To test if husbands' variables accounted for more variance in wives' global well-being than wives' variables in relation to husbands' well-being, multiple regression analyses were performed on the husbands' and wives' data within couples. The variance in spousal predictor variables attributable to marital defensiveness was controlled by including defensiveness in the regression analysis and interpreting it as a covariate. Husbands' variables were entered as predictors for wives' global well-being (see Table 3) and accounted for 29 percent of the

Table 1. Zero-Order Correlations among Husbands' Variables (*n* = 60)

Variables	Age	Education	Vocabulary	Illness	Extroversion	Neuroticism	Marital Defensiveness	Marital Adjustment	Positive Dimension	Negative Dimension	Global Well-Being
Age		-.06	.13	.04	-.04	-.07	.11	.01	-.17	.09	-.15
Education			.53***	-.30*	-.14	-.11	-.29*	.04	.11	-.05	.10
Vocabulary				-.16	.10	.13	-.29*	-.01	.02	.03	-.01
Illness					-.10	.45***	-.09	-.33**	-.41***	.46***	-.48***
Extroversion						.14	.12	.07	.24	-.13	.21
Neuroticism							-.38**	-.40***	-.26*	.47***	-.39**
Marital defensiveness								.63***	.07	-.20	.21
Marital adjustment									.24	-.48***	.38**
Positive dimension										-.60***	.92***
Negative dimension											-.87***
Global well-being											

Notes: Coefficients indicated by *** indicate significance at .05 according to Bonnferroni's criteria for multiple comparisons.
*p < .05
**p < .01
***p < .001

26

Table 2. Zero-Order Correlations among Wives' Variables ($n = 60$)

Variables	Age	Education	Vocabulary	Illness	Extroversion	Neuroticism	Marital Defensiveness	Marital Adjustment	Positive Dimension	Negative Dimension	Global Well-Being
Age		.04	.07	.09	-.07	-.06	.16	.12	.12	-.23	.21
Education			.54***	-.31*	-.01	-.20	-.04	.29*	.11	-.36**	.28*
Vocabulary				-.16	-.01	-.14	-.15	.05	.04	.32**	.22
Illness					.11	.32**	.17	-.20	-.11	.17	-.16
Extroversion						.12	.09	.01	.14	-.06	.11
Neuroticism							-.14	-.39**	-.31*	.57***	-.51***
Marital defensiveness								.58***	.33*	-.37**	.40**
Marital adjustment									.49***	-.53***	.59***
Positive dimension										-.53***	.84***
Negative dimension											-.90***
Global well-being											

Notes: Coefficients indicated by *** indicate significance at .05 according to Bonnferroni's criteria for multiple comparisons.

 *$p < .05$
 **$p < .01$
 ***$p < .001$

27

variance in the criterion scores or 18 percent when variance was adjusted for the effects of sample size, ($F = 2.60$, $p < .025$). Husbands' marital adjustment, closely followed the positive dimension of well-being, emerged as significant predictors. Husbands' illness also contributed significantly to the prediction but appeared to function as a suppressor variable. While illness had no direct relationship with wives' well-being, it did share variance with the significant predictor variables, as shown in the correlation matrix of husbands' variables (see Table 1).

In order to determine if the spousal variables which predicted wives' global well-being were differentially related to separate positive and negative dimensions of well-being, two multiple regressions were performed, regressing the combination of spousal variables on the positive and the negative dimensions of well-being. The regression analysis of husbands' variables predicting the positive dimension of wives' well-being accounted for 28 percent of the variance or an adjusted R^2 of 16 percent ($F = 2.44$, $p < .05$). Husbands' marital adjustment, the only predictor variable to reach statistical significance, accounted for most of the variance. Husbands' variables predicted 27 percent of the variance or 15 percent of the variance adjusted for the effects of sample size in the negative dimension of their wives' well-being ($F = 2.31$, $p < .05$) with husbands' marital adjustment again emerging as the strongest predictor, followed by the positive dimension of husbands' well-being.

Wives' characteristics did not significantly predict husbands' global well-being ($R^2 = .08$, $F = 1.18$, p is n.s.), positive dimension of well-being ($R^2 = .10$, $F = 1.58$, p is n.s.) or negative dimension of well-being ($R^2 = .07$, $F = .97$, p is n.s.). Finally,

Table 3. Multiple Regression Coefficients for Wives' Global Well-Being, with Their Husbands' Variables as Predictors ($N = 60$)

Predictor Variables	Beta #	r	Sr^j
Education	.10	.13	.08
Illness	.32	.03	.25*
Extroversion	−.14	−.13	−.13
Neuroticism	−.18	−.20	−.14
Positive dimension	.40	.22	.29**
Negative dimension	.28	−.10	.18
Marital adjustment	.50	.35	.30**
Marital defensiveness	−.12	.20	−.08

Notes: $R = .54$, $R^2 = .29$, $F(8.51) = 2.60$, $p < .025$.
Standardized regression coefficients.
*$p < .05$
**$p < 0.1$

Fisher's Z test statistic [28] was applied to the three pairs of equations relating spousal variables to husbands' and wives' well-being (global, positive, and negative dimensions). For all three pairs of regression equations, the amount of variance in the criterion accounted for by the predictor variables was significantly greater for the predictions of wives' well-being than for the predictions of husbands' well-being.

Discussion

In this study it was postulated that traditional marital roles (caregiving versus financial providing) promote greater emotional responsiveness to spousal characteristics in women than in men. Lower emotional responsiveness by husbands should presumably help explain the lower levels of affective support received by older women within marriage. Thus, differential emotional responsiveness, along with other marital role elements, may explain the discrepancies in the mental health of married men and women, which generally favor men. The results provide strong support for the hypothesis of differential emotional responsiveness since spousal characteristics predict wives' but not husbands' psychological well-being. Furthermore, gender differences were found for couples on psychological well-being and marital adjustment which are consistent with findings of previous investigations, i.e., women experience more negative affect and less satisfaction in their marriage than do men.

The husbands' perception of the marriage is the most influential spousal variable for wives' well-being. Not only is the wives' own positive assessment of the marriage beneficial to their psychological well-being, as indicated in the correlation matrix of wives' variables (see Table 2) and as reported in the literature, but so is their husbands' positive assessment of the marriage. As mentioned above, the core roles of most married women are those of wife and mother, while the core role of married men is that of provider. The psychological welfare of husbands and children, and by extension, the quality of the relationships within the family, have traditionally rested on women's shoulders. To the extent that one identifies with one's primary roles, the partner's satisfaction or dissatisfaction with the way these roles are fulfilled may enhance or threaten self-esteem and self-confidence. If the wives in this study were held or held themselves responsible for the quality of the marital relation, then their husbands' happiness or unhappiness with the marriage may have been perceived as a reflection of their competency, and consequently have affected their psychological well-being. Furthermore, having a husband who is unhappy with his marriage may be perceived by wives as a threat to the marriage itself, on which they are generally financially dependent.

The second most important spousal variable, associated with the negative dimension of wives' well-being, is the positive dimension of husbands' well-being. This implies that women who live with pleasant, energetic, and enthusiastic men tend to experience less negative affect. Conversely, women married to men who have low levels of energy, positive affect, and enthusiasm tend to be unhappy. Again, the impact of husbands' level of happiness on their wives' well-being may be a consequence of the traditional assumption that wives are responsible for their mates' comfort and happiness. In addition, unhappier husbands may make greater demands for emotional support on their wives. Studies have shown that with age, men do become more dependent on their wives for nurturance and have fewer other sources of social support [29], thus reinforcing wives' caregiving role. However, as Barnett and Baruch [9] have commented, since one has little control over the happiness of another person, wives find themselves in a potentially stressful situation.

Husbands' physical health is the third most important contributor among the spousal variables predicting wives' well-being, but apparently acting through its correlations with the first two significant spousal predictors, i.e., marital adjustment and the positive dimension of well-being. These results complement the findings of previous investigations that showed that the detrimental effects of husbands' ill health on their wives' well-being are experienced by the latter only to the extent that illness affects the husbands' morale [12]. In this study, husbands' illness is negatively related to their perceptions of the marriage and is the variable most strongly associated with their own level of psychological well-being (see Table 1). In contrast, while wives are sensitive to the negative effects of illness on their husbands' well-being, their own ill health is not related to their level of marital satisfaction or general sense of well-being (see Table 2). Similar findings had been reported by Haftrom and Schram [30].

No evidence of a direct relationship was found between the personality traits of spouses and their partners' psychological well-being. It may be that having lived together for decades, older spouses become habituated to each other's idiosyncracies. It is also likely that this cross-sectional sample was somewhat biased since very maladjusted, neurotic individuals may have divorced before reaching retirement age, and very unhappy couples may have refused to participate together in a study on marriage. The relationship between spousal variables and well-being should be examined in future research in longitudinal designs. Finally, education and verbal intelligence are not correlated, as spousal variables, with well-being. It appears that how the marital partner feels, physically and emotionally, contributes more to personal happiness than the partner's intellectual skills or level of education.

In considering the variables which are related to husbands' and wives' own well-being (see Tables 1 and 2), it is interesting to note that marital adjustment is a strong correlate of global happiness for wives, which is consistent with previous research findings [4, 5], but is less highly correlated with well-being for husbands. Among this sample of older men, enjoying good health or suffering from disease appears to be more important for their psychological well-being than the quality of their marital relationship. Since the groups of husbands and wives did not differ in physical health status in this study, it is plausible that the gender differences found in the physical health-psychological well-being relationship are attributable to the different interpretations made by older men and women about health issues. In view of the shorter life expectancy of men, the importance of good health for men's sense of well-being may reflect a concern about death and disability. For older women, the importance of the marital relationship is not overshadowed by personal health concerns, perhaps because the meaning of illness carries for them less negative and drastic connotations.

Some implications, for theory and for further research, can be derived from these findings. First, in relation to the original problem of discrepancies in the mental health of married men and women, which favor men, the results provide support for the role of differential emotional responsiveness to spousal variables. However, sensitivity to spousal variables does not inevitably lead to poorer mental health. If married women are more responsive to their spouse's characteristics, then marriage to a healthy, competent, and supportive spouse should have a more positive and greater effect on well-being for women than for men. Differential responsiveness implies a greater receptivity and a potential to be influenced by the other's characteristics. Depending on the characteristics of both spouses, it can be a source for development and growth as well as a source of distress. Further investigation of men's and women's responsivity to spousal variables would benefit from the inclusion of other related measures such as scales of emotional awareness and emotional expressivity within the marital relationship.

Second, while the results provide some understanding of the relationships and relative importance of spousal variables for the psychological well-being of older wives, they reveal no information about characteristics of wives that might influence older husbands' well-being. It can be speculated that this particular set of spousal variables influence women's well-being because women are socialized to be responsible for and to respond to their spouses' emotional and physical welfare. However, men are socialized to be responsible primarily for their wives' material or financial security rather than for their personal happiness. Consequently the spousal variables measured in this study might not be salient predictors of husbands' well-being. Variables assessing wives' financial well-being might be more strongly related to husbands' global well-being. Nevertheless, it is surprising that, contrary to other studies [12, 13], wives' physical and emotional well-being is not associated with husbands' well-being. These relations should be examined in further research.

In summary, this study supports previous empirical evidence suggesting that older married women are more responsive to their spouses' global, marital, and physical well-being than are older married men. It also provides new information on the relative contribution of spousal variables to the psychological well-being of wives, revealing the particular importance of husbands' perception of the marital relation.

REFERENCES

1. I. H. Gotlib and J. M. Hooley, Depression and Marital Distress: Current Status and Future Directions, in *Handbook of Personal Relationship*, S. W. Duck (ed.), Wiley & Sons, New York, pp. 543-580, 1988.
2. W. R. Gove and J. F. Tudor, Adult Sex Roles and Mental Illness, *American Journal of Sociology, 78*, pp. 812-832, 1973.
3. S. S. Taillefer, *Etat Civil, Sexe et Santé Mentale au Québec*, unpublished master's thesis, Université de Montréal, Montréal, Québec, 1987.
4. N. D. Glen and C. N. Weaver, The Contribution of Marital Happiness to Global Happiness, *Journal of Marriage and the Family, 43*, pp. 161-168, 1981.
5. W. R. Gove, M. Hughes, and C. B. Style, Does Marriage Have Positive Effects on Psychological Well-being of the Individual?, *Journal of Health and Social Behavior, 25*, pp. 122-131, 1983.
6. H. Akiyama and T. C. Antonucci, An Examination of Sex Differences in Social Support in Mid and Late Life, *Sex Roles*, (in press).
7. C. E. Depner and B. Ingersoll-Dayton, Conjugal Social Support: Patterns in Later Life, *Journal of Gerontology, 40*:6, pp. 761-766, 1985.
8. S. Weishaus and D. Field, A Half Century of Marriage: Continuity or Change?, *Journal of Marriage and the Family, 50*, pp. 763-774, 1988.
9. R. C. Barnet and G. K. Baruch, Social Roles, Gender, and Psychological Distress, in *Gender and Stress*, R. C. Barnett, L. Biener, and G. K. Baruch (eds.), Free Press, New York, pp. 122-143, 1987.
10. J. Bernard, *Women, Wives, Mothers: Values and Options*, Aldine Publishing Co., Chicago, 1975.
11. G. J. Methorst, Partners of Psychiatric Outpatients: The Difference between Husbands and Wives on Psychological Well-being and Its Implications for Marital Therapy, in *Marital Interaction: Analysis and Modification*, K. Hahlweg and N. S. Jacobson (eds.), pp. 375-386, 1984.
12. R. C. Atchley and S. J. Miller, Types of Elderly Couples, in *Family Relationships in Later Life*, T. H. Brubaker (ed.), Sage, Beverly Hills, pp. 77-90, 1983.
13. N. Krause and K. Markides, Illness of Spouse and Psychological Well-being in Older Adults, *Comprehensive Gerontology B, 1*, pp. 105-108, 1987.
14. P. T. Costa and R. R. McCrae, Influence of Extraversion and Neuroticism on Subjective Well-being: Happy and Unhappy People, *Journal of Personality and Social Psychology, 38*, pp. 668-678, 1980.
15. E. L. Kelly and J. J. Conley, Personality and Compatibility: A Prospective Analysis of Marital Stability and Marital Satisfaction, *Journal of Personality and Social Psychology, 52*, pp. 27-40, 1987.
16. D. H. Eichorn, J. V. Hunt, and M. P. Honzik, Experience, Personality, and IQ: Adolescence to Middle Age, in *Present and Past in Middle Life*, D. H. Eichorn, J. A. Clausen, N. Haan, M. P. Honzik and P. H. Mussen (eds.), Academic Press, New York, pp. 89-116, 1981.
17. A. L. Gruber-Baldini and K. W. Schaie, *Longitudinal-Sequential Studies of Marital Assortativity*, paper presented at the annual meeting of the Gerontological Society of America, Chicago, Illinois, 1986.

18. B. R. Blishen and H. A. Roberts, A Revised Socioeconomic Index for Occupations in Canada, *Canadian Review of Sociology and Anthropology, 13*, pp. 71-79, 1976.
19. H. J. Locke and K. M. Wallace, Short Marital-Adjustment and Prediction Tests: Their Reliability and Validity, *Marriage and Family Living*, pp. 251-255, 1959.
20. J. A. Jemail and J. LoPiccolo, A Sexual and a Marital Defensiveness Scale for Each Sex, *The American Journal of Family Therapy, 10*, pp. 33-40, 1982.
21. A. Kozma and M. J. Stones, Re-validation of the Memorial University of Newfoundland Scale of Happiness, *Canadian Journal on Aging, 2*, pp. 27-29, 1983.
22. E. Diener and R. A. Emmons, The Independence of Positive and Negative Affect, *Journal of Personality and Social Psychology, 47*, pp. 1105-1117, 1984.
23. J. P. Robinson, P. R. Shaver, and L. S. Wrightsman, *Measures of Personality and Social Psychological Attitudes*, Academic Press, New York, 1991.
24. H. J. Eysenck and S. B. G. Eysenck, *Manual: Eysenck Personality Inventory*, Educational and Industrial Testing Service, San Diego, California, 1968.
25. W. R. N. Blair, *Normative Data for Revised Examination "M"*, personal communication, Ottawa, Ontario, 1959.
26. A. R. Wyler, M. Masuda, and T. H. Holmes, Magnitude of Life Events and Seriousness of Illness, *Psychosomatic Medicine, 33*, pp. 115-122, 1971.
27. T. Y. Arbuckle, D. P. Gold, and D. Andres, Cognitive Functioning of Older People in Relation to Social and Personality Variables, *Psychology and Aging, 1*, pp. 55-62, 1986.
28. D. C. Howell, *Statistical Methods for Psychology*, Duxbury Press, Boston, 1987.
29. J. D. Grambs, *Women over Forty*, Springer Publishing Company, New York, 1989.
30. J. L. Hafstrom and V. R. Schram, Chronic Illness in Couples: Selected Characteristics, Including Wife's Satisfaction with and Perception of Marital Relationships, *Family Relations, 23*, pp. 195-203, 1984.

Chapter 3

THE LONG-TERM MARRIAGE: PERCEPTIONS OF STABILITY AND SATISFACTION

Robert H. Lauer
Jeanette C. Lauer
and
Sarah T. Kerr

Research has shown that marriage is associated with a number of benefits for both men and women. If the marriage works well, it fulfills the intimacy needs of the partners. Marital happiness contributes more than anything else to a general sense of happiness [1]. Glenn and Weaver found that surveys conducted from 1972 to 1986 indicated a decline in the relationship between marital status and happiness [2]. Nevertheless, their data show that married men and women in the 1982-1986 period were proportionately happier than those in any of the other groups.

Marriage is also conducive to physical and mental health. Death rates are lower for the married than the unmarried in all age brackets [3]. Married people are less likely to have problems with loneliness [4]. Finally, married people are less likely to commit suicide or to be under psychiatric care, either as inpatients or out-patients [5].

While older adults are likely to benefit from being married, current trends in marriage, divorce, and remarriage rates mean that increasing numbers of older Americans will live alone. Census figures show that, in 1986, 1.68 million men and 6.64 million women over the age of sixty-five lived alone [6].

These considerations raise the question of what factors might be involved in those marriages that succeed over the long term. What holds people together in a marital relationship that is both stable and satisfying? It is, of course, necessary to have both stability and satisfaction in order to derive the benefits noted above. But as Cuber and Haroff pointed out in their study of over 400 married people [7], some people remain in a marriage that is "devitalized" and some even refuse to leave one that is "conflict-habituated." Thus, a marriage that is stable is not necessarily satisfying.

Studies on marital satisfaction have identified a number of factors important to that satisfaction, including such things as effective communication patterns [8], perceived equity in the relationship [9], and a long rather than very brief courtship period so that the couple know each other well and are subject to fewer surprises after the ceremony [10].

There have been few studies that directly examine long-term marriages to identify the variables that may account for both stability and satisfaction, however. Sporakowski and Hughston reported a study of forty couples who had been married for fifty years [11]. They found that the long-term couples were similar to couples who are satisfied at earlier stages of marriage—they scored high on the Locke-Wallace scale of marital satisfaction and tended to agree in their perceptions of the relationship. Roberts surveyed fifty-five couples who had been married an average of 55.5 years [12]. He did not measure satisfaction, but the couples indicated that their enduring relationship was based on their commitment to each other, their companionship, and qualities of caring. Mudd and Taubin reported a longitudinal study of fifty-nine families over a twenty-year period [13]. Such things as commitment, altruism, egalitarianism, and affection characterized the couples that were still together.

Apart from the few studies noted, the great bulk of the research has been on variables that disrupt marriages; there is little on those that contribute to an enduring and satisfying union [14]. Lauer and Lauer studied 351 couples who had been married fifteen years or more [15]. The median years of marriage of the couples in their sample was 25.5 years. Their respondents indicated that such factors as viewing the spouse as a best friend, liking the spouse as a person, and being committed to the spouse were most often mentioned as factors holding the marriage together. The present study raises the question of whether the same factors are important among those who are at least sixty-five years of age and who have been married at least forty-five years. What do they see as the most important factors in the stability and satisfaction of their relationship?

METHOD

One hundred couples were recruited from retirement communities in California, New York, Florida, Pennsylvania, Arizona, Illinois, Oregon and Nebraska. The couples had been married from forty-five to sixty-four years, with a median length of 54.5 years. All were ambulatory. Six of the couples were childless. The rest had between one and six children. Ninety-seven percent of the couples had some kind of religious affiliation; 69 percent were Protestant, 7.5 percent were Roman Catholic, 7.0 percent were Jewish, and the rest were distributed among various kinds of religious groups. More than half said they attend religious services at least once a week. The couples were mainly upper-middle class, with 74 percent having at least some college education and 84 percent reporting annual incomes over $20,000.

To measure marital satisfaction, we used the same questionnaire employed in the Lauer and Lauer study [14]. Their questionnaire incorporated the Dyadic Adjustment Scale [16] as the first thirty-two items. The DAS was built on the LockeWallace scale and has become one of the more widely used measures of marital satisfaction. The scale's items tap into the factors of consensus, satisfaction, cohesion, and expression of affection. Based on their experience with long-term marriages, Lauer and Lauer [14] added seven Likert-type questions on attitudes toward the spouse (appreciating spouse's achievements; viewing spouse as best friend; liking spouse as a person; and believing that spouse has grown more interesting over time) and toward marriage (viewing marriage as a long-term commitment, a sacred obligation, and an important factor in societal stability). Finally, they used open-ended questions that asked the respondents to indicate which of the previous thirty-nine items were most important in explaining the stability of their own marriage; to graph their satisfaction with the marriage over time, and explain high and low points in the graph; to describe how each spouse had changed over time; and how they handled problems and conflict.

Following the procedure of Lauer and Lauer [14], husbands and wives were given the questionnaires separately. In order to compare the results of the two studies, we tabulated the proportion of those who perceived agreement with their spouses on the various items in the questionnaire. We also tabulated the frequency with which the thirty-nine items were named in order to ascertain which of the variables were perceived by those in long-term marriages to be most important in explaining the stability of satisfying unions.

RESULTS

Since the benefits of marriage depend upon the quality of the relationship, we first looked at how many of the respondents indicated that their marriage was a happy one. Lauer and Lauer reported that 300, or 85.5 percent, of their couples were happy [15]. In the rest, one or both partners indicated some degree of unhappiness. In the present study, 91.5 percent of the respondents said that they were happy, very happy, or extremely happy with their marriages. Thus, they had the kind of marriages that lasted and that were gratifying to them.

The respondents did acknowledge high and low points in their marriages. Most of the graphs showed a tendency for increasing satisfaction over time but with fluctuations (many of which followed the well-known dip during the child-rearing years).

In the following results, the comparable figures from the Lauer and Lauer study (for those couples happily married) are shown in brackets. On fifteen items, 78 percent [73.4%] of the respondents said they always or almost always agree on:

family finances, matters of recreation, religious matters, demonstrations of affection, friends, sexual relations, proper behavior, philosophy of life, ways of dealing with in-laws, aims and goals in life, amount of time spent together, making major decisions, household tasks, leisure, and career decisions. Eighty-six percent [85.1%] said that they confide in their mates all or most of the time, and 87 percent [98%] said they kiss their spouse every day or almost every day. Eighty percent [73.6%] said they laugh together once a day or more. Interestingly, 87 percent [70.9%] said that sex caused no problem or difference of opinion in the "last few weeks." While true for only a small percentage, and a much smaller percentage than for younger couples, sex continues to cause some problems after forty-five years or more of marriage.

As far as attitudes toward the spouse are concerned, 98.5 percent [98.2%] said they like their spouse as a person (the rest were neutral; not a single person in a satisfying marriage in either study disagreed with the statement), and 94.5 percent [92.9%] agreed that their spouse is their best friend. About 85 percent of the respondents in both studies also agreed that their mates were more interesting to them now then when they were first married. With regard to attitudes toward marriage, 98.9 percent [98.2%] agreed with the statement, "Marriage is a longterm commitment." About 84 percent in both studies agreed that marriage is a sacred institution.

Finally, when asked about the most important reasons for the success of the marriage, husbands and wives came up with very similar responses in terms of the frequency with which various reasons were mentioned (Table 1). The Spearman

Table 1. Perceived Reasons for Successfull Long-Term Marriages
(Top Ten, Listed in Order of Frequency of Naming)

Husbands	Wives
Mate is best friend	Marriage a long-term commitment
Like mate as person	Like mate as person
Marriage a long-term commitment	Mate is best friend
Marriage a sacred institution	Laugh together frequently
Agree on aims and goals	Agree on aims and goals
Laugh together frequently	Marriage a sacred institution
Proud of mate's achievements	Agree on expression of affection
Mate more interesting now than when first married	Agree on philosophy of life
Engage in outside interests	Proud of mate's achievements
Agree on major decisions	Mate more interesting now than when first married

rank/order correlation for the ten most frequently named reasons was 0.79 ($p < .02$). The rankings are similar to those reported by Lauer and Lauer [15]. The Spearman rank/order correlation between husbands in the two studies was 0.81 ($p < .01$), for wives the correlation was 0.76 ($p < .02$). In other words, the reasons identified as important to stable and satisfying marriages were very similar in the two studies.

DISCUSSION

Clearly, there is a great deal of perceived agreement between husbands and wives in long-term, satisfying marriages. In both the Lauer and Lauer study and the present study, about three-fourths or more of the respondents perceived agreement with their spouses on all items of the Dyadic Adjustment Scale. There is also a good deal of actual agreement, as shown by the similar rankings shown in Table 1. Moreover, it is apparent that men and women tend to value the same kinds of things in long-term marriages. Even if it is true that men and women speak different languages [17], and that it is appropriate to speak of "his" marriage and "her" marriage [18], it is also true that the men and women in this study perceived the same variables as critical for the long-term success of marriage. It is possible, of course, that a somewhat different set of variables might be identified by those in the earlier years of marriage. But for those in long-term unions, there is consensus on the kinds of things that underlie a stable, satisfying marriage.

In essence, then, our respondents indicated that the most important reason for the success of their marriage was that they were involved in an intimate relationship with someone they liked and enjoyed being with. As in the case of the Lauer and Lauer study, the respondents identified attitudes about the spouse and toward marriage as more important to their relationship than the items on the Dyadic Adjustment Scale. The sense of friendship, the enjoyment of being with each other and sharing in various activities, are a most important component of the glue that provides older as well as younger people with a satisfying marital relationship.

The second most important reason perceived by the respondents is commitment. The commitment has a twofold aspect. It is commitment to the partner and to the institution of marriage. Many of the respondents viewed marriage and the marriage vows as sacred, but they also were committed to the partner as a person. As Lauer and Lauer reported in their study, unhappy couples in a long-term relationship are differentiated from happy couples by the fact that the former are committed to the institution but not particularly to the partner [15, p. 51]. Unhappy spouses believe that the relationship should not be broken even though they do not find it to be gratifying. Those in happy marriages, by contrast, were committed to the partner as well as to the institution.

Third, humor was regarded as important to the marriage. In some cases, respondents talked about how they would deliberately look for things to laugh about together. Humor is known to enhance people's well-being; it also enhances the well-being of relationships.

Finally, we have noted that the respondents perceived agreement on a wide variety of issues. In addition, they indicated that agreement on some matters is important to the success of the marriage. Consensus in a marriage is tied up with feelings about the partner. As many social-psychological studies have found, we tend to like people who are similar to us in various ways. It is understandable, then, that the respondents would indicate both a good deal of perceived agreement and a high level of liking for each other. Of course, we do not know whether our couples had homogamous marriages to begin with, or whether they grew more alike over the years. In any case, consensus is as important for older couples as for younger.

We believe that our results may be valid for a considerable portion of the American population, at least for that portion that is reasonably healthy and is not impoverished. While both samples were nonrandom, both the Lauer and Lauer survey and the present study had respondents from various areas of the country. Moreover, the agreement between the two studies is striking. To the extent that the conclusions are generally valid, they suggest the kinds of factors that younger couples need to work on, and older couples need to work to maintain, in order to secure the benefits of a lasting and satisfying marriage.

REFERENCES

1. N. D. Glenn and C. N. Weaver, The Contribution of Marital Happiness to Global Happiness, *Journal of Marriage and the Family, 43,* pp. 161-168, 1981.
2. N. D. Glenn and C. N. Weaver, The Changing Relationship of Marital Status to Reported Happiness, *Journal of Marriage and the Family, 50,* pp. 317-324, 1988.
3. F. E. Kobrin and G. E. Hendershot, Do Family Ties Reduce Mortality? Evidence from the United States, 1966-1968, *Journal of Marriage and the Family, 39,* pp. 737-745, 1977.
4. C. Rubenstein and P. Shaver, *In Search of Intimacy,* Delacorte Press, New York, pp. 90-91, 1982.
5. M. Argyle, The Skills, Rules, and Goals of Relationships, in *The Emerging Field of Personal Relationships,* R. Gilmour and S. Duck (eds.), Lawrence Erlbaum Associates, Hillsdale, New Jersey, p. 33, 1986.
6. U.S. Bureau of Census, *Statistical Abstract of the United States, 1988,* Government Printing Office, Washington, D.C., p. 51, 1988.
7. J. F. Cuber and P. B. Harroff, *The Significant Americans: A Study of Sexual Behavior Among the Affluent,* Appleton-Century, New York, 1965.
8. T. B. Holman and G. W. Brock, Implications for Therapy in the Study of Communication and Marital Quality, *Family Perspective, 20,* pp. 85-94, 1986.
9. B. Davidson, A Test for Equity Theory for Marital Adjustment, *Social Psychology Quarterly, 47,* pp. 36-42, 1984.

10. K. J. Grover, C. S. Russell, W. R. Schumm, and L. A. Paff-Bergen, Mate Selection Processes and Marital Satisfaction, *Family Relations, 34,* pp. 383-386, 1985.

11. M. J. Sporakowski and G. A. Hughston, Prescriptions for Happy Marriage: Adjustments and Satisfactions of Couples Married 50 or More Years, *The Family Coordinator, 27,* pp. 321-327, 1978.

12. W. L. Roberts, Significant Elements in the Relationships of Long-Married Couples, *International Journal of Aging and Human Development, 10,* pp. 265-271, 1979.

13. E. H. Mudd and S. Taubin, Success in Family Living—Does It Last? A Twenty-Year Follow-Up, *American Journal of Family Therapy, 10,* pp. 59-67, 1982.

14. R. H. Lauer and J. C. Lauer, Factors in Long-Term Marriages, *Journal of Family Issues, 7,* pp. 382-390, 1986.

15. J. C. Lauer and R. H. Lauer, *'Til Death Do Us Part: How Couples Stay Together,* Haworth Press, New York, 1986.

16. G. B. Spanier, Measuring Dyadic Adjustment: New Scales for Assessing the Quality of Marriage and Other Dyads, *Journal of Marriage and the Family, 38,* pp. 15-25, 1976.

17. C. Gilligan, *In a Different Voice,* Harvard University Press, Cambridge, Massachusetts, 1982.

18. J. Bernard, *The Future of Marriage,* World Publishing, New York, 1972.

Chapter 4

HUSBANDS' AND WIVES' PERCEPTIONS OF MARITAL FAIRNESS ACROSS THE FAMILY LIFE CYCLE

Candida C. Peterson

Marital fairness, or the subjective balance between two spouses' gains and losses, was evaluated by a cross-sectional sample of 134 married Australian men and women representing five phases in the family life cycle: preparental, childbearing, the full house, launching, and the empty nest. Husbands' perceptions of their own marital equity described a U-shaped curve across these phases, with significantly more men feeling equitably treated both initially and after children's departure than during any of the three phases with children in the home. Wives' perceptions, by contrast, showed little variation with life cycle phase. Overall, a slight majority (52%) of husbands and wives perceived their marriages as equitable. Both sexes were inclined to agree, however, that whenever deviations from strict marital equity arose during family life, these were most likely to overbenefit husbands and to underbenefit wives. Results are discussed in relation to 1) equity theory, 2) marital satisfaction research, and 3) Bernard's model of the intrinsic sexual inequality of marriage as an institution [1].

Equity theory presents a model of couplehood in which husbands and wives negotiate over time and through the domestic upheavals brought about by childbirth, offsprings' adolescence, the empty nest crisis, and so on, to achieve the subjectively fair balance between each spouse's contributions and benefits known as marital equity [2]. A number of empirical studies have tested the relevance of this equity model to specific phases in marriage [3, 4]. In general, the results of these studies are consistent with the theoretical premise that equitable marriages are valued more highly and perceived as more stable by both spouses than are marriages in which the husband, the wife, or both feel unfairly treated. The one previously published study [5] that attempted a life span test of the additional premise by equity theorists that: ". . . all things being equal relationships should become more and more equitable over time" [2, p. 114], yielded little clear support for this idea. In fact, the theoretical prediction of a steady linear increase in marital equity over each successive phase in marriage from courtship through old age [2, p. 123: Figure 4.3] received no empirical support up to the age of seventy. Instead, a majority of the individual ratings by Traupmann and Hatfield's [5] respondent wives under the age of seventy indicated no change at all in marital equity over time. Instead the collective replies indicated that "older women do report that they felt slightly underbenefited from their thirties to their seventies" [5, pp. 99-100]. An increase of equity after age seventy was suggested, though the sample of wives above this age was small ($n = 16$).

While these data did not provide overwhelming support for an incremental model of marital equity over successive stages of family life, further research seems warranted for several reasons. First, as Traupmann and Hatfield themselves pointed out [5], the use of a retrospective reporting method may have introduced motivational, memory, or computational errors into their data, especially given that "intimates may find the calculation of equity-inequity a mind-boggling task" [6, p. 109] even at a single point in the immediate present. Second, the mapping of equity assessments onto the women's chronological age may have masked some of the variation that has been argued theoretically to link not so much with age as with such "crisis" stages in family life as "when the first child arrives, when the children leave home," etc. [2, p. 114]. Third, as the earlier study included wives only, it is possible that husbands' equity perceptions over family life might conform to the incremental model, even if wives' do not. A major aim of the present study was, therefore, to provide a further empirical test of these possibilities.

While a linear increase is one possible relationship between marital equity and passage through successive stages in family life, another possibility is a U-shaped curve. The latter is the pattern that has typically emerged in the numerous studies that have assessed husbands' and wives' marital satisfaction in relation to the family life cycle [7-9]. Marital satisfaction, as a broad subjective index of overall contentment with being married is clearly distinct from equity. The latter simply describes the perceived fairness of spouses' balance of net benefits from marriage. There are at least two reasons to predict that the two constructs could display similar patterns of change across married life, however. For one, equity theorists argue that marital satisfaction requires equity as a precondition [2]. Also, the same life cycle transitions (childbirth, launching, etc.) that have been put forward to explain the U-shaped satisfaction curve are likely to disrupt marital equity, possibly for similar periods of time and with similar eventual outcomes. One main research question asked in this study was "What pattern would emerge when husbands' and wives' perceptions of the equitability of their marriages was plotted over successive phases in married life?" The following three patterns were considered possible.

Pattern 1

A steadily increasing proportion of the husbands and wives will describe their marriages as strictly equitable at each advancing stage through the family life cycle. (This pattern derives from a theoretical prediction by Hatfield et al., [2, p. 123: Figure 4.3].)

Pattern 2

From the preparental, through childbearing, to the full house phases of marriage, the proportions of equitably treated husbands and wives will decrease. After this, equity will increase over subsequent phases to equal the initial phase by the time of the empty nest. (This pattern is drawn as a parallel to the results of empirical studies of marital satisfaction.)

Pattern 3

No significant change in the proportions of equitably treated husbands or wives will emerge over successive phases in family life from pre-to postparenthood. (This pattern is based on the empirical results of Traupmann and Hatfield's retrospective study of wives' global equity perceptions over the life cycle [5].)

A second exploratory research question for this research was whether the two sexes' equity perceptions might differ at any phase(s) in the life cycle. Since no previous study included husbands, no specific directions of difference was forecast.

PARTICIPANTS

A final sample of 134 married Australian adults participated in this research. Participants were chosen from a pool of volunteers recruited by their student friends and relatives. Participants were instructed to complete the questionnaire privately and not to discuss or show their answers to anyone, including their spouse. To safeguard confidentiality, questionnaires were completed anonymously and sent back to the university in a sealed, unmarked envelope. When received, these were culled to exclude respondents who reported: 1) any previous marriage, 2) any current domestic situation other than intact marriage (e.g., divorced, widowed, separated, *de facto*, cohabiting, commuting between households, etc.), 3) having been married for more than ten years with no offspring as yet. Long term childless or cohabiting couples and remarried spouses were excluded largely for the sake of maintaining the present design's uniform match between family and marital life phases. But, in addition to avoiding the phase confounds that would have arisen if, for example, newlywed remarrieds rearing adolescent stepchildren had been sampled, these exclusions also helped prevent the distortion of participants' present equity perceptions by contrast effects or cumulative disappointments built up in former marriages. After these exclusions, the final sample consisted of fifty-nine males and seventy-five females who had been married an average of twenty years, had a mean age of forty-three years of age, and an average of 2.4 children. In addition to the common requirement of currently being in an intact first marriage, the following additional criteria were used to subdivide the sample by family life-cycle stage [7].

Phase 1: *Preparental:* Married ten years or less with no offspring as yet.

Phase 2: *Childbearing:* Has at least one child twelve years or less and no offspring aged thirteen or older.

Phase 3: *Full House:* Eldest child is thirteen years or older, all offspring are still living at home.

Phase 4: *Launching:* One or more grown offspring have moved out of the respondent's household, but at least one child still lives at home.

Phase 5: *Empty Nest:* Respondent has one or more grown children, all of whom now live away from home.

Application of these criteria resulted in five life cycle subgroups of husbands and wives. A summary of the characteristics of each subgroup is included in Table 1.

Table 1. Participants' Characteristics in Each Life Cycle Phase

Characteristics	Phase:				
	Pre-parental	Child-bearing	Full House	Launching	Post-parental
Number of participants	15	27	48	27	17
Percent male	40	41	46	41	53
Mean age	30.33	34.26	44.40	47.27	60.00
(S.D.)	(4.98)	(6.99)	(5.68)	(5.72)	(8.25)
Mean years married	4.53	10.37	20.80	27.65	35.24
(S.D.)	(3.60)	(4.45)	(3.25)	(5.25)	(10.03)
Mean number of children	0	2.04	2.81	3.04	3.18
Mean age of children	N.A.	6.61	16.42	20.38	31.32
Mean number of offspring still living at home	0	2.04	2.81	1.64	0

EQUITY MEASURE

The instrument used to assess perceptions of marital fairness was a variant of the Global Measure of Equity that, developed and validated by Hatfield [6], has been proven comprehensible and meaningful to older married respondents in both the United States [5] and Australia [4]. The instructions and response alternatives read as follows:

Considering your marriage *as a whole*, including everything you gain and lose from it, and also thinking of everything your spouse puts into it and all he/she gains and loses from it, how does your total relationship stack up? (choose *one*):

( ) a) I get a very much better deal than my spouse
( ) b) I get a deal that is quite a bit better than my spouse's
( ) c) I get a somewhat better deal than my spouse
( ) d) I get a slightly better deal than my spouse
( ) e) We both get exactly the same deal, equally good or bad
( ) f) My spouse gets a slightly better deal than I get
( ) g) My spouse gets a somewhat better deal than I get
( ) h) My spouse gets a deal that is quite a bit better than mine
( ) i) My spouse gets a very much better deal than I get.

There were three minor differences between this and Hatfield's original Global Measure [6]. First, we substituted the words "marriage" for "relationship," [6], and "spouse" for "partner," on the basis of piloting indicating the former terms were both clearer and more congenial to older Australian married couples. Second, we added an extra response category to each arm of the scale ("quite a bit better," denoted b) and h) above). The goal of this change was to encourage participants to pinpoint their subjective evaluations of marital fairness as exactly as possible, especially in light of a tendency for some participants from a similar population tested earlier to place their marks either between choices or on two adjacent categories when the original seven-point Global Measure had been used. The third change, specifying that respondents should "choose *one*" response alternative, was introduced for the same reasons.

Scoring followed Hatfield's categorical procedure [6]. The middle point on the response scale [e) above] denoted strict equity, which choices a) through d) describing varying levels of overbenefit, and choices i) through f) corresponding levels of underbenefit. The choice of categorical scoring was made for several reasons. First, it is not theoretically appropriate to quantify the full range of response choices along a single numerical continuum since equity is conceptually a distinct state of strict fairness that is not necessarily subjectively intermediate between overbenefit and underbenefit. Second, the psychometric intervals between overbenefit, equity, and underbenefit have been shown to be varying and unequal [10]. Third, given Traupmann et al.'s conclusion that, "The treatment of equity scores as categorical rather than continuous has been the tradition among equity theorists" [10, p. 472], the ability to compare the present data with previous research was a further justification for continuing the same categorical scoring tradition.

RESULTS

Table 2 shows the numbers and percentages of participants who rated their marriages as strictly equitable E versus those who felt that they either gained relatively more O, or relatively less U, than their spouse did from the marriage. Collapsed across phases, there was no significant difference in the overall frequencies of equity responses by husbands versus wives, $\chi^2 < 1$. The combined life

Table 2. Numbers and Percentages of Equitably and Inequitably Treated Spouses in Each Life Cycle Phase

Equity Status[a]	Males n=59			Females n=75		
	E	O	U	E	O	U
Phase						
1. Preparental						
N:	5	1	0	5	3	1
%:	83	17	0	56	33	11
2. Childbearing						
N:	4	7	0	6	2	8
%:	36	64	0	38	12	50
3. Full House						
N:	11	10	1	15	4	7
%:	50	45	5	58	15	27
4. Launching						
N:	3	5	3	9	0	7
%:	27	45	27	56	0	44
5. Postparental						
N:	8	1	0	4	0	4
%:	99	11	0	50	0	50
6. Total						
N:	31	24	4	39	9	27
%:	52	41	7	52	12	36

[a]E=equity, O=overbenefited, U=underbenefited

phase data, however, did show a significant sex difference in frequencies of E, O, and U responses, χ^2 (2) = 23.2, $p < .001$. Among those perceiving inequity, 86 percent of husbands were overbenefited while 75 percent of wives were underbenefited. In view of this sex difference, husbands' and wives' responses were analyzed separately in relation to individual life cycle phases.

For husbands, the tendency to feel equitably versus inequitably treated (over- and underbenefit combined) was found to vary significantly across the five phases of family life, χ^2 (4) = 11.1, $p < .05$. Inspection of Table 2 reveals that thirteen of the fifteen husbands in the two childfree phases (preparental and postparental) described their relationships as strictly equitable. But during the three intermediate phases of childbearing, full house and launching, less than half (41%) of this sample of husbands perceived themselves as gaining strictly equitably from marriage. In most cases of inequity, the imbalance was perceived as favoring the husband himself, in line with Bernard's model of the sexual inequalities inherent in traditional styles of marriage and childrearing [1]. While the number of husbands in the present sample is small, the U-shaped pattern reflected in their descriptions of the equity of their marriages is in close keeping with the numerous studies of marital disenchantment [1] that have revealed a similar curve when spouses' satisfaction with marriage is plotted against the same sequential phases in family life.

For this sample the U-shaped pattern described changes in marital equity over time only for males. In fact, there was no significant difference across the five phases from pre- to postparenthood in the frequency with which wives reported equity versus inequity, χ^2 (4) = 1.8, $p > .20$. The overall frequency of feelings of equity among wives was also much lower than equity theorists predicted in the case of long term marriage. Indeed, across all five phases of married life, close to half of the women in the present sample rated their marriages as inequitable. Furthermore, and again in contrast to the male group, among the inequitably treated wives those who felt underbenefited outnumbered the overbenefited by three to one. In fact, when gender contrasts were computed for each individual life cycle phase between the categories of underbenefit versus equity and overbenefit combined, significantly more females than males felt underbenefited during childbearing, χ^2 (1) = 7.8, $p < .01$, the full house, χ^2 (1) = 4.3, $p < .05$, and the postparental phase, χ^2 (1) = 5.9, $p < .02$. But there were no significant differences during launching, $\chi^2 < 1$, or the phase before the birth of children, $p > .05$— Fisher's exact test. Likewise, when ratings of overbenefit were correspondingly contrasted with equity plus underbenefit combined, the difference between males and females was statistically significant during childbearing, χ^2 (1) = 7.6, $p < .01$, the full house, χ^2 (1) = 5.2, $p < .05$, and launching, $p < .05$—Fisher's exact test—but not the first or last phases, both $ps > .05$—Fisher's exact test. In other words, the period of greatest difference between husbands' and wives' perceptions of their global balance of marital gain coincided with the years when some or all of the couple's offspring were still living at home. During these phases, the husbands' evaluation of his balance of gain from marriage was found to depart not only from the stricter fairness of his preparental and postparental male counterpart's impressions, but also from wives' collective impressions of their own equity situations. However these data do also indicate that the two sexes are in basic agreement about the overall balance of benefits accruing to husband versus wife in cases where marriage becomes inequitable during the childrearing years. Both males and females are inclined to view wives as gaining less, and men more, than their equitable share from any imbalances that happen to arise during the parental phases of marriage.

Studies of marital satisfaction have sometimes suggested that family size depresses marital happiness over and above any influences due to marital duration. To test such a notion in relation to equity perceptions, we began by 1) separating husbands from wives (because of the sex differences noted earlier) and 2) eliminating preparental and postparental spouses (who no longer had children at home to influence marital equity). The remaining husbands were then subdivided into those with one, two, or three or more children. When proportions perceiving equity versus inequity (O and U combined) were contrasted, no significant difference emerged, χ^2 (2) = 3.69, $p > .10$. A similar analysis for wives revealed a significant difference in perceptions of equity versus inequity as a function of family size, however, χ^2 (2) = 8.43, $p < .05$. Inspection of the frequency data showed that during the childbearing, rearing and launching stages, wives with larger families were the ones most likely to experience equity. In fact, 67 percent of the mothers of three or more children reported strictly equitable marriages as compared with only 29 percent of the mothers of two, and 33 percent of those with one child. Since a majority of the inequitably treated mothers of one (100%), two (67%), or three or more (80%) children were experiencing underbenefit, the disproportionately greater experience of equity in large households is conceptually opposite to that postulated in the case of marital satisfaction, where a large family was seen to detract from spouses' happiness with marriage.

Numbers of women in the childbearing and launching subdivisions of the present sample were too small to justify separate analyses by family size. Among the present group of twenty-six wives in the full house phase, however, fourteen had only one or two children while twelve had three or more, enabling a within-phase comparison. Results showed that 83 percent of full house wives with families as large as three were experiencing marital equity, as compared with only 36 percent of those with smaller families. Again, this difference was found to be statistically significant, χ^2 (1) = 6.01, $p < .05$.

DISCUSSION

When compared with the collective results of the many studies of marital satisfaction that have sampled husbands and wives at successive phases in the family life cycle, the present pattern of global ratings of marital equity by a cross-sectional sample of spouses across similar life phases reveals both similarities and differences. Perhaps the most striking similarity is the parallel between the U-shaped pattern of the present sample of husbands' perceptions of their marital equity over family life stages and a similarly U-shaped course of marital happiness from the newlywed period to empty nest [7]. Such a parallel is also consistent with the postulate by equity theorists that states both overbenefit and underbenefit are more distressing than strict equity, so a sense of being equitably treated by marriage is a precondition for optimal subjective marital enjoyment [2].

However, while the marital satisfaction literature indicates that wives' life cycle changes closely match husbands' [7] this was not true of the equity perceptions sampled here. Instead, wives' equity ratings showed no important changes across family life phases. Overall, a slight majority of women (52%) described their marriages as strictly equitable, while most of the remainder were experiencing underbenefit. Conversely, since most of the inequitably treated husbands reported overbenefit, these data testified to a basic agreement between the sexes that the male was most likely to gain and the female to lose from any fairness imbalances arising during married life.

The present Australian women's concurrent equity reports were in close keeping with those of Traupmann and Hatfield's earlier retrospective sample of American wives, which indicated that ". . . older women do report that they felt slightly underbenefit from their thirties to their seventies" [5, p. 100]. Taken in conjunction with theirs, the present findings also help to shed light on two of the ". . . intriguing and . . . unanswerable questions" [5, p. 100] raised by Traupmann and Hatfield. First, their fear that artifacts of the retrospective method of assessing marital equity may have limited their data appears unwarranted. The close similarity between our wives' replies and Traupmann and Hatfield's suggests that theirs was not biased either by women's inability to recall the distant past nor by any unwillingness to admit to ongoing marital injustices. Furthermore, these similarities also show that wives' experiences of marital equity appear to transcend any cultural contrasts between marriage patterns or attitudes in Australia versus the United States. Second, since Traupmann and Hatfield had not included husbands in their sample [5], they lacked the data to test their postulate, derived from Bernard's theory that after the dating period ". . . it is men who have the advantage, who reap the most benefits from their marriages" [1, p. 100]. Responses by the present group of husbands to the Global Measure of equity lends empirical support to this hypothesis. Throughout the marital life cycle, nine out of every ten of the married men we questioned felt either equitably treated or overbenefited by marriage. Their significantly greater overbenefit during the family-occupied stages of married life of both pre- and postparental husbands and the underbenefit of wives at corresponding stages is in keeping with Bernard's notion that traditional marriage as an institution is sexually unequal, offering greater benefits overall to the male than to the female, especially when combined with childrearing [1]. However, the present finding that during the childbearing, full house and launching phases, greater marital equity was experienced by mothers of three or more offspring than by wives with smaller families, is difficult to rationalize with Bernard's theory. Nor is there any obvious alternative explanation for this surprising result.

Further study of husbands' and wives' perceptions of marital equity across the life course is therefore clearly needed, not only to shed light on this puzzling apparent link between family size and wives' equity, but also to confirm that our other findings were not biased by the relatively small size and cross-sectional nature of our sample nor by any of this study's other limitations. A longitudinal replication would be especially desirable in order to clarify the extent to which cohort differences in underlying beliefs and expectations about marriage may have contributed to the patterns that emerged in this study when cross-sectional samples from successive family life phases were considered.

The present data, though suggestive, should be treated cautiously pending replication with larger samples of husbands and wives. Furthermore, the present sample was not completely representative of the married adult population both because respondents were all volunteers and as a result of the exclusion of remarried and childless spouses. These latter exclusions were deliberate, as we wished to explore the possibility of life cycle contrasts between spouses all sharing the common experience of a single, traditionally timetabled, parental marriage. It is hoped that future studies will extend sampling to include random selection, remarried spouses and couples in nontraditional marriages. These extensions are desirable both for the sake of representative generalizability and also in order to help clarify the underlying basis for the intriguing links suggested in this exploratory study between life-cycle phase, gender, family size and marital equity.

REFERENCES

1. J. Bernard, *The Future of Marriage*, World, New York, 1972.
2. E. Hatfield, M. K. Utne, and J. Traupmann, Equity Theory and Intimate Relationships, in *Social Exchange in Developing Relationships,* R. L. Burgess and T. L. Huston (eds.), Academic Press, New York, 1979.
3. E. Hatfield, D. Greenburger, J. Traupmann, and P. Lambert, Equity and Sexual Satisfaction in Recently Married Couples, *Journal of Sex Research, 18,* pp. 18-32, 1982.
4. C. C. Peterson and J. L. Peterson, Older Men's and Women's Relationships with Adult Kin: How Equitable Are They? *International Journal of Aging and Human Development, 27*:3, pp. 221-231, 1988.
5. J. Traupmann and E. Hatfield, How Important is Marital Fairness Over the Lifespan? *International Journal of Aging and Human Development, 17*:2, pp. 89-101, 1983.
6. E. Hatfield, *Global Measure*, unpublished manuscript from University of Wisconsin, Madison, 1978.

7. S. A. Anderson, C. S. Russell, and W. R. Schumm, Perceived Marital Quality and Family Life-Cycle Categories: A Further Analysis, *Journal of Marriage and the Family, 46*, pp. 127-139, 1983.

8. B. Rollins and K. Cannon, Marital Satisfaction Over the Family Life Cycle, *Journal of Marriage and the Family, 36*, pp. 271-283, 1974.

9. R. Smart and M. Smart, Recalled, Present and Predicted Marital Satisfaction, *Journal of Marriage and the Family, 32,* pp. 20-27, 1970.

10. J. Traupmann, R. Petersen, M. Utne, and E. Hatfield, Measuring Equity in Intimate Relationships, *Applied Psychological Measurement, 5*, pp. 467-480, 1981.

Chapter 5

AGING COUPLES AND DISABILITY MANAGEMENT

A. Grand
A. Grand-Filaire
and
J. Pous

Numerous studies by both epidemiologists and sociologists have revealed the varying nature of aging. They have put into question the oversimplified image of the aging process as being divided into two phases: an active phase characterized by a high level of consumption—travel, vacations, and cultural activities [1], followed by a regressive phase dominated by the loss of autonomy [2].

This chronological division has little to do with reality. It conceals the fact that the aging process is extremely heterogeneous, multifactorial, and reveals to a marked degree all possible social divisions. Health indicators, notably, bring out the inequality that can be observed in this group as regards illness and death [3]. Economic indicators also show that disparities in income grow stronger after retirement [4].

Old age should not therefore be considered as a stereotyped process divided systematically into two rigid phases. It is rather the result of a whole life history, and the manner of its unfolding must necessarily be analyzed in the light of this history [5].

A decisive stage in the aging process occurs when disabilities arise. The way these disabilities are dealt with has an important effect on the future of the elderly. Warren [6] and Donaldson [7] showed that it is closely related to mortality. The results of a longitudinal survey carried out in southwest France confirmed that disability is one of the most predictive factors of mortality in a rural population [8]. Its age-adjusted relative risk was 5.3 while reported morbidity (as measured by the number of reported diseases) was unrelated to any predictions about mortality. This study has confirmed the key role played by disability on elderly people's longevity.

The more handicapped an old person is, the less control he has over the effective management of his disabilities. As his freedom of action diminishes his entourage becomes more important [9].

The entourage is therefore vital for understanding what happens when disability occurs or becomes worse. The key person in the entourage is, of course, the partner. The partner plays an essential role in assuming responsibility for the handicapped old person. The limits in assuming this role are determined by personal factors such as the state of health, the autonomy, the level of activities, etc. These factors have already been analyzed and the existing literature on this subject is rich in studies focused on the specific features of the partner [10]. Most of them do not take into account an essential determining factor, which is the nature of the relationship between the partners at the moment when the handicap occurs. Hence, rather than focusing on the partner's individual aptitudes we intend to study the way the couple, as a unit, copes with handicaps that arise.

REVIEW OF THE LITERATURE

The sociology of the family offers a useful theoretical framework for understanding the couple's internal dynamic. Given the diversity of family histories and functionings, sociologists have attempted to draw up various typologies. In a recent study, Kellerhals analyzed the different typologies developed over the last twenty years [12]. He has found that they have been constructed around four fundamental group processes: establishment of internal cohesion, role and task distribution, definition of priorities, and integration in the social environment.

The two first processes: establishment of internal cohesion and role and task distribution, can be used so as to understand better how disability is coped with inside the couple.

Disability usually disturbs the way a couple functions by increasing constraints, but it does not occur in a totally neutral situation. The way the couple was organized before its onset inevitably influences the way it is coped with. In fact the way disability is integrated and managed inside the couple depends on role and task distribution as well as on internal cohesion.

Attempts have been made to systematize the process of internal cohesion by defining the notion of an "unspoken contract" between the partners. There is an "unspoken contract" whenever the observed organization is the result of a strong consensus, whatever this organization may be. Thus, two types of couple can be opposed: the contractual couples on the one hand and the noncontractual couples on the other.

Role and task distribution can also be systematized according to the egalitarian or inegalitarian character of the distribution. Thus the egalitarian couples can be contrasted with the inegalitarian couples. These two concepts developed by the sociology of the family (internal cohesion, role, and task distribution) will be used in our study so as to define different types of couples and to understand how these different types cope with disability.

But in order to fully understand the couple's dynamic, an analysis of its previous trajectory is necessary. The relationship that determines the way disability is dealt with has been built up throughout the whole period of the couple's existence. In this respect the understanding of the couple's history is fundamental for the understanding of its present situation.

This analysis, which takes into account the trajectories and life histories of both members of the couple, can be related to the sociological concept of socialization.

Socialization is the process whereby the individual becomes a social being by means of various long apprenticeships that are specific to him [13]. Thus the couple's trajectory and dynamic result from the confrontation of the socialization processes of both its members. We need, then, to analyze not only the present state of the couple but also the biographical structure that emerges from its trajectory.

The analysis of the couple's reactions to the onset of disability can be enriched by the following theoretical considerations: studies on the organization of medicine and on the treatment of diseases have led to the emergence of the hypothesis that the every day life of hospital patients could be considered as consisting of a negotiated order [14]. Pursuing their research in this direction, the authors were able to demonstrate that, at least in the case of chronic diseases, various negotiation processes were in operation at different levels and at different moments: negotiations about the drawing up of diagnoses, about the forms of treatment (at home/in hospital), about the personal management of symptoms and their treatment and, finally, about obtaining modifications in professional life (working hours, job changes, etc.) [15]. Might not this approach be used in the case of aging? Might it not be possible to hypothesize that the methods and processes of socialization involved in aging could also be considered as forms of negotiation?

The onset of disability brings about an increase of constraints that the two members of the couple will have to deal with. Thus they will have to negotiate a new role and task distribution between them, and this negotiation will be more or less easy according to the profile of the couple.

If it can be supposed that dealing with disability is, at least partially, a negotiated process, what consequences can be drawn from the methodological point of view? Commenting on research in this field, I. Baszanger notes that many reports fall into the trap of reconstituting the negotiations from the single point of view of the interviewee without considering the various partners in this negotiation [16]. The spouse is obviously a prime figure in this respect and his or her point of view must systematically be compared to that of the person under study in order to grasp the internal dynamic of the couple at the point when the disability arose. But other partners can be involved in the negotiation (offspring, professionals . . .) and their testimony must also be collected so as to fully understand the dynamic of the disability management.

To sum up, the purpose of the present study is to identify in a population of elderly people different types of couples and to link the resulting typology to the way handicaps are dealt with. Starting from questions arising from research in the field of gerontology, it makes use of the theoretical contribution of various sociological concepts: cohesion of the couple, roles and tasks distribution, socialization, and negotiation, in order to understand the complex interrelations that exist between the internal dynamic of the couple and coping with a handicap.

METHODOLOGY

The Population

The elderly people involved in this study were selected out of a population of 470 individuals aged sixty-five and over. This population was representative of the elderly population of five rural districts in Haute-Garonne (southwest France). Previous data collected by questionnaire in relation to this population enabled us to identify different variables leading to the selection of the present sample [17].

Our choice was guided by a desire to obtain sample coherence on a certain-number of variables such as age, sex, professional category, economic profile, district of origin and especially, in our case, matrimonial status and family situation.

The different disability profiles defined during the previous study that took into account type, seriousness, and duration of the incapacity were also represented. After this selection process, the final population came down to seventy-four old people, forty-three women and thirty-one men, whose age distribution was as follows:

Age Category	65-69	70-74	75-79	80-84	85-89	>90	Total
Men	4	2	10	12	0	3	31
Women	3	5	13	10	9	3	43
Total	7	7	23	22	9	6	74

The average age was 78.4 years for the men and 79.6 years for the women. This relatively advanced average age can be explained by the sampling method that was aimed at selecting old people suffering from disabilities, and these are naturally concentrated among the very old. Distribution according to professional category was also included.

Category	Farm Workers	Manual Workers Clerical Staff	Self-employed (Shopkeepers Tradesmen)	Rural Elite[a]	No Profession	Total
Men	11	10	4	6	0	31
Women	14	10	8	3	8	43
Total	25	20	12	9	8	74

[a]This category includes old people having practiced various professions. The common factor is a much higher educational level than that of the general population.

In this rural milieu the strong presence of farmworkers (both owner-occupiers and laborers) is not surprising. The low percentage of women with "no profession" is due to the fact that in the case of farmworkers and self-employed, the wives often share in the activities of the husbands.

Data Collection

Our qualitative approach consisted of writing a monograph for each old person. This monograph was based on a first interview, the object of which was to:

- collect data enabling us to reconstitute the person's biography, according to the following dimensions: family origin, scholar and professional trajectory, couple and family history, health and functional capacity evolution, disability management (past, present, and future), daily life (housing, activities, sociability . . .)
- identify members of the entourage whose accounts could be relevant to the constitution of the monograph (usually two individuals per old person)

After transcription of the first interview, the monograph was completed by:

- a second interview with the old person in order to fill in the gaps left by the first interview
- one or several interviews with the entourage in order to compare their different accounts with that of the principal interviewee

The Analysis

Each monograph, composed of the registered and transcribed interviews, was analyzed according to a standard grid taking into account the different dimensions previously mentioned. It was then summarized on an index card. Synthesizing the material in this way allowed each researcher to get to know his population better. It also made access to certain types of information much easier for the whole team since the sheer quantity of data collected during the interviews and then set down in the monographs would have been too much for each individual member to come to grips with. In each case, the whole process, from the interviews to the writing of the index card was carried out by the same researcher so as to ensure a certain degree of homogeneity in the processing of each of the seventy-four monographs.

A thematic index was drawn up in order to set forth the dimensions according to which the analysis was to be carried out. Conjugal dynamics was one of these dimensions as well as disability management. Thus it was possible to analyze their interrelation.

The principles of ideal type analysis developed by German sociologists working in the field of illness careers were used to interpret the monographs [18]. Since our corpus was composed of information dealing with the contemporary state of elderly people as well as with their past trajectories (school, working life, marriage), it was both possible and useful to make use of this model of career analysis in order to bring out relevant contrasts in the monographs according to the different dimensions studied. The purpose of this analysis was to define typical profiles of elderly people by confronting disability management with conjugal dynamics.

RESULTS

The object of the study was to identify different profiles of couples and to analyze the capacity of each of them to deal with disability. The identification of the different profiles was made according to the two concepts previously exposed: internal cohesion and role and task distribution.

Concerning internal cohesion, we have confirmed the existence of two opposed types of couple: contractual couples and noncontractual couples.

Contractual couples are characterized by the existence of a strong "unspoken contract" between the partners. This contract leads to an organization that is totally accepted by both partners even if it appears to be extremely inegalitarian to the outside observer. In this category, two subgroups can be distinguished, based on the roles and tasks distribution between the partners. Thus, we can distinguish unilateral advantage contractual couples and mutual advantage contractual couples. In the former, one of the partners, usually the women, assumes responsibility for the greater part of the domestic chores to the advantage of the other partner (usually the man). These couples are characterized by a high degree of rigidity. In the latter, task sharing is more equitable, flexible, and adaptable.

The noncontractual couples are characterized by the absence or the weakness of an "unspoken contract" between the partners. The observed organization pattern can therefore consist of:

- conflicts in cases where a dominating relationship prevails, these conflicts being provoked by the resentment of the dominated partner who is emotionally more dependent

- a "soft consensus" in cases of couples composed of two "individualists." Each of the partners pursues his or her own life dynamic, the couple as such being far less important than the separate development of each of its members. In these cases we can speak of associative couples [19].

Typology

Seventy-four elderly people (43 women and 31 men) were each the subject of a monograph. Seventy-three out of the seventy-four lived or had lived as a member of a married couple. When our study was carried out (1988), thirty-nine interviewees were members of an existing couple. Twenty-five were widows or widowers. In the latter case, it was still possible to have access to the dynamics of the couple they had previously been part of.

The typology concerns a population of sixty-four people corresponding to sixty-two couples, since, in two cases, both members of the couple were the object of a monograph.

Ten interviewees were not able to be classified according to the different types elaborated. Among these ten can be found the only single person of the sample, five widows and four widowers. In these cases, the death of the partner had occurred before 1945, hence the dynamics of the couple were no longer perceptible. In most cases, they have reconstituted their social support and the management of their disabilities can only be studied in relation to this support (notably children and siblings).

As previously mentioned, we studied coping with everyday life: role and task distribution, negotiation between the partners, before, during, and after the onset of disability, for each type of couple presented.

Noncontractual Couples

No "unspoken contract" seems to exist between the partners. Two subgroups can be observed:

Noncontractual couples composed of two "individualists" (associative model)

Five out of the sixty-four interviewees fall into this category. All of them are widows. The history of their married life displays no joint project. Four of the five marriages were arranged or were the result of a reasoned choice. Marriage was not a key stage in the itinerary of these interviewees, each of whom developed a personal dynamic usually centered on a professional occupation that constituted the principle structure in their life.

The continuing existence of the couple depends on the compatibility between the personal strategies of each of the partners. When they are compatible, the "individualists" remain united. In the opposite case separation occurs.

In all cases, the personal project of each "individualist" is maintained over a long period. Its termination marks a greater rupture than widowhood, which does not appear to be a destabilizing life event. When the key activity is reduced or stopped, the replacement activities that are introduced belong usually to the same domain as the former. Most of the interviewees of this group maintain a high level of activity and a strong extra-familial social life. How, then, are illness and disability coped with by this type?

All the interviewees are widows. It is, therefore, not easy to understand how disability was coped with in their couples. It would seem, however, that the emotional autonomy of these "individualists" has lead them, throughout their lives, to manage their health problems themselves. Hence, it is reasonable to assume that, when disability affects one of the two partners, the disabled one will try to maintain his/her autonomy as much as possible. Having recourse to the partner is minimal given the emotional distance between them. On the other hand, the intense social life he or she has developed can lead to help from this strong sociofamilial network.

Disability is therefore coped with, as far as possible, by the individualist himself in his desire for independence. When his independence is threatened, he has recourse to a wide sociofamilial network, in which the partner will only have a marginal role to play.

Noncontractual couples characterized by the existence of a dominating relationship: "the conflictuals"
This type includes fourteen interviewees:

- six "dominated": four widows, one widower, one woman living in a couple.
- eight "dominators": three widows, one widower, one woman and three men living as a member of couples.

The dominated:
Five out of six of these are women, in the majority from a farming background. Their itinerary is characterized by a total absence of control over their lives. They have moved from the authority of their parents to that of their husbands without any possibility of choice and have experienced the most negative aspects of the situation of women in farming: hard physical labor (rewarded by a minimal retirement pension), tension-ridden cohabitation with parents-in-law, and harsh, authoritarian husbands.

These women sometimes state quite clearly that "if they had their time over again" they would not remarry but, since they were from strict backgrounds, divorce was out of the question.

Four characteristics can be identified in this category:

- a concentration on the home environment, in which only household chores are maintained (mainly cooking)
- an early end to professional activity
- practically no social life outside the family
- frustration expressed as regards life in the couple

When widowhood (or separation) occurs, two trends emerge:

- widowhood does not constitute a rupture. Life continues in cohabitation with the children. The authority exercised by the dead husband (five cases of widowhood concern four women) is transformed into authority exercised by the children. Any yearning for independence is made totally impossible by cohabiting with the children. This is even more the case with female farmworkers who only receive an extremely modest retirement pension (approximately 32,000 francs per year). Moreover, in many cases, the transfer of property has been managed by the dead husband to the detriment of his wife.
- widowhood constitutes a positive rupture. The dominated individual recovers a certain degree of independence and autonomy.

To sum up, this category consists mainly of women of farming background with little latitude in any aspect of their lives. Widowhood either continues this state of affairs (the children replacing the husband as figures of authority) or brings about a positive rupture which allows the old person to find a degree of freedom and autonomy (facilitated by not living with children).

The dominating:
Three widows, one widower, one female and three males living in couples.
Two categories can be observed:

- The first one shows resemblance to the "individualists." They display most of the characteristics present in the "individualist" profile we have already described:
  - They have generally given a lot of energy to their professional life. But unlike the individualists, they have forced their partners to bow to its constraints.
  - They keep up a high rate of activities.
  - Their extrafamilial social life is considerable.
  - These "individualistic" dominating partners are usually autonomous in their lifestyle. Whereas their partners had started off with plans and projects for them as couples, they managed their own personal life dynamics. This type of couple, bringing together "individualism" and domination, is

characterized by the presence of a strong distortion between the partners, one of whom is "left behind" and suffers from emotional frustration.

• The second category among the dominating is made up of "dominators."

They are different from the "individualists" both in their attitude to their own past life and in their extrafamilial social life. Unlike the "individualists" who are usually satisfied with their past life, the "dominators" display a certain amount of dissatisfaction. Their extrafamilial social life is generally underdeveloped. More often than not, they are thrown back on home life and their relationships with the outside world are conflictual. They exert a considerable degree of tyranny over their entourage through their demands and complaints (over their partner in the first place, then after his or her death, over the son or daughter who offers support).

For them, widowhood is not a life event likely to set off another dynamic. The feeling of dissatisfaction persists beyond the death of the partner. It influences negatively the relationship with the person who is looking after them (usually an offspring). The "dominators" are thus characterized by an extremely conflictual relationship within their own couple and a familial and extrafamilial social life that makes all relationships with any source of support unlikely.

Coping with disability in the dominating-dominated "conflictual" couples varies according to which partner is affected. When it is the dominated, the other partner is hardly called upon since this would be in open contradiction with the dynamic of their couple. Finding someone to look after him or her is therefore a big problem. When, however, it is the dominating member who is affected, the dominated partner usually takes charge of things efficiently. This state of affairs corresponds logically to the inegalitarian dynamic of the relationship between the partners and, in addition, it may also offer the possibility for the dominated partner to take a form of revenge over the dominator.

Thus, coping with disability inside the couple is much more likely when disability strikes the dominating partner. When widowhood arises, the situation of the dominated partner is much better since the type of relationship he or she has established with the entourage and notably with offspring makes the support much easier.

Contractual Couples

In this category, there are two forms of contract: the unilateral contract that exists to the sole advantage of one partner and the mutually advantageous contract.

Unilateral contractual couples

Six interviewees in our sample correspond to this type: two widows and four married men. These couples are made up of a "beneficiary" and a "provider." All six interviewees are "beneficiaries." The accounts of their "providers" were also obtained and thus constitute the other side to their monographs. The way these couples function can be summarized as follows: the beneficiary relies almost totally on the provider who, according to an implicit contract, takes responsibility for everyday life.

Four characteristics can be associated with this group of beneficiaries:

- Most of them have benefitted from an inheritance at a relatively young age.
- Their professional dynamic is not particularly emphasized. They display no signs of trying to achieve upward social mobility. They rely to a great extent on their partner.
- They gave up their professional activities relatively early, justifying this decision through health problems.
- On retiring, these beneficiaries take up no further activity apart from pastimes and entertainment.

The provider's accounts of themselves give the following profile:

- They have often taken charge of one or several members of their family in the past. This responsibility has often been extremely heavy, both in the type of care provided and in its duration.
- The way they assume their role as providers depends on whether they manage to maintain a margin of autonomy in their lives. Thus, in spite of taking charge of everyday life, which often includes helping offspring, the provider can apparently tolerate this situation without difficulty by developing an activity that gives him or her a degree of autonomy.
- They often express anxiety about the future and about who will look after them when the need arises.

These extremely inegalitarian couples can be defined as contractual because of the high degree of cohesion between the partners. The provider's role helps the other to live according to a hedonistic model. Although the beneficiary's orientation is egocentric, he is clearly differentiated from the "individualist." The latter manages his life actively and generally looks after himself. The "beneficiary" offloads constraints on to his partner. A real degree of intimacy can be observed in the couple. If the beneficiary is individualistic, it is not out of a need to manage his life autonomously, rather it takes the form of passive resistance (justified by health problems) in the face of the demands of everyday life.

Management of disability depends very much on which partner is affected. The beneficiary is usually cared for unhesitatingly by his partner whereas the opposite is far from being the case.

There are no cases of disabled providers in our sample (nor of any who see themselves as such). Nevertheless, the anxiety that they manifest, when the possibility of incapacity is mentioned, clearly shows their lack of confidence in the capacity of their partner to take care of them. The pressure exerted by the "beneficiaries" on their "provider" partners usually takes the form of a dramatization of their health discourse with the object of obtaining more and more attention from their partners. On the contrary, they often play down the health problems of the "providers" and go so far as to deny them totally, if they run the risk of appearing more serious than their own.

If widowhood occurs, the "beneficiary" will seek out another "provider" in his entourage. Thus when disability strikes the beneficiary, it will be easily coped with because it inscribes itself in the inegalitarian nature of the couple's relationships. On the contrary, when the "provider" is affected the support is impossible, making of the "provider" the vulnerable member of this kind of couple.

Mutually advantageous contractual couples

Most of the interviewees fall into this category: thirty-nine out of whom thirty are married (13 women and 17 men), eight widows and one widower.

The notion of a tacit contract of mutual assistance between the partners appears clearly. In most cases, this contract predates the onset of old age, having formed the basis of the couple's dynamic during the whole of their active life. Thus, we can find contracts centered on "upward social mobility," "giving the children a good start in life," and "family solidarity." It can also consist of formal contracts drawn up by a notary in which the aging couple, in agreement with their children, settle the inheritance and the way they themselves will be looked after at a later stage.

Two broad categories can be defined:

- *Couples forming part of an extended family and taking part in the dynamics of this family*:

Here we find the traditional farming family, owner occupiers, with several generations working on the same property. The couple's relationship appears to be submerged in this family dynamic. The group's life project is organized around the work on the farm. These "complex" families are, according to H. Le Bras, particularly numerous in southwest France [20]. In this category, we also find certain shopkeepers who run their businesses on family lines. In these cases, we can observe a continuity between the generations centered on the family business.

In both cases, the couple's relationship takes second place behind the larger relationships of the family group. When widowhood occurs, there is no real fracture. The surviving partner continues to be looked after inside the family.

- *Couples who cope together*:

"Coping together" can include various situations according to the socioprofessional status. Nevertheless, an "unspoken contract" exists between the partners implying mutual help when incapacity arises and coping together with the difficulties. "Coping together" can be related to two types of project: survival or professional career.

• The survival project corresponds to those couples who started off with serious economic, social, or health disadvantages and who were determined to break out of them.

This is the case with couples from farming backgrounds who owned no (or little) land. Working in agriculture implied a life of hard toil in which the husband and wife coped together, all the more so as they often had to leave the parental home.

This is also the case with immigrants who, in their life histories, insist on the project of "earning their bread," working hard to "get ahead." Achieving these objectives depended, above all, on the couple's relationship.

The disadvantage can also be connected to health. "Coping together," in this case, is based on the determination of the couple to remain autonomous, often in spite of long-standing disabilities in one of the partners.

• The professional career project concerns couples whose starting point was more favorable. They have put into practice a strategy of upward social mobility, often involving a high degree of geographical mobility. These couples display a great capacity for adaptation, even in the face of traumatic life events (illnesses and the death of children, in particular).

Three common characteristics are present in these diverse situations:

• Negotiation about tasks. This takes the form of a redistribution of constraints according to the disabilities of each of the partners leading to the sharing of activities formerly carried out exclusively by one of the partners. This is the case with household tasks, usually the women's domain, and which are, at least partially, redistributed when the wife is unable to carry them out.

• The desire to remain together in the home. The couples are attached to their place of residence and to their independence. Relationships with other members of the family, especially children, are usually close but there is also the desire to "manage by themselves" and to deal with their difficulties inside the couple. This need for independence from the rest of the family can lead to calling upon services providing home help when the couple can no longer cope. However, this mutual assistance can have its limits. This occurs when the supporting partner has to take care of another person (notably a relative). Coping with two disabilities at the same time constitutes a critical situation for the supporting partner who has to choose between the two cases. This is also the case when the supporting partner's own situation deteriorates to such an extent that he or she can no longer look after the dependent partner.

• When widowhood occurs, it is obvious that it has an extremely destabilizing effect on these close-knit couples. This is all the more the case when:
  • widowhood is late
  • the disability of the surviving partner is serious
  • the care was previously given by the deceased partner
  • the emotional relationship was strong

In these cases, various types of reaction can be observed, going from total recovery when none of the above conditions is present to a state of complete vulnerability.

Satisfaction with the past is usually expressed by couples of this type. This is probably because the couple's solidarity in the face of life's difficulties has made coping with them easier. The positive nature of the couple's relationship must also play its part in their feelings of satisfaction. It was also observed that relationships with offspring are better in this group than in the others. In profiles of this type, coping with disability is at its most efficient, being integrated fully into the couple's dynamic.

DISCUSSION

The notion of an "unspoken contract" between the partners enables us to understand various phenomena arising when disability occurs.

• Cases where there is no contract: "associative" or "conflictual" couples. The disability is:

- coped with autonomously by each partner in the "associative" couples.
- coped with diversely in "conflictual" couples, depending on the affected partner:
  - if the latter is the dominant one, the dominated partner will assume responsibility and may even derive a degree of satisfaction from the new balance of power
  - if he is the dominated one, the dominant partner will, in most cases, assume no responsibility, and recourse to the informal or formal solidarity network will be necessary.

• Cases where there is a contract:

- if this is unilateral, the disability will be well coped with if it fits in with the internal dynamic of the couple. The way responsibility is assumed will very much depend on the affected partner:
  - if the latter is the "beneficiary," this will be taken on "naturally" by the "provider"
  - if the "provider" is the affected partner, recourse to the formal and informal solidarity network will be necessary because of the shortcomings of the partner
- When there is a mutually advantageous contract, the disability is totally taken in hand by the couple, whichever partner is affected. This can lead to each partner using the other as a "crutch" and thus keep up their conjugal independence even in extreme situations.

As previously mentioned, this typology can be integrated into the perspective defined by Kellerhalls which explores the cohesion and the role and task distribution of the family group [21]. The cohesion of the couple depends on the existence of an "unspoken contract" of varying strength and the roles and tasks distribution is based on two types of power relationship: egalitarian in the cases of the mutually advantageous contracts and the associative couples, inegalitarian in the cases of the one-sided contracts and the conflictual couples.

However, the types defined in this study must be considered as ideal types [18]. Thus, they are not rigid. Certain couples clearly correspond to one particular type. Others display aspects of several different types at one and the same time. Hence, a continuum can be observed between the total absence of an "unspoken contract" and the existence of an extremely solid one as well as between an extremely inegalitarian balance of power and an egalitarian one.

Each couple can be situated along these two axes and the ideal types that we have described represent, in fact, the four most extreme cases we have observed.

egalitarian balance of power

associative couples

mutually advantageous contractual couples

no "unspoken contract"

"unspoken contract"

conflictual couples

unilateral contractual couples

inegalitarian balance of power

Several limits must be mentioned in this research:

• The first limit concerns the definition of the population of seventy-four elderly individuals whose monographs were the material of the analysis. Contrarily to the population of 470 elderly persons from which it was taken, this sample of seventy-four individuals cannot be considered as representative of the elderly population of the rural area concerned by the study. This sample in fact results from a reasoned choice taking into account the necessary balance between the variables previously mentioned: age, sex, professional category, family situation, level of disability. Thus our results cannot be projected onto the general population. However, this was not our purpose. This study was mainly interested in the processes, in the mechanisms explaining the different ways of dealing with disability in the couple. Thus the statistical representativity of the sample was not necessary. We were interested in taking into account the greatest variety of situations so as not to miss the most important ones. That is why the figures given in the results are just an indication. A more extensive survey would be necessary to check the validity of our findings on a bigger sample and to quantify the profiles observed.

• The second limit concerns the way data were collected. Since the research was carried out by means of personal interviews about individual life histories, the resulting typology is based on discourses. These discourses can be suspected of being "subjective" and thus not faithfully expressing reality. The interviewee may have forgotten important information. He can also conceal or alter this information in a conscious or unconscious attempt to reconstruct his history. However, by collecting the points of view of the partner and the wider entourage (offspring, professionals . . .), we were able to adjust the interviewee's testimony and thus approximate to the truth. In this respect, the better way to apprehend the reality would certainly be to carry out observations enabling the inquirer to analyze the couple's dynamics in its daily life.

• The third limit concerns the data analysis and particularly the construction of the typology. Defining typologies in the sociology of family interactions leads to several problems analyzed by Kellerhals and Troutot, among which is the generally static nature of the approaches developed so far [22]. "Establishing how and by means of what internal and external influences a family group moves from one mode of functioning to another and through what transition crises has only been rarely attempted."

The discourse of our interviewees is above all concerned with contemporary issues and it has been difficult to locate possible evolutionary processes in the functioning of the couples. Thus the resulting typology can be suspected of just being a snapshot of the situation at the moment of the study. The lack of longitudinal perspective could undermine the understanding of the evolution process. For instance one can imagine that the same couple can move from one type to another during its history, according to various events such as illness, accident, retirement, children's departure. . . . However, our analysis, by attempting to reconstitute the life histories of the elderly people, has enabled us to pinpoint certain "transition crises" and notably those brought on by the onset of disability in one of the members of the couple.

The only way to fully comprehend the evolution process would be to carry out a longitudinal survey enabling the observer to follow up the couple during its whole history. Such methodology is too heavy to be implemented but one can imagine carrying out several cross-sectional studies on the same population so as to perceive at least partially the evolution process.

CONCLUSION

This study, despite its limits, enables us to emphasize the importance of taking into account, when analyzing the situation of a disabled old person, not only the physical state of health of the partner (which, of course, affects directly his capacity to help) but also, and especially, the couple's dynamic, which plays a determining role in the way the disabilities of each member are coped with.

Before organizing help for the old person, this dynamic must be analyzed since this is the only way of telling whether the partner is capable of or willing to assume responsibility.

The approach that we have carried out has also enabled us to demonstrate the importance of taking into account the situation of the old person as regards his past life, especially the married part of it. This, it would seem, is an example of the important contribution that the human sciences, especially sociology, can make in the field of health. By placing health problems in their social context, by making them "come alive," they enrich a field dominated by the bio-medical approach. As we have seen, tackling problems of disability is never merely a medical matter. Attention must be given to the entourage of the old person, particularly the partner, otherwise the solutions proposed may be doomed to failure.

REFERENCES

1. R. Lenoir, L'invention du 3éme âge, *Actes de la Recherche en Sciences Sociales*, pp. 26-27, 1979.
2. M. Clark, Cultural Values and Dependency in Later Life, in *Aging and Modernization*, D. Cowgill and L. Holmes, (eds.), Appleton Century Crofts, New York, 1972.
3. D. M. Zuckerman, S. V. Kasl, and A. M. Ostfeld, Psycho-social Predictors of Mortality Among the Elderly Poor, *American Journal of Epidemiology, 119*, pp. 410-423, 1984.
4. X. Gaullier, *La Deuxième Carrière*, Seuil, Paris, 1988.
5. Lalive d'Epinay, *Vieillesse. Situations, Itinéraires et Modes de vie des Personnes Âgées Aujourd'hui*, Georgi, Saint Saphorin, 1983.
6. M. D. Warren and R. Knight, Mortality in Relation to the Functional Capacity of People with Disabilities Living at Home, *Journal of Epidemiology and Community Health, 36*, pp. 220-223, 1982.
7. I. J. Donaldson and C. Jagger, Survival and Functional Capacity: Three Years Follow-up of an Elderly Population in Hospitals and Homes, *Journal of Epidemiology and Community Health, 37*, pp. 176-179, 1983.

8. A. Grand, P. Grosclaude, H. Bocquet, et al., Disability, Psychosocial Factors and Mortality Among the Elderly in a Rural French Population, *Journal of Clinical Epidemiology, 43*:8, pp. 773-782, 1990.

9. E. Corren, J. Tremblay, P. Sherif, and L. Bergeron, Entre le Services Professionnels et les Réseaux Sociaux: les Stratégies D'existence des Personnes Âgées, *Sociologie et Sociétes, 16*:2, 1984.

10. G. Favrot, Vieillir Chez soi: un Idéal pour Tous, une Contrainte pour les Familles, *Prévenir, n°14, 1987.*

11. A. Grand, *Les Réseaux Informels de Soutien de la Personne Âgée*, L'année Gérontologique, Toulouse, Maloine, 1988.

12. J. Kellerhals, *Les Types D'interactions dans la Famille*, L'Année Sociologique, pp. 154-159, 1987.

13. M. Drulhe, Socialization, Situation, Corps: Esquisse d'une Axiomatique, *Cahier du CeRS, 4*, pp. 9-20, 1985.

14. A. L. Strauss, S. Fagerhaugh, R. Bucher, D. Ehrlich, and M. Sabshin, The Hospital and its Negotiated Order, in *The Hospital in Modern Society*, E. Freidson (ed.), Free Press, New York, 1963.

15. A. L. Strauss and B. G. Glaser, Chronic Illness and the Quality of Life, C. V. Mosby Co., Saint Louis, 1965.

16. I. Baszanger, Les Maladies Chroniques et leur ordre Négocié, *Revue Française de Sociologie, 17*:1, 1986.

17. A. Grand, P. Grosclaude, H. Bocquet, et al., Predictive Value of Life Events, Psychosocial Factors and Self-rated Health on Disability in an Elderly Rural French Population, *Social Science and Medicine, 27*, pp. 1337-1342, 1988.

18. L. U. Gerhardt and K. Kirchgässler, Analyse Idéaltypique de Carrières de Patients, *Sciences Sociales et Santé, 5*:1, 1987.

19. G. Menahem, Les Mutations de la Famille et les Modes de Reproduction de la force de Travail, *L'homme et la Société*, n° *51-54*, pp. 63-101, 1979.

20. H. Le Bras, Les Trois France, Jacob, Paris, 1986.

21. J. Kellerhals, Les Formes de l'équité dans les Échanges Familiaux, Analyse d'une structure normative, travaux CETEL, n° 27, Genève, 1986.

22. J. Kellerhals and P. Y. Troutot, Une Construction Interactive de types Familiaux, Actes de la Chaire Quetelet, Louvain-la-Neuve, 1986.

23. A. Grand, A. Grand-Filaire, J. Pous, J. F. Barthe, S. Clément, and M. Drulhe, Modes de Socialisations et Handicaps dans une Population Âgée en Milieu Rural, Rapport de Recherche à l'INSERM et au CTNERHI, Toulouse, 250 pages, 1989.

Section II

A Union Broken

Chapter 6

WIDOWHOOD IN ELDERLY WOMEN: EXPLORING ITS RELATIONSHIP TO COMMUNITY INTEGRATION, HASSLES, STRESS, SOCIAL SUPPORT, AND SOCIAL SUPPORT SEEKING

Julie Pellman

Widowhood is considered to be a highly stressful experience [1]. The widow is no longer an object of love [1]; she loses status [2]; she experiences grief [1, 3, 4]; role changes [5], and social losses [2]; and she loses income [6]. She may experience a lack of community integration, many major hassles, a psychological [7-9] and/or a physical [8-10] stress response, a decline in social support, and she may, therefore, engage in social support-seeking behavior.

The relationship between the adjustment of widows and their integration in their community may be seen as part of an ecosystem. Widowhood brings with it changes not only for the survivor, but also for the community. Widows who are integrated in their community are likely to have strong ties in terms of friendship and/or kinship bonds. If these ties are broken as a result of bereavement, the degree of community integration the widow experiences may decline unless these bonds are reformed or new contacts are made.

Widowhood is a stressful experience that causes the survivor to change her lifestyle and the nature of her social relationships. The widow can no longer identify herself as half a pair. She may avoid the members of her social network or these significant others may withdraw from her. She may feel like a fifth wheel. She may be viewed as a sexual threat and may lack experience in building new bonds, find tension in old social contacts, and experience the loss of former relationships [2]. If the widow begins to restructure her life, she may have a need for new social contacts and information that will assist her to live her life as a single person [11]. Social support-seeking behavior may be important to her at this time. Furthermore, a strong support system may alleviate stress [7, 12 13] and daily hassles.

Lazarus, DeLongis, Folkman, and Gruen [14] discuss eight daily frustrations. Widows may experience hassles in all of these areas. The somatic complaints associated with grief may be seen as health hassles. Inner concern hassles may occur during grief. When her spouse dies, the widow no longer has a person with whom to structure and organize her time [2]. Thus, she may experience time pressure hassles. Loss of income may cause the widow to experience financial responsibility and future security hassles. Widows who start a new career or are for some reason unemployed may experience work hassles. Household hassles may occur due to new or increased responsibilities in the area of household management. Environmental hassles may occur if the widow lacks money for transportation, is unable to drive [6], or is fearful to travel or be alone due to safety concerns [14, 15].

The grief process, stress, and hassles experienced by the widow as she restructures her life may affect her community integration. Her support system, if she has one, may be helpful to her at this time. If the widow successfully copes, she may seek social support and may again become integrated in her community. On the other hand, she may become so stressed by her experiences that she may fail to participate at all and becomes fairly isolated.

In order to conduct this research, the following hypotheses were tested: widows 1) would be less integrated in their community, 2) would experience more daily hassles and would have a higher level of stress than non-widows, but 3) that those widows who were integrated in their community would experience less stress and fewer hassles than those who were not integrated. 4) Social support would prove to be a stress-buffering agent in widowhood. 5) As a result of their loss, widows may have less supportive networks than non-widows and 6) may therefore be more likely than non-widows to seek social support.

METHOD

Participants

This convenience sample consisted of women sixty years of age or older; eighty were widows and eighty were non-widows. Non-widows were women who are single, divorced, or married. Half of the participants attended one of several nutrition sites in Kansas City, Missouri. The other half were obtained through other organizations or through the use of a "truncated snowball" technique. The women who were interviewed at nutrition sites were asked to refer others who they knew who did not eat lunch at a nutrition site. About one-quarter of the non-nutrition site participants were obtained in this manner. The remainder of the non-nutrition site participants were women who participated in various clubs or activities for senior citizens in the Kansas City area.

Within the senior centers, respondents were selected at random and asked to participate. Of the 160 participants, forty were nutrition site widows, forty were non-nutrition site widows, forty were nutrition site non-widows, and forty were non-nutrition site non-widows. The willingness of the administrator at the specific senior center to participate and the location of the center influenced the selection of both the nutrition and non-nutrition sites. An attempt to obtain racial and ethnic diversity also influenced the choice of centers. While the sites were not chosen at random, randomization of participants within sites was done. At each site, respondents were selected at random and asked to participate. No participants were used twice, therefore, many of the individuals at each setting were asked to participate.

Measures

The scales given to the participants operationalized the major variables: widowhood (loss of a spouse), hassles (frustrations of daily living), stress (physiological and psychological reaction to strain), and community integration (which involves availability of a reference group, involvement in formal and informal social activities, and psychological identification with the local area), social support (the emotional and instrumental give and take among individuals), and social support seeking (attempts to obtain information and instrumental and emotional support).

All participants were given the following instruments: the Hassles Scale [15] which has 118 items concerned with daily frustrations and on which scores range from 1 (Somewhat Severe) to 3 (Extremely Severe); the Comprehensive Scale of Stress Assessment, Version II [9] which examines the intensity and frequency of the participants' stressors, their stress resistance resources, and their physical manifestations of stress [16], and which consists of twenty-five items with five response alternatives, in at least half of which the first choice is valued at +4 and the last is 0, while remaining items are scored with the first response valued at 0 and the last at +4 [16]. Community Integration [17] is a measure consisting of ten items concerned with three aspects of community integration: community attitudes and sentiments, local social bonds, and formal and informal organizational contact on which participants receive scores ranging from either 1 to 2 or 1 to 3, with the higher the score indicating a greater level of community integration; the Support Systems of Widows [18] consists of ninety-four items which measure emotional-sentimental support, feeling states, economic, service, and social support. The scale was designed to be administered to widows and modified so that it could be given to the non-widows as well. On the sentimental and feeling state sections, the widows noted on thirteen items which person(s) provided them with emotional support now and when their husbands were alive. The non-widows were asked who currently provides this support. The widows' responses to who provided support when their husbands were alive were scored: husband, other, or no response. The widows' responses to who provided support upon the death of their spouses were scored male, female, indeterminate sex, and no response. The non-widows' responses to their sources of current support were scored; husband or other; Seeking Social Support is one of eight scales from the Ways of Coping Checklist (Revised) [19] which were derived from factor analytic procedures [20]. Each item had four response alternatives: not used (weighted 0), used somewhat (weighted 2), used quite a bit (weighted 5), and used a great deal (weighted 10). Folkman et al. present factor loadings for each item in each scale [20]. The weight given to each question was multiplied by the factor loading for each question. The numbers obtained for all the items on each scale were then added to obtain a total score on that scale.

PROCEDURE

Settings

The nutrition sites selected were located in eight of twenty-six Mid-American Regional Council Senior centers. These centers are funded on the federal level by the Administration on Aging and were established on a community level by the Mid-America Regional Council (MARC) and the MARC Commission on Aging.

Unlike the nutrition sites which serve lunch to the elderly five days per week, organizations in the non-nutrition site category involve attending weekly, bimonthly, or monthly meetings for the purpose of community service, teaching and/or participating in classes and/or discussion groups, and socialization.

The interviews took place at the nutrition site where the participants ate lunch, at the organizations of which the participants were members, or in the participants' homes or other mutually convenient settings of the participants' choice. The interviews lasted about one hour, and all of the interviewing was done by the author.

Statistical Analysis

The research design is a 2 × 2 factorial design. It is quasi-experimental and ex post facto in nature. There are two independent variables, widowhood (2 levels: widowed and not widowed) and setting (2 levels: nutrition site and non-nutrition site). On each of the dependent variables, community integration, stress, hassles, social support, and support seeking, a series of 2 × 2 ANOVAS was conducted. In addition, multiple regression was used to include in the analysis the possible effects of selected background characteristics.

RESULTS

Demographic Characteristics of the Sample

Fifty percent of the participants were widows and 50 percent were not widowed. The widows and non-widows were over sixty years of age (mean = 73.46 years, range = 60-97 years). The majority were white (76.3%). The remainder of the participants were black (20.6%) or of other races (3.1%). Most of the respondents were Protestant (65.1%). The rest were Catholic (20.6%), Reorganized Church of Latter-Day Saints (8.1%), and other religions (6.3%). Fifty-eight percent of the participants had incomes of less than $10,000, 25.6 percent had incomes between $10,000 and $25,000, 10 percent had incomes greater than $25,000, and 10.6 percent did not reveal their income. With reference to education, 30.1 percent had achieved less than a high school diploma, 33.1 percent were high school graduates, 27.5 percent had formal education beyond high school, 3.7 percent had no formal education, and 5.6 percent had a special diploma. Forty-four percent had been white collar workers, 25 percent had been blue collar workers, 14.4 percent had been homemakers, 11.3 percent had been professionals, and 5 percent had been skilled craftspersons.

Results of Statistical Analyses

Table 1 illustrates the results of the ANOVAs. The non-widow group was better integrated than the widow group but this difference was not significant. However, the non-widow, non-nutrition site participants had a significantly higher level of community integration than the other three groups ($F(1,156) = 6.752, p < .010$). There were no significant differences between widows and non-widows across all of the locations in the average amount of daily hassles or stress they experienced. However, nutrition site and non-nutrition site participants irrespective of widow-hood differed significantly in the amount of stress they experienced ($F(1,156) = 14.217, p < .000$): non-nutrition site respondents were less stressed than nutrition site respondents.

Table 1 also shows that non-widows sought more social support than widows ($F(1,156) = 6.081, p < .015$). Non-nutrition site participants sought more social support than nutrition site participants ($F(1,156) = 12.045, p < .001$). The inter-action was marginally significant ($F(1,156) = 3.79, p < .057$). A Newman-Keuls test carried out on the means indicated that the non-widow, non-nutrition site participants engaged in more social support-seeking behavior than the other three groups.

The age, income, and education of the participants appeared to influence the results. In order to ascertain the relative contribution of widowhood, age, income, and education to the variance, four stepwise multiple regressions were performed. The above mentioned variables were seen as independent variables. The dependent variables were community integration, hassles, stress, and social support seeking, respectively. The use of age, income, and education as inde-pendent variables was done strictly as a post-hoc test. These findings may be seen in Table 2.

Education was a highly significant predictor of community integration (Mul-tiple $R = .16761, F(1,158) = 4.56699, p < .0341$). Age was a highly significant

Table 1. Results of ANOVAS

Scale	df	F(1,156)	Significance of F
Community Integration			
A[a]	1	2.320	.130
B[b]	1	.091	.764
A×B[c]	1	6.752	.010[d]
Stress			
A[a]	1	.205	.651
B[b]	1	14.217	.000[d]
A×B[c]	1	.081	.777
Seeking Social Support			
A[a]	1	6.081	.015[e]
B[b]	1	12.045	.001[d]
A×B[c]	1	3.679	.057[f]

[a]Main Effect A: Widowhood
[b]Main Effect B: setting
[c]Interaction: Widowhood × Setting
[d]F is significant at .01 level.
[e]F is marginally significant at .01 level.
[f]F is marginally significant at .05 level.

Table 2. Results of Multiple Regression of Widowhood, Age, and Education on Community Integration, Hassles, Stress, and Social Support Seeking Respectively

IV	DV	Multiple R	F(1,158)	p<
Education	Community Integration	.16761	4.56699	.0341
Hassles	Age	.49081	50.13886	.0000
Stress	Age	.30051	15.68500	.0001
	Age Widowhood	.34036	10.28544[a]	.0001
Seeking Social Support	Widowhood Widowhood	.26027	11.48108	.0009
	Age	.31130	8.42354[a]	.0003

[a]df = 2, 157

predictor of daily hassles (Multiple R = .49081, $F(1,158)$ = 50. 13886, $p < .0000$). Age was the strongest predictor of stress (Multiple R = .30051, $F(1,158)$ = 15.68500, $p < .0001$). However, the additional contribution of widowhood to the variance in stress was also statistically significant (Multiple R = .34036, $F(2,157)$ = 10.28544, $p < .0001$). Widowhood was the strongest predictor of social support seeking (Multiple R = .26027, $F(1,158)$ = 11.48108, $p < .0009$). The additional contribution of age to the variance in social support seeking was also significant (Multiple R = .31130, $F(2, 157)$ = 8.42354, $p < .0003$).

DISCUSSION

Hypothesis 1, that widows would be less integrated in their community than non-widows, was not supported. The widows and non-widows did not differ significantly in their level of community integration. The widows had been without their husbands for a mean of 12.51 years. They may have adjusted to their new life and reintegrated themselves in the community. As married women, the widows may have received support from their husbands. As single persons, they may have looked to the community as a source of support.

Education was the only significant predictor of community integration (Multiple R = .16761, $F(1,158)$ = 4.56699, $p < .0341$). The non-widow, non-nutrition site participants were significantly more integrated in their community than the other three groups of participants ($F(1,156)$ = 6.752, $p < .010$), possibly because they were better educated than the other interviewees. This group accounted for the greatest proportion of participants who had attained more than a high school diploma (10.7%). These individuals participated in activities that involved community service, teaching and/or participating in classes and/or discussion groups. They appeared to be concerned citizens who were aware of and interested in the world around them.

Hypotheses 2 stated that widows would experience more daily hassles and would have a higher level of stress than non-widows. This hypothesis was not supported. No significant differences were found in the average amount of hassles experienced by the widows and non-widows at nutrition sites and non-nutrition sites. The participants may not have perceived their daily experiences as hassles [21]. The widows had been without their spouses for 12.5 years. Perhaps they had adjusted to the daily frustrations and hassles they had experienced due to this loss. The only significant predictor of "hassles" was age (Multiple R = .49081, $F(1,158)$ = 50.13886, $p < .000$). The correlation between "hassles" and age is −.491 which was significant. Older participants experienced fewer "hassles" than younger participants. Older participants may have had more years to adapt to their daily frustrations and hassles. There were no significant differences between the widows and non-widows in the average amount of stress they experienced. Again, the widows may have adapted and were no longer experiencing stress.

The non-nutrition site participants experienced a lower degree of stress than the nutrition site participants ($F(1,156) = 14.217, p < .000$). Age was the strongest predictor of stress (Multiple $R = .30051$, $F(1,158) = 15.68500, p < .0001$) and age and stress were significantly positively correlated ($r = .301$). Younger participants experienced less stress than older participants. The non-nutrition site participants were slightly younger (mean age = 72.35 years) than the nutrition site participants (mean age = 74.57 years). Interestingly, hassles correlates negatively with age while stress correlates positively with age. Hassles and stress do not appear to be measuring the same thing. Older people may experience fewer hassles because less is happening in their lives due to losses. The losses themselves and/or the lack of stress-buffering agents may produce stress.

The non-widow, non-nutrition site participants were the most integrated in their community and experienced low stress. Thus, Hypothesis 3, which held that irrespective of widowhood, participants who were more integrated in their community would experience fewer hassles and less stress than those who were not integrated in their community, was partially supported. The group of participants with the greatest amount of community integration experienced low stress. This was not true for hassles. The groups did not differ significantly on the average number of hassles experienced, again indicating that stress and hassles do not necessarily go together.

Hypothesis 4 stated that social support would be a stress buffering agent in widowhood. Evidence for this hypothesis was not upheld. There were no differences among the participants in the amount of social support they received.

Hypotheses 5 and 6 stated that as a result of their loss, widows may have less supportive networks than non-widows and may seek more social support. Evidence for these hypotheses was not upheld. The widows sought less social support than non-widows ($F(1,156) = 6.081, p < .015$). Perhaps this was due to their age and physical declines associated with aging. The widows may have been prevented from seeking as much social support as the non-widows. However, it is possible that they may not have perceived their social networks to be any less supportive nor may they have perceived themselves to be any less integrated in their community. Non-nutrition site participants sought less social support than nutrition site participants. There was a marginally significant correlation between age and seeking social support ($r = -.226$). Older participants sought less social support than younger participants. The non-widows were younger (mean age = 70.91 years) than the widows (mean age = 75.93 years). The non-widows, non-nutrition site participants were the youngest group and may have had the greatest number of supportive persons around them. Due to their advanced age, widows may have lost not only their spouse but other sources of social support. They may not have replaced these supportive persons at the same rate as they lost them. They may, therefore, have had fewer persons on whom to rely.

SUMMARY AND CONCLUSIONS

This study examined the degree to which widows were integrated in their community, the daily hassles and stress they may have experienced, and their social networks and support-seeking behavior. A sample of 160 women, sixty years of age or older, eighty widows and eighty non-widows, were interviewed. Half the sample participated in senior centers in Kansas City, Missouri, while the other half belonged to other organizations or were obtained through a truncated snowball technique. The findings indicated that widowhood in and of itself does not appear to be a predictor either of community integration or the lack of it or of the experience of stress and hassles. Those who experienced hassles were not the same persons as those who experienced stress. It was surprising to find that those who sought social support did not seem most in need of it. Age and education, along with community integration, were better predictors of variables studied than was widowhood.

Only one of the six hypotheses tested was partially supported. This was that individuals who were integrated in their community would experience less stress and fewer hassles than those who were not integrated. This was found to be true for stress but not for hassles. Widows were no less integrated, and experienced no more stress or daily hassles than non-widows. Their networks were no less supportive and they sought no more social support, than non-widows.

Widows were no less integrated than non-widows. Though at first it seemed that the non-widows at the non-nutrition sites were the best integrated, this was explained by the influence of education in the multiple regression analysis. This finding may be explained by the fact that the mean years of widowhood is 12.5 years, which means that adaptations may have been made earlier when they first became widows.

Widows did not experience more hassles. On the other hand, they did experience more stress. In a multiple regression analysis, this was explained by the age of the widows in the nutrition sites. Viz, the older the widow the more stressed. Stress may have occurred when widows had been newly-widowed, but that did not show up in the findings possibly because of the long duration of widowhood.

Those who were more integrated were found to be less stressed. This finding, too, was attributable to both age and education. A very interesting finding was that age related negatively to hassles and positively to stress. Possibly hassles attributable to widowhood do not occur in the lives of the very old but this does not keep this population from being stressed. The very partners that were lost earlier could conceivably have served as stress buffers in the very old.

No differences in availability of social supports were found among widows and non-widows. Again, age was more of an explanatory factor than widowhood. Older participants had fewer supports and sought less social support. It is of great interest that support seeking seems independent of degree of community integration and social supports available. It is entirely possible that beyond a certain age, the need to seek social support is decreased either because of satisfaction with available supports or because of awareness that it requires more expenditure of effort or energy than it is worth.

Clearly, widowhood does not in and of itself appear to be a predictor either of community integration or the lack of it, or of stress and hassles. Perhaps by conducting a path analysis one might find that it is a factor but the analyses used in this study did not obtain that finding. Widowhood does not appear to have an impact on social support or social support-seeking behavior. Possibly, length of widowhood and age are contributory factors. In future studies, it would probably make sense to consider duration of widowhood, age, marital status, education, social support, and community integration as independent variables. Such a controlled comparison study might yield more of the hypothesized results.

REFERENCES

1. B. Raphael, *The Anatomy of Bereavement,* Basic Books, New York, 1983.
2. H. Z. Lopata, Loneliness: Forms and Components, *Social Problems, 17,* pp. 248-262, 1969.
3. E. Lindemann, Symptomatology and Management of Acute Grief, *American Journal of Psychiatry, 101,* pp. 141-149, 1944.
4. J. W. Worden, *Grief Counseling and Grief Therapy: A Handbook for the Mental Health Practitioner,* Springer, New York, 1982.
5. J. M. Gibbs, *Role Changes Associated with Widowhood among Middle and Upper Class Women: A Thesis in Sociology,* University of Missouri, Kansas City, 1974.
6. R. C. Atchley, Dimensions of Widowhood in Later Life, *The Gerontologist, 15*:2, pp. 176-178, 1975.
7. B. S. Dohrehwend, Social Stress and Community Psychology, *American Journal of Community Psychology, 6*:1, pp. 1-14, 1978.
8. R. S. Lazarus, *Psychological Stress and the Coping Process,* McGraw-Hill, St. Louis, 1966.
9. C. L. Sheridan, *The Comparative Scale of Stress Assessment: Global Inventory, Version II,* unpublished manuscript, Department of Psychology, University of Missouri, Kansas City, 1986.
10. H. Selye, *The Stress of Life,* McGraw-Hill, St. Louis, 1976.
11. K. N. Walker, A. MacBride, and M. L. S. Vachon, Social Support Networks and the Crisis of Bereavement, *Social Science and Medicine, 11,* pp. 35-41, 1977.
12. S. Cobb, Social Support as a Moderator of Life Stress, *Psychosomatic Medicine, 38*:5, pp. 300-314, 1976.
13. A. Dean and N. Lin, The Stress-Buffering Role of Social Support, *The Journal of Nervous and Mental Disease, 165*:6, pp. 403-417, 1977.
14. R. S. Lazarus, A. DeLongis, S. Folkman, and R. Gruen, Stress and Adaptational Outcomes: The Problem of Confounded Measures, *American Psychologist, 40*:7, pp. 770-779, 1985.

15. A. D. Kanner, J. C. Boyne, C. Schaefer, and R. S. Lazarus, Comparison of Two Modes of Stress Management: Daily Hassles and Uplifts Versus Major Life Events, *Journal of Behavioral Medicine, 4*:4, pp. 1-39, 1981.
16. C. L. Sheridan and L. K. Smith, *Toward a Comprehensive Scale of Stress Assessment: Development, Norms, and Reliability,* unpublished manuscript, Department of Psychology, University of Missouri, Kansas City, 1987.
17. J. D. Kasarda and M. Janowitz, Community Attachment in Mass Society, *American Sociological Review, 39,* pp. 328-339, 1974.
18. H. Z. Lopata, Support Systems of Widows, in *Research Instruments in Social Gerontology: Vol. 2: Social Roles and Social Participation,* D. J. Mangen and W. A. Peterson (eds.), University of Minnesota Press, Minneapolis, pp. 106-111, 1977.
19. S. Folkman and R. S. Lazarus, If It Changes, It Must be a Process: Study of Emotion and Coping During Three Stages of a College Examination, *Journal of Personality and Social Psychology, 48*:1, pp. 150-170, 1985.
20. S. Folkman, R. S. Lazarus, R. S. Dunkel-Schetter, A. DeLongis, and R. Gruen, Dynamics of a Stressful Encounter: Cognitive Appraisal, Coping, and Encounter Outcomes, *Journal of Personality and Social Psychology, 50*:5, pp. 992-1003, 1986.
21. B. P. Dohrehwend and P. E. Shrout, "Hassles" in the Conceptualization and Measurement of Life Stress Variables, *American Psychologist, 40*:7, pp. 780-785, 1985.

Chapter 7

THE IMPACT OF RELIGIOUS ORIENTATION IN CONJUGAL BEREAVEMENT AMONG OLDER ADULTS

Christopher H. Rosik

In view of the increasing importance religion appears to have for a large number of individuals as they grow older [1-3], one might legitimately wonder if religiousness has any beneficial impact for them in adapting to the loss of a spouse. A small body of research suggests that religion can constitute an important resource in the aged person's adaptation to widowhood [4-11].

The significance of these studies, however, is weakened by a few conflicting findings [12, 13], and by the fact that many define religion rather crudely in terms such as church attendance or activity [14]. Better methods are available, particularly the intrinsic-extrinsic (I-E) religious orientation dimensions [15, 16]. Intrinsic religion is defined as religion as an ultimate goal for its own sake. In contrast, extrinsic religion is religion used by the person as a means to some other self-determined end. This perspective allows for the categorization of two other religious approaches, the indiscriminately proreligious (where items from both dimensions are endorsed) and the nonreligious (where items from either dimension are not endorsed). The advantages of the I-E dimensions are well documented [15, 17], although only Carey has utilized I-E in a study of the widowed [12].

RELIGIOUS FAITH AND GRIEFWORK

The initial or acute grief experience characteristically involves denial and feelings such as shock and abandonment [7, 18, 19]. This acute phase, which lasts a few weeks to no more than about six months [7, 20-22], is marked by the bereaved's gradual realization of the death and intense experiencing of pain [23].

At this point, the role of religious faith is expected to be minimal, as the bereaved is reacting to the fact of the loss. The widowed person is primarily occupied with experiencing the emotional pain associated with the acceptance of the loss, not with attempting to make sense of the situation. Presumably, this emotional hurt is very intense regardless of the extent and nature of one's religiousness.

The acute period is followed by a "working through" phase, proposed to last anywhere from a year to several years for successful completion [7, 21]. With the commencement of this phase, the individual begins *acting upon* the fact of the loss. Having accepted the reality of the death, the bereaved must now locate the loss within a context of meaning which facilitates entry into a life without the deceased [24]. During this time, the adaptive value of an intrinsic religious orientation should be evident, as it provides an overarching, integrated framework within which the loss can be understood. This framework is definitionally not provided by religion in the extrinsic and nonreligious orientations. In the indiscriminately proreligious orientation, the advantages of the intrinsic dimension are likely to be moderated somewhat by the concomitant emphasis on extrinsic items, though some adaptive benefits should still be present.

HYPOTHESES

This perspective on the interplay of the bereavement process and religious faith suggests the following set of hypotheses to be tested in this study:

1. intrinsicness is negatively related and extrinsicness positively related to grief and depression ratings;
2. an indiscriminately proreligious orientation is negatively associated with grief and depression; in contrast, the nonreligious orientation is positively correlated; and
3. the anticipated associations between religious orientation and the grief and depression ratings will increase as the time since the death increases.

No effect of sex was postulated. This was due in part to the lack of consistent findings concerning sex and bereavement adjustment [25], as well as sex and religious orientation [17].

METHOD

Participants and Procedures

The participants were obtained through twelve support groups for widows and widowers in the Los Angeles and Ventura county areas between February and April 1986. One hundred and seventy-nine Caucasian widows and widowers agreed to participate in the study. Useable materials were obtained from 145 widows and twenty widowers. The average age was 63.8 years for widows and 68.3 years for widowers.

Thirty-one of these respondents were missing scores for three or less variables. Missing intrinsic and extrinsic scores ($N = 18$) were replaced with a score derived from a linear regression of the other variables. Other missing variable scores ($N = 16$) were set as the median score on that variable for that group.

Materials

Religious faith was operationalized according to the I-E dimensions [16]. Gorsuch and Venable's "age-universal" I-E scale, designed to widen the readability of the original measure, was utilized in the present study [26]. Measurements of several I and E items were thus obtained utilizing a nine-point Likert type scale. These respective groups of responses were summed and averaged to yield separate I and E scores for each participant.

Adjustment to bereavement was measured in two ways. Since indices of depression have been frequently used as a means of determining adjustment, the thirty-item Geriatric Depression Scale (GDS) was included to allow for comparison. The GDS has been shown to be particularly valuable in assessing depression in an elderly population [27, 28]. However, as depression and grief are probably not synonymous states [29], a revised version of Faschingbauer, Devaul, and Zisook's Texas Inventory of Grief was also administered [30].

In order to protect against the potential confounding effects of socioeconomic status (SES), and physical health, these variables were also assessed [4, 6, 31, 32]. Hollinghead's two-factor index of social position was employed to obtain SES data [33], and a thirty-item physical health checklist measuring the occurrence of pre- and post-bereavement illnesses was given to assess health functioning [34]. Length of bereavement was assessed by having participants report the amount of time (in months) since the death.

Analyses

The hypotheses were tested by means of a hierarchical multiple regression analysis. Analyses were conducted utilizing the GDS scores and the grief ratings from the Texas Inventory of Grief as separate dependent variables.

Time after the spouse's death was entered into the regression equation first, followed by the square of the time after death to assess curvilinearity between the dependent variables and time after death [35]. SES and the widowed's health before and after the death were respectively added to the equation for control purposes.

Finally, intrinsicness, extrinsicness, the interactions of time after death with the I-E dimensions, and the interaction between the I-E dimensions were regressed. The latter variable, computed by multiplying intrinsic and extrinsic scores, was included to assess the proreligious and nonreligious orientations. A high score, reflected by a positive raw correlation with the dependent variable, is indicative of an indiscriminately proreligious stance. Similarly, a lower score suggests a non-religious orientation and would be evidenced by a negative raw correlation.

A significant curvilinear relationship between grief and time after death ($F(1, 135) = 11.43$, $p < .001$, two-tailed) for widows occurred in the total sample but was found to be based upon six subjects whose husbands had died over sixteen years previously. Because this group was not immediately relevant to the purposes of the study, these subjects were dropped allowing for linear interpretation of time after death with a sample of 139 widows.

RESULTS

The means and standard deviations for the main effect independent variables and the dependent variables are presented in Table 1. The average depression score for both widows (11.4) and widowers (13.5) indicates mild depression [27]. Linear estimates suggest that the widows' self-reported depression level returns to the normal range (below 10) at about the five year mark after the death of their husbands. The widowers' depression scores remained in the mildly depressed range throughout the entire range of the time after death variable, that is, up to about 10.5 years. However, this could be an artifact of the small sample and the widowers' low average time following their spouses' death as compared to the

Table 1. Means and Standard Deviations for Dependent Variables and Main Effect Independent Variables

Variable	Possible (Actual) Range	Widows (N = 139)		Widowers (N = 20)	
		Mean	SD	Mean	SD
Grief	15–65	42.8	12.1	47.6	11.3
Depression	0–30	11.4	7.1	13.6	8.8
Age	(47–84)	63.5	11.3	68.3	8.7
After Death[a]	(0–168)	41.5	36.7	27.2	24.5
SES	1–5	2.8	.9	2.6	.7
Health Before	0–30	3.0	3.1	2.1	1.4
Health After	0–30	3.4	3.2	2.3	2.1
Intrinsicness	1–9	6.7	15.5	5.6	17.1
Extrinsicness	1–9	4.5	15.6	4.7	11.8

[a] Time in months after the spouse's death.

widows. In any case, it appears that the depression associated with bereavement was not severe in nature.

In terms of grief, the average for widows (42.8) was lower than that of the widowers (47.6), though both groups were much closer to the extreme high end of the possible range for grief (i.e., 65) than they were for depression. Estimates of widows' grief fell from 47.8 at the time of their husband's death to 33.2 ten years later. Widowers' estimates fell nonsignificantly from 50.2 to 42.2 seven years later. Taken together, these statistics do at least suggest that measures of depression alone may not be sufficient when studying the nature of bereavement for widows and possibly for widowers.

The average religious orientation scores and their accompanying standard deviations suggest a fairly heterogeneous sample. SES averages were indicative of middle-class status.

Hypothesis 1 received partial confirmation. Higher extrinsicness was consistently and significantly associated with more grief and depression. Table 2 indicates that, for the full sample of widows, greater grief and depression were also significantly related to less time after the death and more health problems

Table 2. Hierarchical Multiple Regression Analysis Summary Table for Widows' Grief and Depression

Variable	Grief			Depression		
	Raw r	Partial r	F Ratio	Raw r	Partial r	F Ratio
Time After Death	-.37	-.37	27.21[++++]	-.30	-.30	14.55[++++]
Time Squared	-.31	.12	2.67	-.24	.11	2.03
SES	-.03	-.01	.02	.13	.15	3.56
Health Before	-.09	-.12	2.67	-.01	-.06	.67
Health After	.06	.20	8.09[+++]	.13	.21	7.38[++]
Intrinsicness	.16	.15	4.41[*]	.05	.02	.08
Extrinsicness	.41	.35	23.78[++++]	.23	.20	6.82[+]
Inds. Proreligious	.40	-.04	.29	.22	.11	2.08

Note: $N = 139$, $df1 = 1$, $df2 = 130$.

[*] $p < .04$, two-tailed.
[+] $p < .005$, one-tailed.
[++] $p < .0035$, one-tailed.
[+++] $p < .0025$, one-tailed.
[++++] $p < .00025$, one-tailed.

after the death. Yet even when these relationships were statistically controlled, the association between extrinsicness and both grief and depression remained strong. Table 3 shows that this hypothesized trend also occurred with the widowers, even after accounting for significant relationships between greater depression and more health problems before and after the death.

The predicted negative relationship between intrinsicness and the distress indices was not confirmed. In fact, for the widows, a modestly significant positive relationship was found between intrinsicness and grief. However, when the ordering of the intrinsic and extrinsic variables was reversed, the effect of intrinsicness became nonsignificant. Extrinsicness, in contrast, was highly correlated regardless of order of entry.

Hypothesis 2 was not supported by the data. Widows' I-E interactions were not correlated with the dependent variables. Moreover, contrary to expectations, greater grief and depression among widowers was significantly correlated with indiscriminately proreligious tendencies.

Hypothesis 3 also failed to receive confirmation. Initial analyses revealed no significant interaction between religious orientation and time after the spouse's death for either sex. These interaction variables were subsequently dropped from the analyses.

Table 3. Hierarchical Multiple Regression Analysis Summary Table for Widowers' Grief and Depression

	Grief			Depression		
	Raw	Partial		Raw	Partial	
Variable	r	r	F Ratio	r	r	F Ratio
Time After Death	-.20	-.20	1.08	.11	.11	.43
Time Squared	-.17	.05	.05	.16	.17	1.09
SES	.13	.14	.48	.08	.14	.79
Health Before	.12	.14	.54	.46	.56	11.92[++++]
Health After	.17	.17	.77	.52	.34	4.35[+++]
Intrinsicness	-.22	-.18	.88	.01	-.11	.50
Extrinsicness	.29	.38	3.83[++]	.15	.27	2.69[+]
Inds. Proreligious	.12	.53	7.23[**]	.21	.38	5.49[*]

Note: $N = 20$, $df1 = 1$, $df2 = 11$.

[*] $p < .04$, two-tailed.
[**] $p < .02$, two-tailed.
[+] $p < .05$, one-tailed.
[++] $p < .035$, one-tailed.
[+++] $p < .03$, one-tailed.
[++++] $p < .003$, one-tailed.

DISCUSSION

The present study indicates that the mildly extrinsically religious elderly widowed show more signs of distress than their non-extrinsically religious peers. The overall results are in keeping with the tendency for extrinsicness to correlate more than intrinsicness with nonreligious variables [17]. Yet how might this be explained in the present case? The majority of extrinsic items reflect a tendency to endorse religion for social (support) and emotional (security, comfort) benefits. In view of this and the ambiguities of attributing causation which accompany correlational studies, two options seem possible.

One explanation is that extrinsicness leads to greater distress during bereavement. It may be that a faith oriented toward gaining support and comfort has fewer resources to alleviate distress when faced with the loneliness and discomforts of widowhood than a faith without this orientation. Donahue has noted the fairly consistent pattern of positive association between extrinsicness and such variables as prejudice, dogmatism, fear of death, trait anxiety, and perceived powerlessness [17]. The correlation between extrinsicness and emotional distress may thus reflect a heightened sense of trepidation and helplessness brought about by the spouse's death.

A second explanation which needs to be considered, however, is that individuals experiencing more difficulty adjusting to widowhood accentuate the extrinsic dimension of their faith in order to cope. Thus, in the midst of great distress, these bereaved turn with renewed intensity to the support and comfort aspects of their faith. Whether or not this turning succeeds in reducing distress is yet another question, but such a perspective does raise the possibility that extrinsicness could have beneficial effects in bereavement.

This author favors the first explanation as most likely to account for the findings, though both options may come into play. There is evidence for the stability of religious beliefs and associations during bereavement, a continuity which seems more in keeping with the first perspective [5, 7, 36, 37]. Such continuity is suggested directly in this study by the lack of an interaction between time after death and extrinsicness. However, Loveland's finding that the bereaved did engage in more prayer underscores the tentativeness of choosing between these two interpretive frameworks [36].

The positive relationship between indiscriminately proreligious tendencies and the distress measures among widowers is the most puzzling result to interpret. A larger sample size would have been desirable, but the trend was consistently significant even with this limitation. Conceivably, however, it could represent

1. an increased openness to an undifferentiated religious position as a response to distress;
2. the inability of an undifferentiated general religious outlook to promote adjustment to widowhood; or

3. an agreeable and candid response set which results in a greater acknowledgment of distress.

The failure to find the predicted interactions between I or E and the time after the spouse's death suggests that the effects of religious orientation, or lack thereof, remain stable across the "phases" of grief. However, the average participant appeared to be well beyond the acute grief period. Thus, this stability may only be applicable to bereavement that is well under way. It is therefore conceivable that a sample with a higher percentage of recently bereaved individuals might still reveal some changes in the effect of I and E over time.

This study also provides additional strong support for the need to assess physical health when examining bereavement among older adults. What may be of particular interest for future research is the fact that higher distress was primarily related to self-reported health status after the death for widows and before the death for widowers. Health status may thus be more valuable in reflecting the adjustment to widowhood among widows and predicting it among widowers.

The present research supports Carey's inability to relate intrinsicness to adjustment [12]. However, Carey's study did not observe the negative correlation between adjustment and extrinsicness found in the present investigation. A number of factors could account for this, such as Carey's inclusion in his sample of some widowers who had remarried, and his operationalization of adjustment more in terms of depression than grief. Another important consideration is Carey's possible sampling bias, which could stem from religious homogeneity in his sample and/or the fact that 17 percent of his respondents refused to participate based on feeling eithcr well adjusted or too poorly adjusted.

While Carey's study may suffer from sample bias as a result of response rates [12], it should be noted that the sample employed in this analysis probably had a bias of its own. Specifically, the sample consisted of those widowed who were actively seeking group support. It is possible that these individuals have more distress, are more socially isolated, and/or are more likely to seek social support than persons not involved in such groups. Thus, one cannot rule out the possibility of a different pattern of associations between religious orientation and distress among those widowed not as prone to seek peer support.

What is clear from the present analysis is that for this sample of bereaved older adults, extrinsicness was highly correlated with greater grief and depression. While this author suspects that the direction of causality is from extrinsicness to the distress, a definitive answer must await further research. The next step would appear to be a longitudinal analysis which would include repeated assessment of religious orientation both prior to and following the death of a spouse.

REFERENCES

1. S. C. Ainlay and R. D. Smith, Aging and Religious Participation, *Journal of Gerontology, 39*, pp. 357-363, 1984.
2. B. Hunsberger, Religion, Age, Life Satisfaction, and Perceived Sources of Religiousness: A Study of Older Persons, *Journal of Gerontology, 40,* pp. 615-620, 1985.
3. R. A. Kalish and D. K. Reynolds, *Death and Ethnicity*, University of Southern California, Los Angeles, 1976.
4. P. E. Bornstein, P. J. Clayton, J. A. Halikas, W. L. Maurice, and E. Robbins, The Depression of Widowhood after Thirteen Months, *British Journal of Psychiatry, 122,* pp. 561-566, 1973.
5. K. F. Ferraro, Widowhood and Social Participation in Later Life, *Research on Aging, 6,* pp. 451-468, 1984.
6. D. E. Gallagher, L. W. Thompson, and J. E. Peterson, Psychological Factors Affecting Adaptation to Bereavement in the Elderly, *International Journal of Aging and Human Development, 14,* pp. 79-95, 1981-82.
7. J. O. Glick, R. S. Weiss, and C. M. Parkes, *The First Year of Bereavement,* John Wiley & Sons, Inc., New York, 1974.
8. D. K. Heyman and D. T. Gianturco, Long-Term Adaptation by the Elderly to Bereavement, *Journal of Gerontology, 28,* pp. 359-362, 1973.
9. H. G. Koenig, L. K. George, and J. C. Siegler, The Use of Religion and Other Emotion-Regulating Coping Strategies among Older Adults, *The Gerontologist, 28,* pp. 303-310, 1988.
10. H. G. Koenig, J. N. Kuale, and C. Ferrel, Religion and Well-Being in Later Life, *The Gerontologist, 28,* pp. 18-28, 1988.
11. B. Spilka, R. W. Hood, and R. L. Gorsuch, *The Psychology of Religion: An Empirical Approach*, Prentice-Hall, Inc., Englewood Cliffs, New Jersey, 1985.
12. R. G. Carey, The Widowed: A Year Later, *Journal of Counseling Psychology, 24,* pp. 125-131, 1977.
13. R. L. Simons and G. E. West, Life Changes, Coping Resources, and Health among the Elderly, *International Journal of Aging and Human Development, 20,* pp. 173-189, 1984-85.
14. M. Herriott and H. A. Kiyak, Bereavement in Old Age: Implications for Therapy and Research, *Journal of Gerontological Social Work, 3,* pp. 15-43, 1981.
15. R. L. Gorsuch, Measurement: The Boom and Bane of Investigating Religion, *American Psychologist, 39,* pp. 228-236, 1984.
16. G. W. Allport and J. M. Ross, Personal Religious Orientation and Prejudice, *Journal of Personality and Social Psychology, 5,* pp. 432-443, 1967.
17. M. J. Donahue, Intrinsic and Extrinsic Religiousness: Review and MetaAnalysis, *Journal of Personality and Social Psychology, 48,* pp. 400-419, 1985.
18. E. Lindemann, Grief and Grief Management: Some Reflections, *The Journal of Pastoral Care, 30,* pp. 198-207, 1976.
19. E. Kübler-Ross, *On Death and Dying*, Macmillan, New York, 1968.

20. A. M. Arkin, Emotional Care of the Bereaved, in A*cute Grief: Counseling the Bereaved*, O. S. Margolis, H. C. Raether, A. H. Kutschner, J. B. Powers, I. B. Seeland, R. DeBellis, and D. J. Cherico (eds.), Columbia University Press, New York, pp. 40-44, 1981.

21. M. Osterweis, Bereavement and the Elderly, *Aging, 348*, pp. 8-13, 41, 1985.

22. D. K. Switzer, *The Dynamics of Grief*, Abingdon Press, Nashville, 1970.

23. J. W. Worden, *Grief Counseling and Grief Therapy*, Springer Publishing Company, New York, 1982.

24. H. L. Jernigan, Bringing Together Psychology and Theology: Reflections on Ministry to the Bereaved, *The Journal of Pastoral Care, 30*, pp. 88-102, 1976.

25. C. Balkwell, Transition to Widowhood: A Review of the Literature, *Family Relations, 30*, pp. 117-127, 1981.

26. R. L. Gorsuch and G. D. Venable, Development of an "Age-Universal" I-E Scale, *Journal for the Scientific Study of Religion, 22*, pp. 181-187, 1983.

27. T. L. Brink, J. A. Yesavage, O. Lum, P. H. Heersema, M. Adey, and T. L. Rose, Screening Tests for Geriatric Depression, *Clinical Gerontologist, 1*, pp. 37-43, 1982.

28. J. A. Yesavage, T. L. Brink, T. L. Rose, O. Lum, V. Huang, M. Adey, and V. O. Leirer, Development and Validation of a Geriatric Depression Screening Scale: A Preliminary Report, *Journal of Psychiatric Research*, 17, pp. 37-49, 1983.

29. T. R. Kosten, S. Jacobs, and J. W. Mason, The Dexamethasone Suppression Test during Bereavement, *Journal of Nervous and Mental Disease, 172*, pp. 359-360, 1984.

30. T. R. Faschingbauer, R. A. Devaul, and S. Zisook, Development of the Texas Inventory of Grief, *American Journal of Psychiatry, 134*, pp. 696-698, 1977.

31. D. A. Arens, Widowhood and Well-Being: An Examination of Sex Differences Within a Causal Model, *International Journal of Aging and Human Development, 15*, pp. 27-40, 1982-83.

32. L. Y. Steinitz, Religiosity, Well-Being, and Weltanschauung among the Elderly, *Journal for the Scientific Study of Religion, 19*, pp. 60-67, 1980.

33. A. B. Hollinghead, *Two-Factor Index of Social Position*, Yale Station, New Haven, Connecticut, 1957 (memo).

34. A. Wyler, M. Masuda, and T. Holmes, The Seriousness of Illness Rating, *Journal of Psychosomatic Research, 11*, pp. 363-374, 1967.

35. F. N. Kerlinger and E. J. Pedhazur, *Multiple Regression in Behavioral Research*, Holt, Rinehart and Winston, Inc., New York, 1973.

36. G. G. Loveland, The Effect of Bereavement on Certain Religious Attitudes, *Sociological Symposium, 1*, pp. 17-27, 1968.

37. C. M. Parkes, *Bereavement: Studies of Grief in Later Life*, International Universities Press, New York, 1972.

Chapter 8

ELDER MALTREATMENT ITEMS, SUBGROUPS, AND TYPES: POLICY AND PRACTICE IMPLICATIONS

Philip A. Hall

Despite assertions that there is general agreement as to what constitutes elder maltreatment, reviews of published reports show that the variety of labels and descriptors employed prevent comparison from one study to the next [1, 2]. This chapter reports a content analysis of 288 maltreatment cases that were validated by the Texas Department of Human Resources. From a review of the literature, several guiding concepts were developed and used to place the types of maltreatment into a broader context.

Examination of the elder maltreatment cases leads to three principal findings. First, although multiple elements of maltreatment occurred in seven of ten cases, there were not enough cases in which similar elements occurred to form clear patterns. Elder maltreatment encompasses a wide range of acts and conditions, which suggests that policy and practice require greater specification. Second, the inclusive concept of maltreatment requires differential criteria to define its major dimensions. The overlapping categories which result from the present analysis represent a focus for policy and practice clarification. Third, the most difficult category to differentiate, neglect, appears to make it easier to commit other forms of maltreatment. Key issues in addressing neglect involve whose standards guide the investigation, whose preferences determine intervention, and what resources are utilized.

Our society's reluctance to intervene in the domestic unit and the limited resources allocated to protective services suggest that only the most patently offensive occurrences will receive attention. It may be that the numerically greater population at risk and in need will continue to fall over the edge on a case by case basis before receiving attention.

THE PROBLEM

The problems encountered in identifying and intervening in child and spousal maltreatment must also be dealt with in cases of elder maltreatment [3, 4]. Current evidence suggests that human service practitioners either do not recognize maltreatment or, when recognizing it, often simply respond by referral [5]. Without formal policies and procedures, such referrals frequently constitute *pro forma* responses [6, 7]. At the present time, state and national legislation has no standard criteria or response for intervention [8]. Understanding elder maltreatment also suffers because the media tends to report only the most flagrant abuses, a phenomenon which may lull practitioners and programs into a sense of confidence that an adequate professional response is available [9].

The appearance of practitioner surveys regarding elder maltreatment [9] now brings a call for study of these conditions, but an important preparatory phase has been missed. More detailed preliminary work is needed to establish the range of acts or situations within which the determination of actionable maltreatment will be made. As important as it may be to determine acts requiring legal intervention, recognition of situations which place elder people at risk and on the verge of needing intervention should underpin primary and secondary prevention efforts and guide their development.

Case Records as Data Sources

This study reports an attempt to classify acts and situations recorded as evidence of maltreatment by the Texas Department of Human Resources (DHR) during its first two years of providing adult protective services [10]. Using case records as the source of data may be criticized because such records represent a service population rather than the general population of interest. However, development of a typology of maltreatment should benefit from examining incidents which are now confirmed by the responsible agency as maltreatment. Further refinement of the typology awaits studies of the general elder population.

The confusion produced by exploratory studies of elder maltreatment makes appropriate the systematic study of case records. Exploratory studies have relied on practitioner memory of particular cases, practitioner reconstruction of a particular case, or practitioner estimates of the relative frequency with which loosely-defined phenomena occur in their experience. Although several studies appear to include large numbers of respondents, their authors do not report on the cases of maltreatment, but instead focus on numerically small subgroups of persons from various professions or rely on a case example to generalize about maltreatment [6, 11, 12]. The few studies of case records involve small samples located in settings likely to be associated with particular forms of maltreatment [13-15].

A study of cases judged valid by practitioners charged with responding to reports of elder maltreatment creates the opportunity to examine who comes to the attention of public authorities, how practitioners and others understand the phenomena reported, the kinds of interventions thought desirable and actually implemented, and the apparent results of interventions attempted. This chapter concentrates on the phenomena used to validate maltreatment.

METHOD

An enumeration of reports validated by DHR staff allowed the formulation of a stratified, systematic state-wide sample. The population was stratified into sixteen groups by type of maltreatment reported, ethnicity, and urban-rural location. Systematic sampling was then conducted across the agency's ten operating regions to achieve geographic representation. The obtained sample of 284 constitutes 19 percent of the enumeration and contains the work of 157 direct-service and sixty supervisory personnel.

DHR personnel receive reports of abuse, usually by phone, and record the alleged maltreatment verbatim. Investigation occurs within twenty-four hours, principally by means of home visits made the same day. The data analyzed in this study were gathered from information entered on an investigation form and recorded in greater detail in the case narrative.[1]

The data were arranged in a list of items which focused on verbs (to identify actions). These were supplemented by nouns and accompanying adjectives. Finally, adverbs were included to capture the quality of the acts [16].

Two readers examined the records and listed discrete acts or conditions of maltreatment. Several issues arose in this process. First, an item might be mentioned in general but lack detail; for example, "A doesn't treat B right." These remained in the initial count but were dropped from further specific analysis. Second, several similar acts might be reported in the same case; for example, "A yells at B and threatens to place her in a nursing home." These were classified according to the most denigrating or dangerous item for the elder person's autonomy. Third, some items were recorded with others so consistently that they were treated as a single joint item; for example, elements 1 and 2 in Table 1.

Guiding Concepts

The overlap of terms associated with elder maltreatment is exemplified by the legislative definitions of abuse and neglect under which DHR operates. Both definitions contain the same phrase: "deprivation or failure to provide by the

---

[1]The records did not yield information to allow completion of our original collection form. That plan anticipated the following format: Who did what to whom, where, when, with what, with what intent, for how long, in what context, and with what result to the parties involved. Even the effort to sort out who participated sometimes proved difficult. The perceived immediacy of action required, and the multiple conditions identified, may explain the absence of explicit detail.

Table 1. Frequency of Forty-three Maltreatment Elements

Element Number	Element	Number of cases
1	Care of the person and immediate living area	71
2	Not caring for health or seeking medical care	62
3	Others take the elder's resources	36
4	Others misuse the elder's resources	29
5	Personal maintenance: hygiene, clothing, food	27
6	Call names, insult, swear at	24
7	Care of immediate living area	21
8	Medication problems	21
9	Elder misuses own resources	16
10	Others coerce elder regarding resources	16
11	Food: Supply, prepare, consume	16
12	Others force elder from quarters	15
13	Beat up	13
14	Physical aggression—not specific	13
15	Leave elder alone for long time, abandon	13
16	Threaten to hit, commit suicide, or poison	12
17	Verbal aggression—not specific	11
18	Push, shove, grab, slap	11
19	Elder helpless, immobile	11
20	Personal care: hygiene, clothing	9
21	Elder cannot manage own resources	9
22	Elder falls, trouble walking	9
23	Kick	9
24	Threaten institution, confine, abandon	9
25	Force elder to other quarters	8
26	Use or try to use a knife or gun, suicide attempt, poison	8
27	Others move into elder's quarters without permission	8
28	Elder refused travel, visits from others	8
29	Won't follow medical advice or have tests	7
30	Restrain, lock up elder	6
31	Hit or try to hit with an object	6
32	Trouble moving and care of living area	5
33	Sexually molest elder	4
34	Elder fears returning home	4
35	Medical emergency	4
36	Resource use problem—not specific	4
37	Throw object at elder	3
38	Force elder to care for another person	3
39	Won't use/can't afford medical device	3
40	Runs away from other persons	2
41	Throw (not at person)/smash object	2
42	Elder takes other's resources	1
43	Elder refuses to talk	1

caretaker or one's self the goods and services necessary to avoid physical harm, mental anguish, or mental illness" [10]. The differentiation and specification of harm, anguish, and illness is sufficiently difficult. Using similar definitions of abuse and neglect becomes confounded in the literature by the shading of acts with the lack of action and their location in the elder person, the caretaker, or both.

Proceeding along the lines of grounded theory, the literature and practice experience suggest that several kinds of maltreatment should be addressed [17-19]. Overt physical abuse constitutes a type universal to maltreatment studies. More detailed identification of injury severity and the frequency or duration of abusive acts remains to be accomplished. However, a rank-ordered approach has been developed by Straus [20]. He identifies eight items in a violence scale which moves from the presumably less to the more physically harmful. Each item references an action of one person against another. Some items identify separate acts (slapped the other person), some combine acts together into a single item (kicked, bit, or hit with a fist), while still others list together an act or an effort to act (hit or tried to hit with something).

Straus's scales also include a verbal aggression component which mirrors items often listed in the maltreatment literature under the label of emotional, verbal, or psychological abuse and neglect. These labels seem quite slippery when applied to the relations of adults within the domestic setting. Straus expanded the literal meaning of verbal aggression to include items such as "sulked or refused to talk about it" and the physical act "threw something (not at the person) or smashed something." Straus's five-item scale appears to offer a descriptively useful device, and his label of verbal aggression seems more empirically useful than the inclusive emotional or psychological abuse and neglect categories.

Exploitation represents a third dimension common to most of the elder maltreatment literature. Most references focus on actually taking the elderly person's property—cash, personal, or real. The misuse of these resources by another, as exemplified by the niece who does an elderly relative's grocery shopping and a substantial portion of her own with the elder's money, receives less explicit attention. Similarly, verbal or emotional coercion, often in terms of threats to confine or abandon the elder person if he/she does not share resources with another, does not appear consistently in definitions of exploitation. Coercion to obtain resources seems more an issue of the tactics used to exploit than of verbal aggression as characteristic of interpersonal transactions.

Lau and Kosberg introduce the violation of older people's rights as an aspect of maltreatment, exemplified by such actions as "being forced out of one's dwelling or into another setting" [13, p. 12]. Other acts of imposing upon an older person or restricting his/her movement would expand on this concept of rights violations, although distinguishing such acts from verbal aggression and exploitation as discussed above may prove difficult. In this study, the notion of rights guided the examination of the data for threats or actions which limited an elder person's independence or interfered with his/her exercise of decision making.

The concept of neglect, whether by others or one's self, so prominent in the child maltreatment literature, receives quite uneven attention with reference to elderly people. Like emotional or psychological abuse, the term neglect seems to be treated as a nebulous, even a residual category. In the absence of relative responsibility laws, neglect by others may be difficult to prove. Self-neglect represents a yet more elusive concept, as exemplified by elderly people who seem competent to handle their affairs but appear unwilling to do so or individuals who desperately want to provide for themselves but, by reasonable standards, are unable to do so.

Hickey and Douglas distinguish passive from active neglect [21]. In their formulation, persons other than the elder are responsible for both types. Passive neglect, as represented by mean scores on a five-point scale, receives the highest acknowledgment from each of ten professional groups representing 228 persons likely to encounter elder maltreatment. Active neglect varies from a position of second rank in three groups to third rank in seven groups among four types of maltreatment studied.

The author's exposure to the Community Care for the Aged and Disabled program of DHR suggests that neglect represents a concept too complex to operationalize clearly.[2] Instead, problems experienced by elder people and/or caregivers tend to coalesce around health maintenance and medical care, personal maintenance (including self-care and condition of the living area), and questions concerning the ability of elderly people to use their resources for their own benefit. These areas, then, joined the more generally identified concern with physical violence, verbal aggression, and exploitation in examining the acts and conditions listed.

FINDINGS

Maltreatment Acts and Conditions

As indicated in Table 1, forty-three acts or situations appear in validating the 284 cases. Diversity characterizes the sample. Only two elements appear in as many as 15 percent of the cases while 69.4 percent of the reports contain two or more maltreatment items. For the remaining elements, thirty-one appear in fewer than 5 percent of the cases, eight in between 5 and 9 percent, and two in 10 to 14 percent, none in as many as 15 to 19 percent, and two in 20 percent or more. A single element characterizes 30.6 percent of the reports, while 44.7 percent contain two elements. Three items occur in 19 percent, four in 4.6 percent, and five in 1.1 percent of the remaining cases.

---

[2]During the summer, 1983, the author participated in a state-wide study to validate a new form to determine need for CCAD services; mental health and activities of daily living presented especially difficult concepts to unravel.

The validation procedure concentrates on determining whether maltreatment exists according to DHR criteria which emphasize the immediacy of danger to the elderly person. One would expect that evidence of life-threatening acts or conditions should dominate the reports. Examination of Table 1, however, suggests that the reports validate a core of problems concerning self-care and health status, as evidenced by the two most frequently occurring items (care of the person and immediate living area, and not seeking medical care). This core receives added emphasis from the fifth, seventh, eighth, and eleventh most frequent elements (personal maintenance, care of immediate living area, medication problems, and food). Together, these six account for 38.2 percent of the 570 elements recorded. These six items appear to fall under the general rubric of neglect. The gerontology literature details numerous difficulties that elderly people encounter in self-care as well as problems of willingness, skills, and resources encountered in others, often adult children or grandchildren, attempting to provide care. The concentration of items in the personal care and health status of the elder people in this study suggests that there may be a core of deterioration or limitation of an elder person which then makes the more extreme forms of maltreatment easier for other people to commit. The ages ranged from sixty-five to ninety-four, with a mean of 78.7 years and standard deviation of 7.3. Those eighty-five or older represented 20.4 percent, those seventy-five to eighty-four accounted for 47.9 percent, and those sixty-five to seventy-four contributed 31.7 percent of the sample.

The third, fourth, and tenth items (others take elder's resources, others misuse elder's resources, others coerce elders regarding resources) refer to exploitation of the elder person and constitute 14.2 percent of the total elements. This set of three items runs the gamut from incidents of outright theft of the cash from a social security check to threatening to beat the elder person if money or property is not given or creating a false need to convince the elder person to share resources, to shopping for the elder person's groceries and charging a large fee for the service. In some instances the elder person actively agrees. For example, an eighty-year old has only supplemental income but wants a niece to have over half of it to support her in college. In other instances the elder person acquiesces. An example involves the person who knows her grandson lives with her the one week at the beginning of each month until her money is gone. She wants the company and states she needs very little. Investigation determines there has been no food in the house for over five days. In all but two reports, the elder declined to seek formal prosecution of the other person. In these cases intervention must rely upon informal processes of persuasion and bargaining.

Three additional items complete the group of twelve which appear in as many as 5 percent of the cases. Item 6 (call names, insult, swear at) involves verbal aggression. Although denigration and infantilization do not constitute desirable phenomena, the injury they cause a person requires further study. Item 9 (the elder misuses her own resources) similarly suggests a need for careful assessment. Item 12 (others force the elder from her own quarters) includes both efforts to move an elderly person to a nursing home against her will and more blatant acts such as locking an elderly woman out of her home with no provision for substitute quarters.

Joint Occurrence of Elements

The fact that 69.4 percent of the cases contain two or more elements prompts examination of the joint occurrence of items to suggest patterns for further study. Only five pairs of items appear in five or more cases (Table 2).

The numerically dominant pair includes items 1 and 2 (care of the person and immediate living area, and not seeking medical care) which suggest the nebulous area of neglect. Item 2 appears in thirty-eight cases in combination with one of the three elements indicating personal care and living area maintenance difficulties. Items 3 and 4 involve other persons gaining access to the elder's resources and are both paired with item 1. Together these represent fourteen cases. Some aspect of personal care and living area difficulty occurs in each of the fifty-two cases.

The joint occurrence of elements involves only 6 of the 12 most frequently appearing items and 18.3 percent of the cases. When the single element cases are included, they together represent almost half the cases, 48.9 percent, but only 17.4 percent of the total items reported. These patterns reinforce the evidence for a core of maltreatment based in personal and health care. The linkage of exploitation with this core, however, involves only fourteen cases.

The elements commonly identified as indicating abuse appear almost exclusively in the 2 and 3 element cases. These do not represent solitary events. By contrast, exploitation occurs both alone and in combination with other problems. The core of personal and health care difficulties occurs alone in many instances but also appears with the popularly recognized phenomena of physical aggression, verbal aggression, and exploitation.

Table 2. Pairs of Items in Five or More Cases

Items	N
Health status plus Living area	9
Health status plus Personal maintenance	10
Health status and Care of person/area	19
Care of person/area plus Others misuse	8
Care of person/area plus Others take	6

Elements Combined: Subgroups and Types

Half of the cases but less than one-fifth of the items were accounted for by the joint and solitary occurrence of the most frequent items. Collapsing the elements into subgroups may provide an indication of more general aspects of elder maltreatment which warrant further study.

Straus's physical aggression scale fits the data well. Additional items include sexually molest and suicide attempt. Although "beat" lacks specificity, it combines with the elements "grab-shove-push-slap" and "kick" to represent *Simple Assault*. A second set of items involves use of an object. "Using a weapon, attempting suicide, poison"; "hit with an object"; and "throw an object at the person" can be termed *Aggravated Assault*. ("Attempting suicide" is included here because it involves using a substance/object against self.) The subgroups have the common characteristic of Assault and occur in fifty cases. The sexually molest item ($N = 4$) and the physical aggression not specific item ($N = 13$) are deleted because of difficulty determining what occurred.

Straus's verbal aggression scale also fits the data in most respects. Few explicit instances of sulking, refusing to talk, or stomping out are recorded. The threat of institutionalization, confinement, or abandonment adds a dimension not contained among Straus's items, one which may be important for this population. Two subgroups cluster around what may be labeled *Insult* and *Threat*. The "call names, swear at, insult" item represents Insult. The combination of threats to institutionalize and to hit indicates Threat. *Verbal Aggression* thus is identified in forty-five cases. The verbal aggression not specific item ($N = 11$) is dropped for lack of specificity. Items 40 and 43 would fall under Straus's scale, but they appear in only three cases.

Violation of the elder's rights, as Lau and Kosberg use the term, refers more to acceptable conduct then to specific legal rights. Three subgroups appear viable. "Refuse travel or visits from others" and "lock-up or restrain" suggest *Restraint*. Similarly, the four items (12, 25, 27, 38) involving imposition on the elder person represent an *Impose* subgroup. Another item consists of leaving the elder person alone and might be termed *Abandon*. The three *Rights* subgroups appear in sixty-one cases.

Misuse of the elder person's resources—cash, personal property, and real property—occurs both by others and by the elder. Three items referring to others who take, coerce, and misuse resources form the *Exploit* subgroup. Three other items (9, 21, 42) reflect the difficulties experienced by elder people when managing their own resources. These are labeled *Self-Management*. Combined further into *Material* maltreatment, these appear in 106 cases. Item 36 involves four cases, but its non-specific nature hinders further analysis.

The remaining elements fall into what may be termed *Activities of Daily Living* (ADL) and *Medical* difficulties. Item 1 leads the ADL subgroups because it includes both personal care and care of the living area. The combination of items

5, 11, and 20 represent *Self Care*. Problems limited to the condition of the immediate Living Area appear in twenty-one cases. Finally, issues regarding the elder's ability to move around by herself represent *Ambulation*. The four subgroups appear in 158 cases.

The Medical dimension includes the second most frequent element which suggests *Not Caring*. Items 8, 29, and 39 coalesce into *Nonuse*. A third subgroup, *Acute,* is formed from items 19 and 35. Medical maltreatment appears in 108 cases.

The collapsing of elements into subgroups and then into types results in a ranking in three tiers. First, ADL comprise the dominant type. The 158 cases in which this element is noted represent 55.6 percent of the cases. Medical ($N = 108$) and Material ($N = 106$) occupy the second rank, appearing in 38 percent and 37 percent of the reports, respectively. The remaining three types—Rights ($N = 61$), Physical Aggression ($N = 50$), and Verbal Aggression ($N = 45$) occur in between 21.5 and 15.8 percent of the investigations. Two items, 34 and 41, join the six previously mentioned as dropped from further analysis. Item 34 remains too vague to classify, and item 41 does not fit readily into the Insult or Threat subgroups of Verbal Aggression. In all, then, forty-one occurrences of eight items require further elaboration before they can be placed in the analytical framework developed.

How useful do the subgroups prove to be in identifying patterns? Combination of the subgroups which appear in five or more cases are presented in Table 3.

Two of the pairs contain the same number of cases because the subgroups contain single elements: Not Caring—Both; Not Caring—Living Area. When compared with Table 2, Self-Care and Not Caring rises by five cases and nine new cases are identified as Self-Care and Nonuse. Both and Exploit increase by only three, but a new link appears between Exploit and Impose. A final new group is

Table 3.   Joint Occurrence of Subgroups in Five or More Cases

Subgroups	N
Medical Nonuse plus Self-Care	9
Medical Care plus Living Area	9
Medical Care plus Self-Care	15
Medical Care plus Care of Person/Area	19
Exploit plus Care of Person/Area	17
Exploit plus Others Impose	15
Simple Assault plus Insult plus Others Impose	5

identified and involves the three subgroups Simple Assault-Insult-Impose. The subgroups labels raise the joint occurrence to eighty-nine cases, an increase of thirty-seven (41.6%) from simply using the elements. Combining the single element and joint occurrence of maltreatment subgroups accounts for 182 (64.1%) of the cases.

A final step consists of searching for the joint occurrence of the six maltreatment types. Table 4 shows these combinations when they occur in four or more cases. The increase is to 114 cases from the eighty-nine in Table 3.

The utility of Table 4 lies in identifying cases containing as many as four maltreatment types and examining the combinations of types. Three of the nine combinations contain three types and account for twenty-three of the 114 cases. Each contains a traditionally recognized form of maltreatment—material, verbal, assault—two also involve ADL, and one includes medical. When the cases represented in Table 4 are combined with the single maltreatment cases, 91.1 percent of the ADL, 83.3 percent of the Medical, 75.5 percent of the Material, and 72 percent of the Assault reported are included. However, these proportions drop to 55.7 percent for Rights and 53.3 for Verbal maltreatment.

Overall, ADL and Medical problems are perceived to constitute important aspects of elder maltreatment. Both ADL and Medical appear separately and jointly in reports involving other forms of maltreatment. Four of the six maltreatment types occur, to a large extent, either alone or in one of the patterns identified in Table 4. The two which do not follow this pattern are among the least frequently reported types.

Table 4. Joint Occurrence of Types in Five or More Cases

Maltreatment Types	N
Material plus Medical	7
Material plus ADL plus Rights	8
Material plus ADL	22
Medical plus ADL	46
Material plus Medical plus ADL	10
Rights plus ADL	6
Assault plus Medical	5
Assault plus Material	5
Assault plus Verbal plus Rights	5

DISCUSSION

Policy Implications

Policy issues arising from the data reported in this chapter include media attention to only blatant maltreatment, limited resources allocated according to competing criteria, and value conflict concerning intervention in domestic settings.

Pedrick-Cornell and Gelles noted the extent to which the mass media seize upon partial and unrepresentative data to popularize the concept of elder maltreatment [9]. They caution that simplistic data will negatively influence the development of policy and practice. The present study indicates that elder maltreatment constitutes a diverse phenomenon, at least as encountered by the 157 workers studied for this chapter. At each level of analysis—act or condition, subgroup of elements, and maltreatment type—pattern identification remains complex. Identification of a core of maltreatment containing daily living and health problems emphasizes the need to differentiate acts or conditions involving the elder person, others, or both, as well as more detailed analysis of the intention of those involved overtly or indirectly.

Faulkner persuasively raised the issue of the presumed availability of services when mandatory reporting of elder maltreatment becomes public policy [8]. Without sufficient quantity and quality of services, too ready reliance on involuntary intervention may result. The data presented in this chapter suggest a community-based system of in-home and possibly respite care services as a major policy emphasis, with reliance on the criminal and civil legal systems to prevent further physical assault or exploitation.

Unfortunately, if Dressel's study of OAA funded services also applies to other human services in aging, cooperation and coordination focused on service delivery will be limited [22]. Block and Sinnott identified referral as a principal response by service personnel [6]. At a time when close cooperation and mutual accommodation to one another seem crucial at the local level, resource conservation and allocation decisions may frustrate attempts to make available the varied resources that are needed.

There remains the possibility that Callahan's call for nonintervention in domestic matters may win out [23], to be overcome only when the volume of frail elderly people at risk and in need produces a public outcry. Unless further preparatory work continues, a public outcry would place elder maltreatment in the position of so many services—resources become available but understanding of the problem remains cloudy, and knowledge of effective intervention suffers from even greater nebulousness.

A final policy implication drawn from these data concerns the extent to which we should rely on public agencies or the growing pattern of public agency contracts with voluntary agency and private practitioners. Elder protective services may constitute a narrow public mandate and voluntary agencies and private practitioners might benefit themselves, over the longer run, by expanding their willingness and skills in addressing the psychosocial and managerial needs of elderly clients.

Practice Implications

Numerous studies document avoidance of elderly people by practitioners. The incidence of self and medical care problems occurring in the cases studied does little to reassure the squeamish. Wide understanding by practitioners of the array of conditions and persons likely to be involved in elder maltreatment could help reduce the reluctance of some practitioners to acknowledge this subject.

Very positive evidence exists of relative willingness to provide intensive primary care to elderly people. Poulshock reported the general level of care provided to frail elders by family members and satisfaction with that care to be high [24]. Practitioners need to learn to distinguish among family units which provide adequate care to the satisfaction of the participants, family units experiencing stress or desiring not to assume responsibility for a frail elder family member, and domestic settings in which clear maltreatment occurs or an older person cannot manage alone. A number of protocols for identifying elder maltreatment can be tailored to a variety of practice settings [25-27].

Awareness and identification, however, count relatively little without procedures for dealing with persons at risk or engaging in elder maltreatment [28]. In the absence of program-level policies and procedures, many practitioners will have to exercise discretion in building personal networks to serve elder maltreatment [29].

Continuing efforts to explicate the content of elder maltreatment should provide practitioners with guidance for intervention and assist in prioritizing maltreatment components. Precise evidence will also benefit planners who must address such issues as when to intervene, what resources to utilize, and how to allocate them.

REFERENCES

1. N. H. Giordano and J. A. Giordano, Elder Abuse: A Review of the Literature, *Social Work, 29,* pp. 232-236, May-June 1984.
2. P. A. Hall and S. Rodriguez-Andrew, Report, *Intervention and Outcome in Elder Maltreatment,* mimeographed, Worden School of Social Service, Our Lady of the Lake University, San Antonio, 1984.
3. B. Star, *Helping the Abuser: Intervening Effectively in Family Violence,* Family Service Association of America, New York, 1983.
4. T. J. Stein, The Child Abuse Prevention and Treatment Act, *Social Service Review,* pp. 302-314, 1984.
5. L. V. Davis and B. E. Carlson, Atttitudes of Service Providers Toward Domestic Violence, *Social Work Research and Abstracts, 17,* pp. 34-39, 1981.

6. M. Block and J. Sinnott, *The Battered Elderly Syndrome,* University of Maryland, Center on Aging, College Park, 1979.
7. P. N. Chen, S. L. Bell, D. L. Dolinsky, J. Doyle, and M. Dunn, Elder Abuse in Domestic Settings: A Pilot Study, *Journal of Gerontological Social Work, 4,* pp. 3-17, 1981
8. L. R. Faulkner, Mandating the Reporting of Suspected Cases of Elder Abuse: An Inappropriate, Ineffective and Ageist Response to the Abuse of Older Adults, *Family Law Quarterly, 16,* pp. 69-91, 1982.
9. C. Pedrick-Cornell and R. J. Gelles, Elder Abuse: The Status of Current Knowledge, *Family Relations, 31,* pp. 457-465, 1982.
10. Texas Human Resources Code, Title 2, Chapter 48.
11. T. Hickey and R. L. Douglas, Neglect and Abuse of Older Family Members: Professionals' Perspectives and Case Experiences, *Gerontologist, 21,* pp. 171-176, 1981.
12. H. O'Malley, H. Segars, R. Perez, V. Mitchell, and G. Kneupfel, *Elder Abuse in Massachusetts: A Survey of Professionals and Paraprofessionals,* Massachusetts Legal Research and Services for the Elderly, Boston, 1979.
13. E. E. Lau and J. I. Kosberg, Abuse of the Elderly by Informal Care Providers, *Aging, 299-300,* pp. 10-15, 1979.
14. E. Rathbone-McCuan, Elderly Victims of Family Violence and Neglect, *Social Casework, 61,* pp. 296-304, 1980.
15. J. Steuer and E. Austin, Family Abuse of the Elderly, *Journal of the American Geriatrics Society, 20,* pp. 372-376, 1980.
16. K. Krippendorff, *Content Analysis,* Sage Publications, Beverly Hills, pp. 57-63, 1980.
17. B. G. Glaser and A. Strauss, *The Discovery of Grounded Theory: Strategies for Qualitative Research,* Aldine, Chicago, 1967.
18. J. I. Kosberg, *Family Conflict and Abuse of the Elderly: Theoretical and Methodological Issues,* paper presented at the 1979 Gerontological Society Annual Meeting, Washington, D.C., November 1979.
19. R. J. Gelles and M. A. Straus, Determinants of Violence in the Family: Toward a Theoretical Integration, in *Contemporary Theories About the Family,* Volume I, W. R. Bun, R. H. Hill, F. I. Nye, and I. L. Reiss (eds.), The Free Press, New York, pp. 549-581, 1979.
20. M. A. Straus, Measuring Intrafamily Conflict and Violence: The Conflict Tactics (CT) Scales, *Journal of Marriage and the Family, 14,* pp. 75-88, 1979.
21. T. Hickey and R. L. Douglass, Mistreatment of the Elderly in the Domestic Setting: An Exploratory Study, *American Journal of Public Health, 71,* pp. 500-507, 1981.
22. P. L. Dressel, Policy Sources of Worker Dissatisfaction: The Case of Human Services in Aging, *Social Service Review, 56,* pp. 406-423, 1982.
23. J. J. Callahan, Elder Abuse Programming: Will It Help the Elderly? *The Urban and Social Change Review, 15,* pp. 15-16, 1982.
24. S. W. Poulshock, *Executive Summary: The Effects on Families of Caring for Impaired Elderly in Residence,* Margaret Bleuker Research Center for Family Studies, The Benjamin Rose Institute, Cleveland, October 1982.
25. D. Ferguson and C. Beck, H.A.L.F.—A Tool to Assess Elder Abuse Within the Family, *Geriatric Nursing, 4,* pp. 301-304, 1983.

26. Hospital Protocol Committee, *The Protocol for the Treatment and Referral of Adult and Elderly Abuse Victims,* The Family and Child Abuse Prevention Center, Toledo, 1983.
27. S. K. Tomita, Detection and Treatment of Elderly Abuse and Neglect: A Protocol for Health Care Professionals, *Physical and Occupational Therapy in Geriatrics, 2,* pp. 37-51, 1982.
28. D. J. Shell, *Protection of the Elderly-A Study of Elder Abuse,* Manitoba Council on Aging, Winnipeg, Canada, 1982.
29. D. E. Biegel, B. K. Shore, and E. Gordon, *Building Support Networks for the Elderly,* Sage Publications, Beverly Hills, 1984.

Chapter 9

A CASE-COMPARISON ANALYSIS OF ELDER ABUSE AND NEGLECT

Michael A. Godkin
Rosalie S. Wolf
and
Karl A. Pillemer

This study was designed to examine the factors which contribute to the abuse and neglect of the elderly by caregivers in a domestic setting. It is part of a larger project funded by the Administration on Aging (AOA), which evaluated three model programs established to identify, treat, and prevent elderly abuse and neglect. The selection of elder abuse/neglect as a priority area by AOA was in response to the concern of the public and legislators about reports of mistreatment and violence in the older population.

Previous research had substantiated the existence of elder abuse and neglect as a significant social problem, provided a partial, conceptual basis for its occurrence, and indicated some strategies for its prevention and treatment. However, the findings were compromised by conceptual and methodological problems related to definitions, methods and sources of data, and the absence of control groups. The purpose of this study was to address one of the major limitations of earlier work by comparing abuse cases with non-abuse cases. Several theoretical explanations drawn from the literature provided the framework for the research.

The project and its findings are reported in *Elder Abuse and Neglect: Final Report from Three Model Projects* by R. S. Wolf, M. A. Godkin, and K. A. Pillemer, Center on Aging, University of Massachusetts Medical Center, 55 Lake Avenue North, Worcester, MA 01605.

THEORETICAL EXPLANATIONS OF
ELDER ABUSE/NEGLECT

Attempts to conceptualize the nature and dynamics of elderly abuse and neglect have been, in large part, based on theories which have emerged from the family violence and social gerontology literature, and have listed a multiplicity of factors as causal agents [1, 2]. Five such explanations have perhaps been the most prominent and offer the most promise in their attempts to improve our understanding of this problem.

Psychological Status of the Abuser

Some researchers of child abuse and spouse abuse have suggested the important role played by the personality problems of abusers. Young, for example, suggests that child abusers have a perverse fascination with punishment as an entity in itself [3]. In the literature on spouse abuse, Shainess indicated that the abuser's feelings of aggression may be fused with erotic thoughts [4]. Lyons suggested that spouse abusers have a need to manifest a false sense of security to mask their actual insecurity [5]. On the other hand, Gelles has been highly critical of the research that emphasized the importance of the pathological traits of perpetrators in abuse situations [6]. In the elderly abuse literature, Douglas et al. included the "flawed development" of the abuser as one cause of abuse [7]. Lau and Kosberg talk about the "non-normal" child (e.g., the mentally ill or alcoholic) who may have been cared for much of his/her life and who is unable to adjust to a caregiving role if those upon whom he/she has been dependent become impaired [8]. In fact, it could be argued that abusers of the elderly are more likely than child or spouse abusers to have a personality disorder. Because societal conditioning instills greater taboos on aggressive acts toward the elderly than other forms of family violence it may be that those who inflict such abuse are manifesting a greater degree of deviant behavior.

Intergenerational Transmission of Violent Behavior

The "cycle of violence" theory has emerged from the child abuse literature [9]. This explanation of elderly abuse suggests that violence as a normative, behavioral response to anger or frustration is learned by children from their parents. Applying this theory to elderly abuse, it could be suggested that abusers are likely to have been victims of child abuse. Presently, there is no evidence to support this premise.

Dependence and Exchange Relationships

Several researchers have concluded that the physical impairments of the elderly and subsequent dependency on the caregiver make them vulnerable to acts of abuse and neglect [10-12]. They are careful to point out, however, that dependency itself is not a sufficient explanation for this type of abuse since not all dependent elders are abused. In fact, the role of dependency relationships could perhaps best be explained by exchange theory which, while not specifically applied to elderly abuse, has been attributed to other forms of family violence [13, 14]. On one level, exchange theory would suggest that as the elderly become more dependent and impaired, an imbalance in the exchange of positive reinforcements occurs in their relationships with the caregivers. The potential would then exist for the costs of caregiving to be perceived as outweighing any benefits, to the extent of inducing anger and violence. Dowd has suggested that perceived power is intrinsic to the concept of exchange [5]. Thus, if an individual perceives a power deficit in the exchange and other sources are not present, attempts may be made to restore a power balance by violence.

External Stress

The literature on child abuse and spouse abuse indicates that externally imposed stresses (e.g., accidents, illnesses, financial problems) are a significant factor [9, 16, 17]. One study has examined the role of external stress in cases of elderly abuse, but only as it affects victims [18]. In cases of elderly abuse, the stresses experienced by the abuser are apt to be more important than those on the victims. It is likely that stress serves only as a precipitant of abuse. Predisposing factors must exist because not all stressed caretakers become abusive.

Social Isolation

Isolation has been found to be a characteristic of abusers and families in child abuse and spouse abuse cases [19-21]. It is hard to determine, however, whether isolation is an antecedent or precedent factor in abuse cases. It may well be that families in which abuse occurs prefer to remain secluded to avoid detection. On the other hand, research which has demonstrated the way in which social supports mitigate family life stresses supports the notion that isolation may precede acts of abuse and neglect [22, 23]. It is also likely that regular interactions with neighbors and friends serve as a deterrent in potential abuse situations because of the likelihood of being detected.

With this literature as background, this chapter investigates the importance of each of the above theories. Specifically, the following hypotheses are examined:

1. Caregivers who abuse or neglect the elderly are more impaired psychologically than caregivers of non-abused elders.
2. Caregivers who abuse or neglect the elderly have a greater history of violence in their background than caregivers of non-abused elders.
3. Abused/neglected elders are more dependent on their caregivers than non-abused/neglected elders.

4. Interpersonal conflict between elders and their caregivers is greater in abuse/neglect cases than for non-abused/neglected elders.
5. Caregivers who abuse or neglect the elderly are experiencing more external stressors than caregivers of non-abused elders.
6. Abused/neglected elders are more isolated socially than non-abused/neglected elders.

METHODS AND PROCEDURES

A quasi-experimental research design was used to compare two groups of elders (60 years and over). The study groups were clients of Elder Home Care Services of Worcester Area, Inc., a large case management agency for the elderly, which also served as an AOA model project site. One group was composed of victims of domestic abuse and neglect, the second of non-abused clients. Both were recipients of case management and social services from the agency. Between July 1981 and June 1983, fifty-nine individuals were identified by the two elder abuse specialists at the agency as victims of abuse/neglect. The comparison group of forty-nine clients was chosen by the agency's case managers who, during two separate time periods (July-October) in 1981 and 1982, selected their next assigned client for inclusion in the study.

A research instrument (Case Assessment Form) was developed by the authors with the assistance of the elder abuse specialists at the agency in light of information from earlier research. A set of definitions was developed for the categories of physical abuse, psychological abuse, material abuse, active neglect, and passive neglect (Table 1). For both the victims and comparison group, data were collected on the sociodemographic characteristics, living situation, social supports, finances, health, cognitive, emotional and functional status, and recent life changes. Data on caregivers and abusers included sociodemographic characteristics, social supports, the relationship of the caregiver to the elder clients, the existence of problems related to health, psychological functioning, substance abuse, significant losses, finances, and recent life changes. Possible stressful interdependencies were also documented. The Case Assessment Form was modified for the comparison group by omitting questions pertaining to the type and manifestations of abuse and neglect. Differences between the cases and comparison group were tested using the chi square test for nominal data and the Mann-Whitney test for ordinal data.

RESULTS

A comparison of the two groups indicated no significant differences with respect to age, sex, race, marital status, and income of the elderly clients. Sixty percent of the abuse victims were over the age of seventy-five. Eighty percent of this group were women, and over 60 percent had annual incomes less than five

Table 1. Classification of Abuse/Neglect

ABUSE:	
Physical	—the infliction of physical pain or injury, physical coercion, (confinement against one's will) e.g., slapped, bruised, sexually molested, cut, burned, physically restrained.
Psychological	—the infliction of mental anguish, e.g., called names, treated as a child, frightened, humiliated, intimidated, threatened, isolated, etc.
Material	—the illegal or improper exploitation and/or use of funds or other resources.
NEGLECT:	
Active	—refusal or failure to fulfill a caretaking obligation, INCLUDING a conscious and intentional attempt to inflict physical or emotional distress on the elder, e.g., deliberate abandonment or deliberate denial of food or health-related services.
Passive	—refusal or failure to fulfill a caretaking obligation, EXCLUDING a conscious and intentional attempt to inflict physical or emotional distress on the elder, e.g., abandonment, denial of food, or health-related services because of inadequate knowledge, laziness, infirmity or disputing the value of prescribed services.

thousand dollars. All but two of the elderly victims were white. Slightly less than half of the victims were widowed (44.8%), and more than a third (36.2%) were married.

Twenty-one of the forty-nine non-abused clients had a caregiver, whereas a caregiver for the fifty-nine abused elders was a necessary precondition. A significantly higher percentage of the caregivers in abuse situations were men (71.2%) compared to the non-abusive caregivers (23.8%). There were no significant differences in their age composition. Over half the abusers (55.9%) were under the age of sixty. Approximately 50 percent of the abusers were either husbands (25%) or sons (23%). One out of every five cases (18.6%) involved a daughter as the abuser. In all but 12 percent of the cases, abusers were a relative. Approximately two out of every five elderly victims were physically abused (44%) and/or materially abused (39%). Psychological abuse was present in nearly three-quarters of the cases (72.9%), and over half of them involved neglect (57.7%).

The following section will examine the significance of the factors hypothesized to be related to the incidence of elderly abuse. The results focus on the mental status of the abuser, dependency relationships, the dynamics of the caregiving relationship, external stressors, and social isolation. Data on intergenerational histories of violence in the abusers' families proved difficult to gather. Consequently, this factor had to be omitted from the study.

Psychological Status of the Abuser

As can be seen in Table 2, a significantly higher percentage of caregivers in abuse/neglect cases had a history of mental or emotional illness (40.7%) or had suffered a decline in their mental health prior to the abuse (45.8%) than the caregivers in the non-abuse sample (5.3% and 5.0%, respectively). At the same time alcohol abuse occurred in one-third of the cases, but not at all in the comparison group. There were no significant differences between the two groups with respect to drug abuse and the manifestation of behavior provocative to the elder.

Dependency Relationships

Mental Health Status of the Elders

The emotional and mental health of the victims of abuse were significantly worse than for the non-abused/neglected elders (Table 3). The emotional status of the elders was considered "poor" in 58.8 percent of the abuse/neglect cases and in 8.5 percent of the comparison group. Conversely, none of the maltreated elderly clients was considered to be in "excellent" emotional health or was rated as having a "very high" self-esteem, compared to about one-quarter (25.5%) of the comparison group. Although nearly half (44.5%) of the abused/neglected elders were reported to have "moderately low" or "very low" self-esteem, only about one-fifth (21.8%) of the non-abused/neglected elders was given the same rating. Sixty-one percent of the elderly cases had suffered a recent decline in mental health prior to their being abused or neglected; for the comparison group the figure was 6.4 percent. A recent increase in provocative behavior by elderly clients toward their caregivers was found in 37.3 percent of the abuse/neglect cases and 2.1 percent of the comparison group.

Health Status of the Elders

There were no significant differences between abused/neglected elderly and non-abused/neglected elderly with respect to the numbers of impairments requiring attention, nor the numbers of prescribed medications. A significant percentage of the maltreated elderly was reported to have experienced a recent decline in physical health (81.4%) in contrast to about one-fifth (21.3%) of the non-victimized elders.

Cognitive Functioning of the Elders

Generally, elders who were abused and neglected had significantly lower cognitive functioning when compared to the non-abused group except in the area of

Table 2. Emotional/Mental Status of Caregivers

Emotional/Mental Status	Cases		Statistic	Controls	
	N	Percent		N	Percent
History of mental health problems:					
No	35	59.3	$X^2 = 8.28$	18	94.7
Yes	24	40.7	$p = .004$	1	5.3
	59	100.0		19	100.0
Substance abuse history: Problems with alcohol abuse					
No	38	64.4	$X^2 = 8.85$	19	100.0
Yes	20	33.9	$p = .003$	0	0.0
Yes, suspected	1	1.7		0	0.0
	59	100.0		19	100.0
Current mental health status:					
A recent decline	27	45.8	$X^2 = 10.85$	1	5.0
No recent decline	32	54.2	$p = .001$	19	95.0
	59	100.0		20	100.0

remote memory where there was no significant difference (Table 4). In the abuse cases the percentage of elders with ongoing problems in orientation (person, place, and time) and memory (immediate and recent) ranged from between 11.1 percent to 17.8 percent. This compares to a rate of between 0 percent and 6.4 percent for elders in the nonabuse group. Similarly, the percentages of cases without orientation and memory problems ranged from 60 percent to 73.6 percent, whereas, in the comparison group, the range was between 73.5 percent and 91.8 percent. Elderly victims of abuse/neglect were able to provide consent in a significantly lower percentage (81.6%) when compared to elders in the non-victimized group (95.8%).

Instrumental Activities of Daily Living of Elders

It is apparent from Table 5 that elderly clients who were abused or neglected had problems with personal care, mobility, meal preparation, safety of property, and management of personal affairs in significantly higher proportions than elders in the comparison group, but were not significantly different with respect to shopping and transportation. For one activity, household management, the comparison group had a significantly higher percentage (89.8%) of problems compared to the abuse/neglect cases (72.9%). Among the elderly victims, 72.4 percent needed help for general personal care, including 66.1 percent for mobility, 74.6 percent for meal preparation, 50 percent for the security of property, and 76.3

Table 3. Emotional/Mental Status of Elders

Mental/Emotional Health	Cases		Statistic	Controls	
	N	Percent		N	Percent
Assessed emotional state:					
Excellent	0	0.0		12	25.5
Good	21	41.2	$Z = -5.77$	31	66.0
Poor	30	58.8	$p = .0001$	4	8.5
	51	100.0		47	100.0
Assessed self-esteem:					
Very low	2	5.6		1	2.2
Moderately low	14	38.9	$Z = 3.11$	9	19.6
Moderately high	20	55.6	$p = .002$	25	54.9
Very high	0	0.0		11	23.9
	36	100.0		46	100.0
Current mental health status:					
Mental health changes:					
A recent decline	36	61.0	$X^2 = 33.58$	3	6.4
No recent decline	23	39.0	$p = .0001$	44	93.6
	59	100.0		47	100.0
Provocative behavior:					
A recent increase	22	37.3	$X^2 = 19.04$	1	2.1
No recent increase	37	62.7	$p = .0001$	46	97.9
	59	100.0		47	100.0

percent for the management of personal affairs. In the comparison group, the corresponding percentages for those needing help were 32.7 percent for general personal care, 38.8 percent for mobility, 53.1 percent for meal preparation, 20.4 percent for the security of property, and 36.7 percent for management of personal affairs.

Specific Dependencies

There were no significant differences between the abuse cases and comparison group with respect to the degree of dependency of elder clients on their caregivers for financial resources, financial management, companionship, transportation, daily needs (e.g., medications), and property maintenance. It must be remembered that only the twenty-one non-abused elders who had a caregiver were included in the comparison group, and this group had dependencies on its caretakers similar to the abused elders. However, given that twenty-eight of the non-abused elders were without a caregiver at all, it can be assumed that as a whole group the non-abused elders were more self-sufficient and less dependent. This finding is indicated by

Table 4. Cognitive Status of Elderly Clients

Cognitive Status	Cases		Statistic	Controls	
	N	Percent		N	Percent
Orientation to person:					
On-going problem	6	11.1		1	2.0
Intermittent problem	13	24.1	$X^2 = 7.72$	5	10.2
No problem	35	64.8	$p = .021$	43	87.8
	54	100.0		49	100.0
Orientation to place:					
On-going problem	6	11.3		1	2.0
Intermittent problem	8	15.1	$X^2 = 6.13$	3	6.1
No problem	39	73.6	$p = .047$	45	91.8
	53	100.0		49	100.0
Orientation to time:					
On-going problem	8	15.1		0	0.0
Intermittent problem	10	18.9	$X^2 = 9.98$	5	10.6
No problem	35	66.0	$p = .007$	42	89.4
	53	100.0		47	100.0
Immediate memory:					
On-going problem	8	16.7		0	0.0
Intermittent problem	6	12.5	$X^2 = 9.33$	10	20.4
No problem	34	70.8	$p = .009$	39	79.6
	48	100.0		49	100.0
Recent memory:					
On-going problem	8	17.8		1	2.0
Intermittent problem	10	22.2	$X^2 = 6.75$	12	24.5
No problem	27	60.0	$p = .034$	36	73.5
	45	100.0		49	100.0
Ability to consent:					
Can give consent	40	81.6	$X^2 = 4.86$	46	95.8
Cannot give consent	9	18.4	$p = .027$	2	4.2
	49	100.0		48	100.0

Table 5. Elders' Problems with Instrumental Activities of Daily Living

Instrumental Activities	Cases		Statistic	Controls	
	N	Percent		N	Percent
Personal care:					
Problem	42	72.4	X^2 = 16.92	16	32.7
No problem	16	27.6	p = .0001	33	67.3
	58	100.0		49	100.0
Mobility:					
Problem	39	66.1	X^2 = 9.04	19	38.8
No problem	20	33.9	p = .005	30	61.2
	59	100.0		49	100.0
Meal preparation:					
Problem	44	74.6	X^2 = 5.43	26	53.1
No problem	15	25.4	p = .020	23	46.9
	59	100.0		49	100.0
Safety of property:					
Problem	29	50.0	X^2 = 10.04	10	20.4
No problem	29	50.0	p = .002	39	79.6
	58	100.0		49	100.0
Management of personal affairs:					
Problem	45	76.3	X^2 = 17.22	18	36.7
No problem	14	23.7	p = .001	31	63.3
	59	100.0		49	100.0
Household management:					
Problem	43	72.9	X^2 = 4.89	44	89.8
No problem	16	27.1	p = .027	5	10.2
	59	100.0		49	100.0

the fact that the abused/neglected elders were reported to have experienced recent increased dependency needs in a significantly higher proportion (61.0%) than the non-abused clients (4.3%). A significantly higher percentage of caregivers involved in abuse, however, was dependent on the elder for its financial needs. Just over 74.4 percent of the former were financially dependent compared to 36.8 percent of the latter. Nearly 42 percent of the abusers were "very dependent" on the elder for finances compared to 15.8 percent of the caregivers in non-abuse cases. There were no significant differences between the two groups with respect to their companionship dependencies, nor the degree to which both sets of caregivers had become increasingly dependent in recent times.

Relationship Dynamics

The data in Table 6 indicate the presence of a significantly greater degree of interpersonal conflict between the elder and the caregiver in the abuse cases. The relationship between elders and caregivers was considered "poor" in 77.2 percent of the cases and 4.8 percent of the controls. In 1.8 percent of the abuse cases the relationship was reported to be "excellent" compared to 52.4 percent of the non-abuse cases. Caregivers were said to have unrealistic expectations of their elderly counterparts in 67.9 percent of the abuse/neglect situations. Unrealistic expectations were reported at a rate of 5.6 percent in the comparison group.

External Stress

There appears to be a greater degree of stress in abusive families from both internal and external sources. The degree of stress imposed by elders on relatives was considered "a lot" in 66.7 percent of the cases compared to 23.5 percent of the comparison sample, whereas no stress was encountered in 19.4 percent of the abuse cases and 47.1 percent of the non-abuse cases. Nearly two-thirds (60.3%) of the abusers had undergone a recent change in their family relationships and two-fifths (41.4%) in living arrangements prior to the onset of abuse or neglect compared to 15.0 percent and 0.0 percent, respectively, for the caregivers in the

Table 6. Interpersonal Dynamics between Elder and Caregiver

Relationship Dynamics	Cases		Statistic	Controls	
	N	Percent		N	Percent
Assessed quality of relationship:					
Poor	44	77.2		1	4.8
Good	12	21.1	$Z = -2.17$	9	42.9
Excellent	1	1.8	$p = .029$	11	52.4
	57	100.0		21	100.0
Caretaker expectations: Caretaker has unrealistic expectations of elder	19	67.9	$X^2 = 17.31$	1	5.6
Caretaker does not have unrealistic expectations of elder	9	32.1	$p = .0001$	17	94.4
	28	100.0		18	100.0

non-abuse situations. However, there were no significant differences between cases and the comparison group with respect to the other events in their lives such as: recent loss of spouse through death or divorce/ separation, recent birth of a child, prior suicide attempts, and long- or short-term financial problems.

Elderly clients in abuse/neglect situations, however, experienced potentially stressful life changes related to their families, such as the death of a spouse (39%), and living situations, such as a new residence (37.3%), at significantly higher rates than the elderly in the comparison group (4.3% and 10.6%, respectively).

Social Isolation

An examination of the living situation and social network of elderly clients indicates that those who are abused or neglected are more likely to live with another person, usually the caregiver, and have significantly fewer social contacts because of recent losses than the comparison group. Eighty-six percent of the abused elders live with others compared to 29.2 percent of the comparison group. Eighty-three percent of the abused/neglected elderly reside with their caregivers compared to 42.9 percent of those elderly with caregivers who are not abused or neglected. Despite the tendency of the non-abused group to live alone, they have significantly more extensive social contacts. Almost 19 percent of the abused elderly have no social contacts, whereas only 6.1 percent of the controls are without contacts. Over one-third (35.6%) of this group have suffered recent losses in their support system, compared to 4.3 percent in the comparison group.

Concerning other factors related to social isolation, there were no significant differences between the two groups of elders with respect to marital status, frequency of social contacts, church or club affiliations, or the availability of an emergency contact, nor were there any significant differences between caregivers in the study and comparison groups with respect to the availability of familial support, the presence of an emergency contact, and the stability of support systems.

DISCUSSION

An analysis of the data indicates that all four factors under study play a role in cases of elderly abuse/neglect: the characteristics of the elder and caregiver, dependency and exchange relationships, external stresses, and social isolation.

To illustrate the conceptualization of the problem, qualitative data from two cases of elderly abuse and neglect will be used. The first client (FAL) is a white widow (of 50 years), about eighty-two years of age, who was subjected to "long-term" physical (pushed around) and psychological (intimidation) abuse by her son. The second client (MDA) is a white, single woman, about sixty-two years of age, who has been physically and psychologically abused and neglected for up to three years by her brother. She has been severely beaten (resulting in bone fractures and bruises), verbally intimidated, and neglected in terms of her need for food, companionship, false teeth, and glasses. The abuse and neglect is considered life threatening.

Their cases indicate that violence against the elderly is more likely to occur if men are the caregivers, particularly if the male caregiver has a history of mental health problems, including recent deterioration in mental health, and when alcohol abuse is present.

> FAL's son is an alcoholic with a history of violent and argumentative behavior including assault and the kidnapping of his daughter during a custody battle. He appears to be a very unstable person who has refused all attempts to get him to seek help.
> MDA's brother has a psychiatric history including fifteen years of institutionalization. Up until three years ago he was receiving outpatient care, but then terminated. He is considered very unstable emotionally and abuses alcohol. After a recent incident of physical abuse in which his sister received blackened eyes and facial bruises, he was arrested for disturbing the peace.

Elders who are abused or neglected are more likely to have emotional and psychological difficulties themselves. They tend to have low self-esteem, poor emotional health, and show evidence of recent deterioration in their mental health. Insufficient information made it difficult to characterize the mental and emotional status of FAL, although her emotional state was "good," and she was "very controlled and clear" when discussing her relationship with her son

> In the last few years the mental status of MDA has deteriorated. This is reflected in her appearance including the use of heavy, inappropriate makeup, frequent dying of her hair, and the constant wearing of a coat. She has difficulty maintaining a coherent conversation: her answers are often unfocused and inappropriate. Her emotional status is considered "poor."

Elders who are abused or neglected in this study are not more physically impaired than non-abused elders with respect to the number of impairments requiring attention or number of medications required for treating physical disabilities. They do tend, however, to be more functionally impaired with respect to instrumental activities of daily living and self-sufficiency with personal care, mobility, meal preparation, safety of property, and management of personal affairs. Abused/neglected elders are more likely to have problems with cognitive functioning evidenced by orientation and memory impairments and the ability to give consent. Surprisingly, in some ways, given the cognitive and functional impairments of abused/neglected elders, they are not seen as more dependent on their caregivers with respect to financial resources and management, companionship, transportation, daily needs, and property maintenance, than the twenty-one in the comparison group who had a caregiver. The fact that abused elders are more likely than non-abused elders to have a caregiver in the first place and that they have experienced a greater recent increase in dependency needs indicates that they are more dependent than the whole comparison group for many of their needs.

FAL has a number of health problems including hearing loss, a heart condition, and incontinence for which she has had recent surgery. These problems have limited her functional dependence. For example, her son does the food shopping and meal preparation. In addition, he fills her prescriptions, takes her to medical appointments, and having refused assistance with household management, is responsible for all household chores. She is, then, quite dependent on her son for many of her needs.

MDA has dental and eye problems, but is essentially in good health. Her poor emotional health and tendency to be disoriented to people and places necessitate her needing considerable help with instrumental activities of daily living. For example, she refuses to undress herself to bathe fearing her neighbors can see. She does not keep her own clothes or the house clean. Her brother takes her clothes shopping and pays all bills. She, too, is quite dependent on her caregiver.

Problems in the exchange relationship between abusers and elders are indicated by the data. Perceived disparities and imbalances in the exchange of benefits are just as likely to be related to the psychological status and interpersonal dynamics of both parties, as to the dependency requirements of the elder suggested by previous research. In fact, abusers tend to have dependency needs of their own, especially with respect to finances, which suggests the presence of interdependencies.

FAL's son is "very dependent" on his mother for financial support and works only periodically.

MDA's brother is also "very dependent" for financial assistance from his sister on whom he is "slightly dependent" for companionship. He does work as a janitor, however, and uses his income to pay for clothing and food expenses. His sister pays the rent.

The tension in the relationship between the abuser and the elderly victim may not be as much related to increasing dependency needs of the elder but more a consequence of their interpersonal problems and likely long-standing conflict. Relationships between caregivers and elders in abuse/neglect situations are more likely to be assessed as poor, evidenced in part by the unrealistic expectations of caregivers and perceived provocative behavior of clients. Such difficulties in the relationship between abusers and elderly victims, however, are predictable given the psychological difficulties of both parties.

FAL and her son have relied on each other since he was divorced approximately fifteen years ago. Their relationship is described as "poor." The mother says her son is constantly yelling and belittling her and the son finds himself provoked by his mother's demands for attention because of her unwillingness to go out of the house without him.

MDA and her brother are also described as having a "poor" relationship. They have a long history together having shared various apartments for approximately twenty years. The brother finds his sister's behavior provocative and feels that she tries deliberately to irritate him. He, in turn, has unrealistic expectations of his sister whom he thinks should be working.

Elders in abuse/neglect cases are seen as imposing a greater degree of stress on caregivers than those in the comparison group because of their physical and psychological problems. Other situational stresses that impact significantly on abuse cases relate to changes for both victims and abusers in family and living situations which result in them living together.

> FAL was seen as being a large source of stress to her brother because of her demands for attention and tendency to soil her sheets. The abuser's divorce and decision to move back with his mother from the West Coast was seen as a significant contributor to a long-term abuse situation.
>
> MDA's behavior, i.e., constant pacing and incoherence was a large source of stress to her brother. Another important stressor on their relationship that contributed to the abuse situation was the decrease in finances that resulted from MDA's loss of her job.

Because of recent losses in their social supports, elders in abuse/neglect cases have a depleted social network. They are more isolated, in an important way, than elders who are not abused or rejected.

> FAL seems to be isolated socially and very dependent on her son for companionship during their fifteen years living together. She has no social life and the only other contact she has is with her sister, on a monthly basis. She has, in fact, refused all attempts to encourage her to seek companionship from other than her son. Her hearing problem has made it difficult to use the telephone as a means for social contact.
>
> MDA is also very isolated, especially since her mental status deteriorated. Her only social activity is a visit from her sister every two or three months. Her brother, the abuser, with whom she has lived for approximately twenty years, is also very dependent upon his sister for companionship. He works nights as a janitor and sleeps during the day. In addition, he has discontinued his treatment as an outpatient at the psychiatric institution where he was once housed.

Elders in the comparison group are, however, more likely not to have a caregiver and to live alone. Given the fact that they have a more extensive social network, their living situation would seem to reflect a healthier independence, higher functional status, and greater overall self-sufficiency.

CONCLUSION

In trying to conceptualize the nature and dynamics of elderly abuse and neglect, especially in terms of the four factors under study, several major points can be made. It needs to be reemphasized, however, that these postulates are restricted in their generalizability and limited to the population sampled in this study.

- The psychological status of abusers (largely men) and elders is an important component of abuse/neglect cases. In particular, both parties have problems with their psychological and emotional health.
- Abused/neglected elders are more impaired functionally and cognitively than non-abused elders, and consequently are less self-sufficient performing instrumental activities of daily living.
- Conflict in the exchange relationship between abusers and elders, related to interpersonal dynamics and underlying personal emotional problems, seems to play an important role in cases of abuse/neglect. Interpersonal problems are reflected in the provocative behavior of some elders which contributes to their being seen as a greater source of stress, and the unrealistic expectations of caregivers, which may be manifested in continued financial dependency.
- Changes in the family and living situations of perpetrators and abused/neglected elderly lead to their lives becoming more interrelated, often in terms of the need to share a common residence.
- Abuse/neglected elderly tend to be more isolated than elders who are not subject to abuse.

To summarize, it appears that both abused elders and the abusers experience emotional problems which contribute to interpersonal difficulties in their relationship. Prior to the abuse, their lives become more inter-related, and they become increasingly interdependent. Both parties experience changes in their family situations, and the abused elder, in particular, becomes more isolated. Interdependence is manifested by a shared living situation and the financial dependency of the perpetrator on the elderly person. Given the emotional and interpersonal problems of both parties, it is perhaps likely that a shared living arrangement becomes a "pressure-cooker" situation that leads to abuse.

On a final note, the results of this study indicate an important need for in-depth research that examines the role of family dynamics in elderly abuse and neglect. Given that a great number of the abusers were adult children or spouses, it is likely that these cases involve complex and long-term family problems and unresolved conflicts. One such issue for which there was insufficient information in this study is the possibility that abusers were themselves abused or neglected as children. An examination of family dynamics would also need to identify differences between spouse abuse and abuse by adult children as well as between the various types of abuse.

REFERENCES

1. E. Villomare and J. Bergman, *Elder Abuse and Neglect: A Guide for Practitioners and Policy Makers,* prepared for the Oregon Office of Elderly Affairs, National Paralegal Institute, San Francisco, 1981.

2. House Select Committee on Aging, *Domestic Violence Against the Elderly,* Hearing before the Subcommittee on Human Services of the Select Committee on Aging, House of Representatives, U.S. Government Printing Office, Washington, D .C., 1980.

3. L. Young, Parents Who Hate, in *Violence in the Family,* S. Steinmetz and M. A. Straus (eds.), Dodd, Mead, New York, p. 187, 1974.

4. N. Shainess, *Psychological Aspects of Wife-Battering,* Birmingham Post, July 12, 1975.

5. J. R. Lion, Clinical Aspects of Wife-Battering, in *Battered Women,* M. Roy (ed.), Van Nostrand Reinhold, New York, p. 126, 1977.

6. R. J. Gelles, Child Abuse as Psychopathology: A Sociological Critique and Reformulation, in *Violence in the Family,* S. Steinmetz and M. A. Straus (eds.), Dodd, Mead, New York, p. 190, 1974.

7. R. L. Douglass, T. Hickey, and C. Noel, *A Study of Maltreatment of the Elderly and Other Vulnerable Adults,* Institute of Gerontology, University of Michigan, Ann Arbor, 1980.

8. E. E. Lau and J. L. Kosberg, Abuse of the Elderly by Informal Care Providers, *Aging, 11,* pp. 299-300, 1979.

9. M. A. Straus, R. J. Gelles, and S. K. Steinmetz, *Behind Closed Doors: Violence in the American Family,* Anchor Books, Garden City, New York, 1980.

10. H. O'Malley, H. Segars, R. Perez et al., *Elder Abuse in Massachusetts: A Survey of Professionals and Paraprofessionals,* Legal Research and Services for the Elderly, Boston, June 1979.

11. T. Hickey and R. L. Douglass, Mistreatment of the Elderly in the Domestic Setting: An Explanatory Study, *American Journal of Public Health, 71,* p. 500, 1981.

12. S. K. Steinmetz, Dependency, Stress, and Violence Between Middle-Aged Caregivers and Their Elderly Parents, in *Abuse and Maltreatment of the Elderly,* J. L. Kosberg (ed.), John Wright PSG Inc., Littleton, Massachusetts, p. 134, 1983.

13. W. J. Goode, Force and Violence in the Family, *Journal of Marriage and the Family, 33,* p. 624, 1971.

14. I. F. Nye, Choice Exchange and the Family, in *Contemporary Theories About the Family,* Vol. II, W. R. Burr, R. Hill, and I. F. Nye (eds.), The Free Press, p. 1,1979.

15. J. J. Dowd, Aging as Exchange: A Preface to Theory, *Journal of Gerontology, 30,* p. 584, 1975.

16. B. Justice and R. Justice, *The Abusing Family,* Human Sciences Press, New York, 1976.

17. S. Sedge, Spouse Abuse, in *The Battered Elder Syndrome*, M. Block and J. Sinnott (eds.), Center on Aging, University of Maryland, College Park, Maryland, p. 33, 1979.

18. M. C. Sengstock and J. Liang, *Identifying and Characterizing Elder Abuse,* Final Report Submitted to NRTA-AARP Andrus Foundation, Institute of Gerontology, Wayne State University, Detroit, 1982.

19. D. G. Gil, *Violence Against Children: Physical Child Abuse in the United States,* Harvard University Press, Cambridge, Massachusetts, 1971.

20. C. R. Hanneke and N. M. Shields, *Patterns of Family and Non-Family Violence: An Approach to the Study of Violent Husbands*, Policy Research and Planning Group, Inc., St. Louis, 1981.

21. R. J. Gelles, *The Violent Home,* Sage, Beverly Hills, California, 1972.

22. S. Cobb, Social Support as a Moderator of Life Stress, *Psychosomatic Medicine, 38,* p. 300, 1976.
23. T. H. Wan, *Stressful Life Events, Social Support Networks and Gerontological Health,* Lexington Books, Lexington, Massachusetts, 1982.
24. M. R. Block and J. D. Sinnott (eds.), *The Battered Elder Syndrome,* University of Maryland Center on Aging, College Park, Maryland, 1979.
25. N. H. Giordano and J. A. Giordano, *Individual and Family Correlates of Elder Abuse,* presented at the 36th Annual Scientific Meeting of the Gerontological Society of America, San Francisco, November, 22, 1983.

Section III

Grandparenting

Chapter 10

RAISING EXPECTATIONS FOR GRANDPARENTS: A THREE GENERATIONAL STUDY

Robert Strom
and
Shirley Strom

Most mothers and fathers believe that raising children today requires more parental involvement than it did in the past. When people moved less, responsibilities for child development were shared by the extended family including grandparents, aunts, uncles, and cousins. A sense of communal obligation for youngsters was also more common. Whereas neighbors used to know one another better and felt comfortable offering advice to other people's children, the tendency is now to view parents as the only proper source of child correction and guidance. Accordingly, some parents conclude "if our child doesn't turn out right, we will be considered at fault."

It seems that, in many families, the responsibility for childrearing has become disproportionate, with parents assuming more obligation than some can effectively manage. The resulting demand for various support services from public agencies continues to increase [1]. At the same time society makes this kind of help available, it is important to recognize that grandparents could become a greater resource. When parents can count on grandparents to share some of the family load for caregiving and guidance, there is less need to seek outside support. By providing America's 50 million grandparents learning opportunities that help them adjust to their changing role, they could contribute more to the development of grandchildren.

Our efforts to increase the involvement of grandparents in family affairs began by offering a free class on child and adolescent development at several senior citizen centers and churches in metropolitan Phoenix. Participants were invited to make known aspects of their experience as grandparents by responding to structured questions during group discussions. Each discussion was recorded. These baseline data were considered essential because the family relations literature revealed a patronizing attitude toward grandparents instead of creative instructional programs to help them grow [2-5]. During two years of data gathering, more than 400 grandmothers and grandfathers attended the weekly classes. The resulting information helped to formulate the nation's first curriculum for grandparents [6-11].

The purpose of the present study is to determine how the curriculum benefits grandparents in terms of relationships with grandchildren seven to eighteen years of age and their parents. Specifically, the program goals are to increase the satisfaction of being a grandparent; improve how well grandparents perform their role; enlarge the scope of teaching provided by grandparents; decrease the difficulties and the frustrations of being a grandparent; and improve grandparent awareness of personal success.

METHOD

Sampling and Intervention

A sample of nearly 400 grandparents reflected the national proportion of people, age fifty and older, who classify themselves as Protestant, Catholic, or Jewish [12]. A list of churches and synagogues in the Phoenix area stratified by religion was developed with assistance from the Arizona Ecumenical Council. In a series of randomly paired drawings within each religion, the first church chosen became an experimental site and the second a control site. Selection continued until the sampling needs were reached. This method avoided the contamination of either group that might otherwise have occurred through grandparent interaction if experimental and control participants were drawn from the same sites.

The 185 self-selected grandparents drawn from control sites were not provided classes but were paid thirty dollars to fulfill the same test schedule as their peers. Classes were provided for 210 experimental participants. Each of the program components were described previously [13]. All twelve of the weekly sessions started with group discussions of topics outlined in the course guidebook. After sharing their views, grandparents observed videotapes of younger people discussing the same issues such as peer pressure, drugs, sexuality, gender roles, self esteem, goals, and education. These unrehearsed conversations with children and parents reveal what it is like to be growing up now and raising youngsters today. Next, a mini-lecture examined some of the changes taking place in the lives of grandparents, parents, and grandchildren. Individuals then commented on their interviews with family members using suggested agenda from the guidebook. Finally, multiple choice homework items focusing on self evaluation were submitted anonymously and used to provide feedback about group norms of behavior. Ninety percent of the experimental participants completed the class and received a certificate.

Three Generational Instrumentation

Each grandparent in the experimental group chose one grandchild and one son or daughter who helped evaluate changes in grandparent attitudes and behavior. Some of the relatives lived nearby and others were from out-of-state. All three generational groups completed separate versions of the Grandparent Strengths and Needs Inventory (GSNI) before classes began, when the instruction ended, and three months after the intervention [14]. Grandchildren and parents were assured that their responses would never be shown to grandparents. Control group members were administered the GSNI according to the same schedule, but the sons, daughters, and grandchildren they identified did not complete the instrument.

The GSNI consists of sixty items, divided equally into six subsets that focus on separate aspects of grandparent development. Respectively, the subsets identify grandparent:

satisfaction—aspects of the grandparent role that provide satisfaction;
success—ways in which grandparents successfully perform their role;
teaching—the scope of family guidance that is expected of grandparents;
difficulty—problems encountered with the obligations of grandparenting;
frustration—grandchild behaviors that are upsetting to the grandparent;
informational needs—things grandparents need to know about grandchildren.

All versions of the instrument are scored in the same way, by assigning a numerical value of 4, 3, 2, or 1 to each of sixty responses. Responses most indicative of grandparent strength are valued 4, with diminishing values assigned to other answers on the basis of their distance from the best response. Scoring may begin from left or right, as in this example from the grandparent version:

		Always	*Often*	*Sometimes*	*Never*
Item 11	I am good at listening to my grandchild	4	3	2	1
Item 34	It is difficult to keep a conversation going with my grandchild.	1	2	3	4

The best indicator of grandparent strength for item 11 is Always while Never reflects grandparent strength in item 34. Both responses would be valued 4. Respondents who circled other answers would receive the lower values as shown. Items 1-30 are constructed so that Always is the best indicator of strength while Never is the best response for items 31-60. After values are assigned to every response, subtotals are derived for each of the subsets.

Three of the subsets (satisfaction, success, and teaching) comprise an index of grandparent potentials. The remaining subsets (difficulty, frustration, and information needs) provide an index of concerns. Together the six subset scores and the two overall index scores offer important information for planning curriculum. High alpha coefficients, above .90, were obtained for all subpopulations on every administration of the GSNI. These indicators are consistent with previous test-retest correlational data.

RESULTS AND DISCUSSION

Effects on Potentials and Concerns

The absolute item mean score of 2.5 for either index serves to differentiate between favorable and unfavorable performance. When a higher score is recorded, the source assigning it has identified an area of strength. Conversely, a score below 2.5 suggests that further growth is needed. The resulting comparison of the way grandparents view themselves and how they are seen by family members offers a more reliable perspective of their strengths and needs.

All three generational groups assigned grandparents favorable pretest scores for both potentials and concerns. When the instructional program ended twelve weeks later, grandparents were assigned higher posttest scores by themselves, the parents, and grandchildren. Grandparents indicated they experienced significant growth in potentials ($p < .001$) and concerns ($p < .047$). This view was corroborated by parents who reported they had observed the grandparent gain in potentials ($p < .006$) and concerns ($p < .019$). Scores assigned by the grandchildren also increased, but these changes were nonsignificant. It is relevant to note however, that the perceptions of grandchildren were significantly more favorable than those reported by parents and grandparents before the program and at the finish. When the inventory was given a third time several months later, the gains each source had identified earlier were sustained. In contrast, the control group made no gains during the project.

Improvement in Subset Scores

The potentials and concerns indicators offer a broad view of change, but they do not reveal the particular realms in which behavior is modified. Because subsets are more specifically defined, the information they offer is more detailed. The absolute total mean score of 25 for any subset distinguishes between favorable and unfavorable ratings. Whenever a higher score is recorded, the source assigning it has identified a strength; subset scores below 25 reveal dimensions of behavior that grandparents may need to change.

Grandparents expressed favorable self impressions on the pretest measures of satisfaction, success, teaching, and ability to deal with difficulties and frustrations. After attending the program, they scored significantly higher on three subsets: satisfaction ($p < .001$), success ($p < .055$), and teaching ($p < .001$). The growth identified by grandparents was confirmed by parents. They assigned significantly higher posttest scores indicating greater grandparent satisfaction ($p < .018$), more active teaching ($p < .055$), and less frustration ($p < .050$). Gains for the success and difficulty subsets approached significance as well. That the grandchildren witnessed similar improvement is shown by the higher but nonsignificant gains they recorded for every subset on the posttest.

The one subset on which grandparents assessed themselves unfavorably at the beginning of the program was information needs. Even though their scores for this set of items improved on the posttest, grandparent self impression remained in the unfavorable range. Grandchildren and parents gave favorable scores but recorded their lowest ratings on this subset.

When the subset scores for satisfaction, success, and teaching are combined and the difficulties, frustration, and information needs scores are united, the resulting totals for potentials and concerns are favorable if they reach 75. It was determined that grandparents, parents, and grandchildren recorded a higher total score for potentials and higher total score for concerns following the instructional program. These findings indicate grandparents learned to improve their influence, and they grew more capable of dealing with family problems. The higher rating for potentials than for concerns shows grandmothers and grandfathers viewed their role in a more positive than negative way. This distinction is important because people who enjoy their role can more readily generate optimism when it is necessary to cope with difficulties.

Influence of Independent Variables

Multivariate analyses were conducted to determine how each of eleven independent variables influenced grandparent performance. Experimental participants did significantly better when one or more of these conditions existed: their son or daughter was married; they spent more than five hours a month with their grandchild; they lived less than 200 miles from their grandchild; their grandchild was a granddaughter; their grandchild was between ages seven and eleven; they were under seventy years of age; and they were grandmothers. The nonsignificant variables were grandparent level of education, grandparent income, grandparent marital status, and whether the grandparent was related to the grandchild through a son or daughter.

IMPLICATIONS AND CONCLUSIONS

This study demonstrated that grandparents are able to benefit from an educational program designed to help them make a greater contribution to the family. Following intervention, grandparents reported they had made significant improvements in attitudes and behavior. These improvements were corroborated by parent inventory scores. Participating grandchildren also observed grandparent gains, but to a lesser degree. More specifically, grandparents benefited by understanding how their role is changing, acquiring a broader perspective, experiencing greater mental stimulation, gaining more confidence and higher self esteem, improving intergenerational communication, and strengthening family relationships.

These feelings expressed by grandparents illustrate the personal impact of the program: "I was comparing my grandchildren to my own children, but it can't be done. This is a different day and age, and I can understand it now. I feel I am more openminded than before." "It helped me realize that I need to keep growing if I want respect from my grandchildren." "It helped me recognize the privileges I have as a grandparent as well as the duties that I owe my grandchildren." " I feel so much better about myself as a grandmother. I also feel more optimistic about our grandchildren."

The benefits cited by grandparents were reinforced by their sons and daughters: "Taking this course has really helped my mom think about her role in my child's life. She is working hard to get to know my children as individuals. She feels accepted." "My parents seem more willing to share with us. I know my children could learn a lot from them." "My mother has always been kind and loving to all of us, but now she is more interesting to be around. It is fun to hear what she is learning." "I'm glad my mom and dad decided to quit being cheerleaders in favor of becoming a more constructive influence in our lives."

The favorable changes that occurred in the lives of these grandparents should be available to other families as well. The emerging concept of grandparent education deserves to be more widely understood, supported, and implemented. Some of the next steps to achieve these broad goals include establishing demonstration sites for grandparent education; developing leadership training for grandparent educators; expansion of the curriculum to include grandchildren of all age groups; orienting parents to the potential of grandparents; adaptation of the curriculum and instructional procedures to fit the needs of men and women living in long-term care centers; and dissemination of the grandparent program to other countries.

REFERENCES

1. P. Benson, D. Williams, and A. Johnson, *The Quicksilver Years: Hopes and Fears of Early Adolescence,* Harper and Row, New York, 1987.
2. H. Kivnick, Grandparenthood: An Overview of Meaning and Mental Health, *The Gerontologist* 22:1, pp. 59-66, 1982.

3. V. Bengston and J. Robertson, *Grandparenthood*, Sage Publications, Beverly Hills, California, 1985.
4. A. Cherlin and F. Furstenberg, *The New American Grandparent*, Basic Books, New York, 1986.
5. M. Link, The Grandparenting Role, *Lifestyles: A Journal of Changing Patterns, 8*:3, pp. 27-34, 1987.
6. R. Strom and S. Strom, Redefining the Grandparent Role, *Cambridge Journal of Education, 13*:3, pp. 25-28, 1983.
7. R. Strom and S. Strom, A Creative Curriculum For Grandparents, *Journal of Creative Behavior, 18*:2, pp. 132-141, 1984.
8. R. Strom and S. Strom, Becoming A Better Grandparent, in *Growing Together: Intergenerational Sourcebook,* K. Struntz and S. Reville (eds.), American Association of Retired Persons and the Elvirita Lewis Foundation, Washington, D.C., pp. 57-60, 1985.
9. R. Strom and S. Strom, Preparing Grandparents for a New Role, *Journal of Applied Gerontology, 6*:4, pp. 476-486, 1987.
10. R. Strom and S. Strom, Intergenerational Learning and Curriculum Development, *Educational Gerontology, 14*:3, pp. 165-181, 1988.
11. R. Strom, H. Bernard, and S. Strom, *Human Development and Learning,* Human Sciences Press, New York, 1989.
12. G. Gallup, *Religion in America*, Gallup Center, Princeton, New Jersey, pp. 6-27, 1987.
13. R. Strom and S. Strom, Grandparents and Learning, *International Journal of Aging and Human Development, 29*:3, pp. 163-169, 1989.
14. R. Strom and S. Strom, *Grandparent Development: Final Research Report to the Andrus Foundation,* Arizona State University, Tempe, Arizona, 137 pp. 1989.

Chapter 11

GRANDCHILDREN AND GRANDPARENTS: ROLES, INFLUENCES, AND RELATIONSHIPS

Karen A. Roberto
and
Johanna Stroes

The changing structure of our population has resulted in a greater number of three and four generation families. Within the family, the opportunity to experience a variety of roles, for a longer period of time, has also increased. An example of an expanding position within the family is that of grandparent. Today, 94 percent of all older adults with children are grandparents and nearly 50 percent are great-grandparents [1].

Several studies indicate that grandparents play a variety of roles within the family and demonstrate different styles of grandparenting [2-7]. For example, Wood and Robertson proposed that grandmothers can have either personal or social relationships with their grandchildren, while maintaining either a) apportioned, b) symbolic, c) individualized, or d) remote styles of grandparenting [7]. Apportioned grandparents are concerned about doing what is morally right for the grandchildren while maintaining the prerogative to spoil and indulge them. In contrast, symbolic grandparents are only concerned about doing what is morally right. Individualized grandparents see grandchildren as a way to keep themselves from becoming lonely and old. Remote grandparents place little emphasis on any aspect of the relationship or grandparenting in general [7, 8]. Grandparent-grandchild interaction styles often change during the course of the relationship and grandparents tend to maintain different types of relationships with different grandchildren [2].

The type of relationship grandparents have with their grandchildren also depends on a variety of personal and situational variables. One factor is age; older grandmothers tend to have significantly less contact with their grandchildren than do younger grandmothers. The latter are more involved in fun-loving activities and view themselves as too young to fit the image of the traditional grandmother [9].

Parental factors can also influence the relationship between grandparents and grandchildren. For example, the amount of contact parents allow grandchildren to have with their grandparents during childhood directly affects the type of relationship they develop and later maintain [10]. Thompson and Walker found that when granddaughters have less than monthly contact with their grandmothers, they tend to adopt their mothers' feelings for their grandmothers [11]. Marital status of the parents is another variable that can modify the role of grandparents. In cases of parental divorce, grandparents have a bigger roles in the lives of their grandchildren when their child retains custody as opposed to their child-in-law [12].

Some studies support the idea that maternal grandparents play a more significant role in the lives of grandchildren than do paternal grandparents [13-15]. Because of morbidity factors and childhood interaction patterns, young-adult grandchildren tend to have the most contact with their mother's mother, followed by their fathers' mother, mother's father, and father's father [15]. The quality of the grandparent-grandchild relationship also varies according to parental linkage. Relationships with maternal grandmothers appear to be the strongest among all grandparent-grandchild dyads [14, 16].

Only a small amount of research exists that focuses on grandchildren's perceptions of the role grandparents play in their lives. Adolescent and young-adult grandchildren report their relationship with their grandparents is of great importance [15, 17]. Frequency of contact does not seem to be a factor in determining relationship importance [18], but grandchildren do feel that it affects the solidarity of their relationship with their grandparents [19]. Grandchildren's strongest motivators for maintaining a relationship with grandparents seem to be enjoyment of the relationship, emotional ties with grandparents, and feelings of obligation [18].

Most of what is known about the grandparent-grandchild relationship is based on interview and questionnaire data from grandmothers. When researchers include grandfathers in their studies, results either report on the grandparent dyad or on comparisons between grandparent dyads, not on relationships specifically with grandfathers. We also know very little about grandparent-grandchild relationships from the grandchild's point of view. This study begins to address these gaps in the research by examining the importance of *both* grandmothers and grandfathers in the lives of their grandchildren, from the perspective of their young-adult grandchildren. By comparing the perceptions of grandchildren with both grandmothers and grandfathers, similarities and differences in grandparent roles, influences, and relationships can be more accurately explored.

The following questions guided the research presented in this chapter:

1. What type of activities do young adult grandchildren participate in with their grandparents?
2. How influential are grandmothers and grandfathers in the value development of their grandchildren?
3. Do grandchildren perceive differences in relationships with their grandmothers and grandfathers?
4. Does participation, influence on values, and the relationship with grandparents differ based on how grandchildren conceptualize the role of their grandmothers and grandfathers.

METHOD

Sample

A convenience sample of 142 college students enrolled in two sections of an introductory gerontology course was selected for this study. This course is part of the university's general education curriculum and is comprised of students from a variety of disciplines. Three-fourths of the students were female and over 90.0 percent were caucasian. They ranged in age from seventeen to fifty-four ($M = 23.1$; $SD = 6.2$). Three percent of the students classified themselves as freshman, 25.0 percent as sophomores, 35.0 percent as juniors, and 38.0 percent as seniors.

Eleven percent of the respondents had no living grandparents. Approximately 63.0 percent of the sample reported having at least one living grandfather and 82.0 percent reported having at least one living grandmother. Seventy-seven respondents (17 males and 60 females) had both a living grandfather and grandmother.

Procedures

During two different semesters, on the first day of class students were invited to complete a questionnaire describing their relationship with their grandparents. Identical questions were asked about grandmothers and grandfathers. When students had more than one living grandparent, they were told to select one and answer all questions with respect to that particular grandparent. Overall, 62.0 percent of the grandchildren answered the questions with respect to their maternal grandmother while 38.0 percent responded in terms of their paternal grandmother. For the students having a living grandfather, 53.0 percent responded in terms of their maternal grandfather while 47.0 percent answered the questions with respect to their paternal grandfather. Of the seventy-seven students with both a living grandmother and grandfather, one-fourth had both sets of grandparents, 32.0 percent had only one grandmother, and 69.0 percent had only one grandfather. Within this group, a greater percentage of respondents focused on their maternal grandparents (55.0% grandmothers; 60.0% grandfathers) versus their paternal grandparents (45.0% grandmothers; 40.0% grandfathers).

Measures

The respondents were asked how frequently, when they were not in school, they participated in the following activities with their grandparents: phone visits, recreation outside the home, brief visits for conversations, discussions of important topics, religious activities, dinner, exchange of gifts, and help with chores. Responses were coded from (1) once a month or less to (5) daily and summed for a total *participation with grandparent* score. The scale had an internal consistency coefficient of .91. The assessment of participation was limited to when the respondents were not in school to maximize the opportunity they had to interact with their grandparents. It was believed that attending college would require the majority of students to live away from their families as well as place greater demands on their resources (e.g., time, money, mobility).

The impact grandparents had on their grandchildren's general belief system was determined by asking the grandchildren how much influence their grandmothers and grandfathers had on eight aspects of their lives: religious beliefs, sexual beliefs, political beliefs, family ideals, educational beliefs, work ethic, moral beliefs, and personal identity. Responses were coded (1) none, (2) a little, (3) some, and (4) a great deal and summed for a total *value development* score. Cronbach's alpha computed for the total value development scale was .91.

Four items, drawn from Bengtson's Positive Affective Index [20], were used to evaluate the respondents' *relationship* with their grandparents. The first two items assessed how well the respondents felt their grandparents understood them and how well they understood their grandparents. The third question asked respondents to indicate how well they and their grandparents communicated. The final question required grandchildren to indicate how similar their life views were in comparison to their grandparents. Responses were coded (1) not at all, (2) somewhat, (3) quite a bit, and (4) a great deal and summed for a total relationship score. The relationship scale had an internal consistency coefficient of .88.

Role conception was determined through the use of the *Grandchild Role Conception Scale* [15]. This ten-item scale is based on the work of Robertson who identified two dimensions of grandparenting: social and personal [18]. The *social dimension* of grandparenting is determined almost exclusively by social or normative forces that meet the needs of society [8]. In the *personal dimension*, the grandparent role is determined almost exclusively by a regard for individuality and personal or self-fulfillment [8]. Five items comprise each dimension. An example of an item from the social dimension is, "It is very important that my grandparent be involved with family activities." "My grandparent has brought a very important sense of perspective to my life" is an example of the type of statement included in the personal dimension. Responses for all items ranged from

(1) strongly disagree to (5) strongly agree. The scale has a reported reliability coefficient of .68 for the social dimension and .83 for the personal dimension. Similar alpha coefficients were found for this sample; .78 for the social dimension scale and .71 for the personal dimension scale. From these scales, Hartshorne and Manaster [15] adapted Robertson's [8] four general categories of role conception: *apportioned* (high social/high personal), *individualized* (low social/high personal), *symbolic* (high social/low personal), and *remote* (low social/low personal). Grandparents were assigned to one of the four categories using the median score. Grandparents with scores at the median level and below were labelled low in role orientation and scores above the median were regarded high in role orientation.

Analyses

In the first stage of data analysis, paired *t*-tests were used to compare the responses of the seventy-seven individuals who had both a living grandfather and grandmother. Slight variations in the final sample size used to answer each research question reflect missing responses. Separate analyses were then conducted by gender to explore differences in grandson's and granddaughter's perceptions of their grandparents. Separate analysis were used because of the disproportional number of granddaughters in the sample.

The literature suggests that relationships with maternal grandparents are stronger than with paternal grandparents. In this stage of the analysis, perceptions of maternal grandmothers versus paternal grandfathers were compared. To maximize the number of respondents, independent *t*-tests were used to analyze responses from all grandchildren with a living grandparent.

A series of one-way analyses of variance were conducted to determine differences in participation, value development, and relationships according to role conception. Using the responses from the seventy-seven grandchildren having both grandparents, separate analyses were completed for grandfathers and grandmothers. When significant differences were found, Duncan's Multiple Range test was used to compare differences among the means. To compensate for unequal group size, the harmonic mean of the two groups being compared was used.

RESULTS

Participation with Grandparents

Grandchildren participated in more activities with their grandmothers ($M = 12.4$; $SD = 5.4$) than with their grandfathers ($M = 11.4$; $SD = 4.5$), $t(70) = -2.40$, $p < .05$. An examination of each type of activity indicates that grandchildren participate in brief visits for conversation, family gatherings, talking over things that are important, and helping with chores more with their grandmothers than with their grandfathers (Table 1). When separated by gender, no significant difference was found in overall participation for grandsons ($t(15) = -1.57, p > .05$) or granddaughters ($t(53) = -1.88, p > .05$). No differences in overall participation were found between maternal and paternal grandmothers ($t(97) = -.18, p > .05$) and grandfathers ($t(78) = -.26, p > .05$).

Value Development

Grandmothers were perceived as having greater influence on the development of their grandchildren's values ($M = 18.8$; $SD = 6.7$) than grandfathers ($M = 17.1$; $SD = 6.9$), $t(77) = -3.99, p > .001$. Grandchildren reported being influenced more by their grandmothers than their grandfathers in all areas assessed except their political beliefs and work ethic (Table 2). No differences between grandmothers and grandfathers were found for these two areas. Both grandsons ($t(16) = -2.44$, $p < .05$) and granddaughters ($t(58) = -3.17, p < .01$) perceived their grandmothers as having more influence on their value development than their grandfathers. The comparison between maternal and paternal grandmothers ($t(104) = .89, p > .05$) and grandfathers ($t(85) = .18, p > .05$) revealed no significant differences in overall value development.

Table 1. Participation in Activities with Grandmothers and Grandfathers

Activity	Grandmother		Grandfather		
	M	SD	M	SD	t-Value
Phone visits ($n = 77$)	1.8	1.2	1.7	1.1	n.s.
Recreation out of home ($n = 77$)	1.2	.5	1.1	.4	n.s.
Brief visits ($n = 76$)	1.8	1.3	1.6	1.1	2.38*
Family gatherings ($n = 7\ 7$)	1.5	.9	1.3	.7	2.01*
Talk over items of importance ($n = 75$)	1.6	1.0	1.4	.8	2.63**
Religious activity ($n = 71$)	1.3	.7	1.2	.6	n.s.
Dinner together ($n = 75$)	1.4	.8	1.3	.7	n.s.
Receive gifts ($n = 74$)	1.2	.4	1.1	.4	n.s.
Give gifts ($n = 73$)	1.1	.3	1.1	.3	n.s.
Help with chores ($n = 75$)	1.5	.9	1.3	.7	2.63**

Note: The variations in sample size are a result of missing responses.
*$p < .05$
**$p < .01$

Relationship

Grandchildren perceived their relationship with their grandmothers (M = 11.9; SD = 2.5) as stronger than with their grandfathers (M = 9.5; SD = 2.9), $t(77)$ = -6.97, $p < .001$. Grandchildren rated each area of their relationship with their grandmothers significantly higher than with their grandfathers (Table 3). Here too, both grandsons ($t(16)$ = -2.74, $p < .05$) and granddaughters ($t(59)$ = -6.43, $p < .001$) perceived their relationships to be stronger with their grandmothers than with their grandfathers. No significant differences were found for grandchildren's relationships with their grandparents according to parental linkage grandmothers ($t(104)$ = .99, $p > .05$); grandfathers ($t(85)$ = .29, $p > .05$).

Role Conception

The respondents rated grandmothers significantly higher than grandfathers on both the social ($t(74)$ = -2.00, $p < .05$) and personal ($t(74)$ = -3.85, $p < .001$) dimensions of grandparenthood. No significant differences were found for grandsons on either the social ($t(15)$ = -1.59, $p > .05$) or personal ($t(15)$ = -1.85, $p > .05$) dimensions. Granddaughters rated their grandmothers higher than their grandfathers on the personal dimension ($t(58)$ = -3.38, $p < .001$), but no significant differences between grandmothers and grandfathers were found on the social dimension ($t(58)$ = -1.28, $p > .05$).

Table 2. Grandmothers' and Grandfathers' Influence on Value Development

Value	Grandmother		Grandfather		
	M	SD	M	SD	
	($n = 77$)		($n = 77$)		t-Value
Religious beliefs	2.3	1.3	1.9	1.2	3.26**
Sexual beliefs	1.7	.9	1.4	.8	3.02**
Political beliefs	1.7	.9	1.6	.7	n.s.
Family ideals	3.1	.9	2.7	1.1	4.15**
Educational beliefs	2.4	1.2	2.2	1.2	2.41*
Work ethic	2.4	1.2	2.4	1.2	n.s.
Moral beliefs	2.7	1.2	2.5	1.2	2.77**
Personal identity	2.5	1.2	2.2	1.2	3.51***

*$p < .05$
**$p < .01$
***$p < .001$

Table 3. Grandchildrens' Relationship with Grandmothers and Grandfathers

| Relationship Item | Grandmother | | Grandfather | | |
| | M | SD | M | SD | |
	($n = 77$)		($n = 77$)		t-Value
Grandparent understands you	3.0	.8	2.3	.8	6.72***
You understand grandparent	3.1	.7	2.5	.8	6.69***
Communication with grandparent	3.2	.8	2.5	.9	6.21***
Similar life views as grandparent	2.6	.8	2.2	.9	4.17***

***$p < .001$

Based on their style of grandparenting, the majority of grandmothers and grandfathers were classified either as apportioned (48.0%; 42.0%) or remote (29.0; 36.0%). Seventeen percent of the grandmothers and 13.0 percent of the grandfathers were classified as individualized. A small percent of grandmothers (6.0%) and grandfathers (9.0%) were classified as symbolic. Significant differences were found for both grandfathers and grandmothers in all three areas studied (Table 4).

Participation

Grandfathers labelled as apportioned participated in a greater number of activities with grandchildren than grandfathers labeled as remote or individualized. Grandmothers categorized as apportioned also rated higher in participation than those labeled as remote or individualized grandmothers.

Value development

Both apportioned and individualized grandfathers contributed more to the value development of their grandchildren than grandfathers classified as symbolic or remote. Grandmothers labeled as apportioned contributed more to the value development of their grandchildren than those perceived as individualized or remote grandmothers.

Table 4. Participation, Value Development, and Relationship by Grandparent Classification

	1 Apportioned		2 Symbolic		3 Individualized		4 Remote		F-Value
	M	SD	M	SD	M	SD	M	SD	
Grandfathers	n = 32		n = 7		n = 10		n = 28		
Participation (1,4) (1,3)	16.1	5.3	13.5	8.1	12.2	5.6	10.2	.7	6.91
Value development (1,2) (1,4) (3,2) (3,4)	22.2	5.5	12.7	5.7	18.5	5.6	12.9	5.1	16.62
Relationship (1,2) (1,4) (3,4)	11.5	2.3	8.0	.9	10.0	3.2	7.9	2.5	11.07
Grandmothers	n = 37		n = 5		n = 13		n = 22		
Participation (1,4) (1,3)	16.8	6.9	16.2	8.7	11.8	5.1	10.8	1.5	5.66
Value development (1,2) (1,3)	22.1	5.9	17.4	8.2	18.0	5.3	14.0	5.9	8.82
Relationship (1,4) (3,4)	13.0	2.0	11.7	2.5	12.1	1.8	19.1	2.6	8.39

Note: The number in parentheses denotes pairs of groups significant at the .05 level. All F-values are significant at the .001 level.

149

Relationship

Similar differences were found for the overall relationship grandparents had with their grandchildren. Again, grandfathers labeled as either apportioned or individualized had stronger relationships with their grandchildren than did those labelled as remote. Apportioned grandfathers also had a stronger relationship with grandchildren than those categorized as symbolic grandfathers. Relationships with apportioned and individualized grandmothers were rated higher than with grandmothers labeled as remote.

DISCUSSION

The results of this study indicate that grandchildren participated in activities with their grandmothers to a greater extent than with their grandfathers. Participation with both grandparents, however, was somewhat low. On average, grandchildren interacted with their grandparents once a month or less. While the scaling of the responses for this measure prohibits obtaining a detailed picture of interactions beyond this point, the findings are similar to Kennedy's study of college students relationship with grandparents [18]. He reports that 29.0 percent of his sample saw their grandparents once or twice a month and 47.0 percent reported having contact several times a year or less. The grandchildren's current lifestage experiences may be a contributing factor. During late adolescence and young adulthood, individuals tend to focus their energy on personal growth and relationships outside the family. Grandchildren do not abandon their grandparents, but their relationship with them takes on a different dimension as both generations grow older [2].

The most frequent types of interaction with grandparents were brief visits for conversation and participating in important discussions. A recent study of high school students also found that grandparents were viewed as confidants and companions by their grandchildren [17]. While it can not be determined whether the grandchildren or grandparents initiated the activities examined in the current study, a strong motivation for college students in maintaining a relationship with their grandparents is their enjoyment in being with their grandparents [18]. Together, these findings suggest that as grandchildren mature they tend to form a more voluntary relationship with grandparents rather than one based solely on family obligation.

A fundamental task of the family is the transmission of values from one generation to another. Grandparents may play a crucial role in this process by serving as arbitrators between parents and children concerning values that are central to family continuity and individual enhancement [21]. The grandchildren in this study perceived their grandparents as influential in their value development with grandmothers having a greater influence than grandfathers in almost every value domain. This finding supports previous research that suggests grandmothers have a broader influence on their grandchildren than grandfathers [14]. The areas where grandmothers had a greater impact focused primarily on interpersonal issues (e.g., family ideals, personal identity, religious beliefs) traditionally associated with a woman's realm of knowledge. Conventional sex role beliefs may influence the perception of grandparents, and of grandfathers in particular, about what constitutes appropriate areas of conversation with their grandchildren [14]. This is not to suggest that grandfathers are not influential in the lives of their grandchildren, but that their presence in these areas may be more subtle. Future research that includes a greater range of values is needed to further explore grandparents role in the value development of their grandchildren.

Grandchildren reported having a stronger relationship with their grandmothers than with their grandfathers. Past research on grandparents suggests that greater involvement with grandchildren [22, 23] and parental linkages [10, 13-14, 16] are associated with greater satisfaction with the grandparent role. In this study, these same factors do not seem to influence grandchildren's perception of the relationship with their grandparents. Further examination of the data revealed only moderate correlations between grandchildren's participation in activities with grandparents and the salience of their relationship. The strength and pattern of association were similar for grandmothers ($r = .38$, $p < .01$) and grandfathers ($r = .30$; $p < .05$). In addition, no differences in the grandchildren's perceptions of their relationships with their grandparents were found between maternal and paternal grandparents. Parental influences on the relationship between grandparents and grandchildren may weaken as grandchildren move through the adult years and establish for themselves their grandparents role. Longitudinal research is necessary to explore how parental attitudes and life circumstances influence the relationship their children have with grandparents. An examination of the grandparent-grandchild dyad is also needed to determine how personal and situational variables affect perceptions of the relationship for both generations.

Differences in each of the areas investigated were found according to the role in which grandchildren conceptualized their grandparents. Grandmothers and grandfathers labeled "apportioned" participated in more activities with their grandchildren, contributed more to their grandchildren's value development, and had a stronger relationship with their grandchildren than grandparents designated as "remote." These two classifications can be viewed as opposite ends of the grandparent continuum. Apportioned grandparents are perceived as highly involved in both the social and personal dimensions of grandparenting while remote grandparents are not very active in either aspect of the grandparent role. As in other studies [8, 15], the apportioned and remote categories represent the largest percentage of grandparents. Perhaps because the expectations for relationships with these two groups of grandparents appear clearer than for the other types of grandparents (i.e., individualized and symbolic), their influence is more (apportioned) or less (remote) encompassing of the entire relationship with their grandchildren. More complex grandparent roles (i.e., high social/low personal or low social/high personal) differentially influence grandchildren's perceptions of their relationship with grandmothers and grandfathers.

The results of this study attest to the presence of grandparents in the lives of their adult grandchildren. The examination of responses of grandchildren having both a grandmother and grandfather provided insight into the variations in type and degree of involvement between grandchildren and grandparents. While the preponderance of women in the sample may have heightened the importance of grandmothers, the responses of the small subset of grandsons also demonstrate stronger ties with grandmothers than grandfathers. Future research that continues to explore similarities and differences in grandchildren's relationships with their grandparents is warranted.

REFERENCES

1. N. Hooyman and H. A. Kiyak, *Social Gerontology: A Multidisciplinary Perspective* (2nd Edition), Allyn and Bacon, Boston, 1991.
2. A. Cherlin and F. Furstenberg, *The New American Grandparent*, Basic Books, New York, 1986.
3. K. Doka and M. Mertz, The Meaning and Significance of Great-Grandparenthood, *The Gerontologist, 28*, pp. 192-197, 1988.
4. H. Kivnick, Dimensions of Grandparent Meaning: Deductive Conceptualization and Empirical Derivation, *Journal of Personality and Social Psychology, 44*, pp. 1056-1068, 1983.
5. B. Neugarten and K. Weistein, The Changing American Grandparent, *Journal of Marriage and the Family, 26*, pp. 199-204, 1964.
6. L. Troll, Grandparents: The Family Watch Dogs, in *Family Relationships in Later Life*, T. Brubaker (ed.), Sage, Beverly Hills, pp. 63-74, 1983.
7. V. Wood and J. Robertson, The Significance of Grandparenthood, in *Times, Roles, and Self in Old Age*, J. Gubrium (ed.), Human Science Press, New York, pp. 278-304, 1976.
8. J. Robertson, Grandmotherhood: A Study of Role Conceptions, *Journal of Marriage and the Family, 39*, pp. 165-174, 1977.
9. C. Johnson, A Cultural Analysis of the Grandmother, *Research on Aging, 5*, pp. 547-567, 1983.
10. S. Matthews and J. Sprey, Adolescents' Relationships with Grandparents: An Empirical Contribution to Conceptual Clarification, *Journal of Gerontology, 40*, pp. 621-626, 1985.
11. L.Thompson and A. Walker, Mothers as Mediators of Intimacy between Grandmothers and Their Young Adult Granddaughters, *Family Relations, 36*, pp. 72-77, 1987.
12. S. Matthews and J. Sprey, The Impact of Divorce on Grandparenthood: An Exploratory Study, *The Gerontologist, 24*, pp. 42-47, 1985.
13. L. Fischer, Transitions to Grandmotherhood, *International Journal of Aging and Human Development, 9*, pp. 293-299, 1982-83.
14. G. Hagestad, Continuity and Connectedness, in *Grandparenthood*, V. Bengtson and J. Robertson (eds.), Sage, Beverly Hills, pp. 31-48, 1985.

15. T. S. Hartshorne and G. J. Manaster, The Relationship with Grandparents: Contact, Importance, Role Conception, *International Journal of Aging and Human Development, 15*, pp. 233-245, 1982.

16. E. Hoffman, Young Adult's Relations with Their Grandparents: An Exploratory Study, *International Journal of Aging and Human Development, 10*, pp. 299-310, 1979-80.

17. M. Dellman-Jenkins, D. Papalia, and M. Lopez, Teenagers' Reported Interaction with Grandparents: Exploring the Extent of Alienation, *Lifestyles, 8*, pp. 35-46, 1987.

18. G. E. Kennedy, College Students' Relationships with Grandparents, *Psychological Reports, 64*, pp. 477-478, 1989.

19. V. C. Downs, Grandparents and Grandchildren: The Relationship between Self-Disclosure and Solidarity in an Intergenerational Relationship, *Communication Research Reports, 5*, pp. 173-179, 1988.

20. D. Mangen and W. Peterson (eds.), *Research Instruments in Social Gerontology: Social Roles and Social Participation* (Vol. 2), University of Minnesota Press, Minneapolis, pp. 132-133; 154, 1982.

21. V. Bengtson, Diversity and Symbolism in Grandparental Roles, in *Grandparenthood*, V. Bengtson and J. Robertson (eds.), Sage, Beverly Hills, pp. 11-25, 1985.

22. V. Kivett, Grandfathers and Grandchildren: Patterns of Association, Helping, and Psychological Closeness, *Family Relations, 34*, pp. 565-571, 1985.

23. J. Thomas, Gender Differences in Satisfaction with Grandparenting, *Psychology & Aging, 1*, pp. 215-219, 1986.

Chapter 12

ADULT GRANDCHILDREN AND THEIR GRANDPARENTS: THE ENDURING BOND

Lynne Gershenson Hodgson

The myth of the isolated nuclear family has been dispelled in classic studies [1-3]. For older people in particular, family ties are of primary importance for socialization as well as informal support [4-8]. Increases in life expectancy and changes in fertility patterns have yielded multigenerational family networks including two, three, four, and sometimes as many as five generations, what Knipscheer [9] has described as the "verticalization" of family relations [10]. Although most studies of intergenerational relationships in later life focus on the aging parent/adult child bond [11], there is increasing interest in broadening our understanding of family patterns with extended kin [12, 13]. Grandparent/grandchild relationships, as one nexus of the family network, are "an emergent social phenomenon" [14, p. 24].

Studies have explored grandparent/grandchild bonds from the perspective of the grandparent [15]; (for an overview see [16] and from the perspective of the young grandchild [17, 18]). These studies generally center on the significance of the role for each generation and the behavioral components of the relationship: frequency of contact, types of contact, and types of aid which are exchanged (for an overview, see [19]). Conclusions point to the dynamic nature of the grandparent/grandchild bond and suggest the tendency for grandchildren to grow up and away from their grandparents. Yet even with the increased interest surrounding the grandparent/grandchild relationship, few studies have extended the analysis to include adult grandchildren and the realities of these particular intergenerational bonds [20, 21]. With the demographic certainty that increasing cohorts of grandchildren will grow to adulthood with at least one living grandparent [22], the issues surrounding these bonds become critical to our understanding of future family constellations.

Barranti has summarized what we know about the bonds between adult grandchildren and their grandparents, highlighting the scarcity of research, particularly from the perspective of the younger generation [23]. Contrary to assumptions based on findings from prior studies of young grandchildren, these studies [24-27] report evidence of a continuing relationship between the generations. Although they focus on different dimensions (e.g., perceived role, satisfaction with relationship, interaction, and support patterns), there is consensus on the salience of the bonds and on the need for additional research to define more precisely the patterns. Most recently, Kennedy analyzed the attitudes of college students toward their grandparents, concluding that grandchildhood is a significant role as one grows to young adulthood [28]. He, too, calls for further research to test his findings on a wider and more representative sample.

This chapter seeks to further understanding of the attitudes and behaviors of adult grandchildren toward their living grandparents. It focuses on two dimensions of the intergenerational bond, association and affect, from the perspective of the adult grandchild. Do adult grandchildren maintain contact with their grandparents? How do they perceive the strength of the emotional bond between the generations? Additionally, this chapter provides insight into some basic research questions raised by studies of young grandchildren and studies of more general extended family networks regarding factors which affect those relationships. Do age and sex of the adult grandchild make a difference in the quality of the bond? Does the middle generation play a role in the cross-generational relationship? Finally, is geographical distance between the generations related to the strength of the bonds?

METHODS

During the spring of 1990, a sample of men and women, ages eighteen and older, responded to a national telephone survey of adult grandchildren. The sampling frame consisted of all residential telephone customers in the fifty states. Numbers were generated on a random basis, and an automatic plus one system was employed, whereby busy signals, no answers, and answering machines were redialed immediately to the next consecutive telephone number. Interviews were conducted by trained interviewers. Approximately one quarter of the 1000 people contacted met the requirements for inclusion in the study—being over eighteen and having at least one living grandparent. "Grandparent" was defined as the biological parent of a biological parent; thus the maximum number of possible living grandparents for any respondent was four. Stepgrandparents were excluded because, theoretically, they introduce another set of parameters into an already complex web of relationships. Of the 226 individuals who met the requirement, 217 agreed to be interviewed and, of those interviewed, 208 completed questionnaires resulted. The final sample included 208 men and women, eighteen and older, who had at least one living grandparent.

The questionnaire was designed to elicit responses about selected characteristics of the relationship between adult grandchildren and their grandparents. Several measures of association were used. A frequency scale (0 = never to 8 = everyday) was employed to determine level of contact; types of contact were assessed (face-to-face, phone, letter); and, finally, a variety of questions regarding specific situational contacts was asked. A Likert-type scale was used to determine the perceived closeness or affect of the relationship between the two generations (1 = not close at all to 4 = very close). Additional information regarding the emotional component of the bond was also elicited (e.g., reasons for perceived closeness; long-term dynamics of the relationship).

Questions were primarily structured with fixed choice responses, although qualitative data were gathered in several portions of the questionnaire (e.g., "Why did you choose this grandparent as the one to whom you feel closest?"). The interview yielded basic information on all living grandparents of the respondents and more detailed data on the one living grandparent to whom the respondent felt emotionally closest. Herein, we focus on the latter.

The interviews ranged from fifteen minutes to half an hour, depending on the number of living grandparents. Interviewers remarked on the high degree of cooperation and enthusiasm of the respondents in discussing their grandparents, making note of the extemporaneous comments frequently offered. A final question asked whether the respondent would be willing to be reinterviewed in the future; more than 90 percent answered affirmatively.

SAMPLE CHARACTERISTICS

The 208 survey respondents exhibit a profile similar to the general young adult population [29]. Table 1 presents the demographic characteristics of the sample. The sample, representing every geographic region of the country, was primarily white, with representative proportions of black and hispanic respondents. The median family income was in the $25,000-50,000 range. More than 60 percent of the respondents reported some college experience and perhaps reflecting that level of educational achievement, 45 percent of the sample who worked outside of the home reported occupations in the classifications of executive/supervisory and professional. The 25 percent who were not working for pay at the time of the interview included students, homemakers, and those looking for work. The relatively young mean age of this sample (27.4 years, S.D. = 6.7, range 18-51) results from the inclusion criterion that required a living grandparent. These respondents were almost evenly split between those who had never been and those who were currently married. Almost half of the respondents were parents themselves.

The 208 respondents reported a total of 340 living grandparents. The mean number of living grandparents per respondent was 1.64 (*S.D.* = .82). The majority (55%) of the sample had only a single, living grandparent; 28 percent had two; 14 percent had three and; 2 percent had all four (natural) grandparents. Figure 1 shows the distribution among the four possible relations of a respondent: father's father; father's mother; mother's father and mother's mother. Approximately one quarter of the sample reported having paternal grandfathers and slightly less than a third had maternal grandfathers. Almost half had paternal grandmothers; even greater percentages had maternal grandmothers. The average age of the respondent's grandparents was seventy-six (*S.D.* = 9.08); maternal grandparents were significantly younger than the paternal side.

The demographic profile of the 340 grandparents of the sample respondents approximates quite closely the demographics of the general population of older Americans. With respect to all major indices—sex ratio, marital status, housing

Table 1. Demographic Characteristics of the Respondents
(*N* = 208)

Characteristic	Percent (*N*)	Characteristic	Percent (*N*)
Age		Education	
18-29	63.0 (131)	8th grade or less	2.4 (5)
30-39	30.3 (63)	Some high school	15.5 (32)
40-49	6.3 (13)	High school graduate	21.4 (44)
50-59	.5 (1)	Some college	37.4 (77)
Gender		College graduate	18.4 (38)
Male	47.6 (99)	Post college	4.9 (10)
Female	52.4 (109)	Family income	
Marital status		Under $10,000	9.0 (16)
Currently married	43.8 (91)	$10-25,000	20.2 (36)
Widowed	.5 (1)	$25-50,000	39.9 (71)
Separated	2.4 (5)	$50-75,000	18.0 (32)
Divorced	7.7 (16)	$75-100,000	5.6 (10)
Never married	45.7 (95)	$100,000 plus	7.3 (13)
Children		Race	
Yes	46.9 (97)	White	81.7 (165)
No	53.1 (110)	Black	9.4 (19)
Work status		Latino	5.9 (12)
Work	74.5 (155)	Other	3.0 (6)
Homemaker	7.7 (16)		
Retired	.5 (1)		
Student	11.1 (23)		
Unemployed	6.3 (13)		

type, living arrangements, and proximity to extended family—the proportions within the study population are representative of the proportions within the population at large [30].

The Closest Grandparents

During the interview, respondents were asked to identify the grandparent to whom they were emotionally closest. If only one grandparent was alive, that grandparent became the "closest." In this group of grandparents, grandmothers outnumbered grandfathers three to one. This imbalance reflects two realities. When only one grandparent was alive, that grandparent was more often a grandmother than a grandfather (77% to 23%); therefore, grandmothers were more likely to be placed in the closest category by default. Second, even when a respondent had more than one living grandparent, grandmothers were often chosen over grandfathers.

Table 2 presents a descriptive profile of the respondents' 208 closest grandparents. The mean age of the grandparents was 77.3 (S.D. = 9.35). Only slightly more than a quarter of the grandparents were married and living with their spouses. That proportion varied greatly by sex, with grandmothers much more

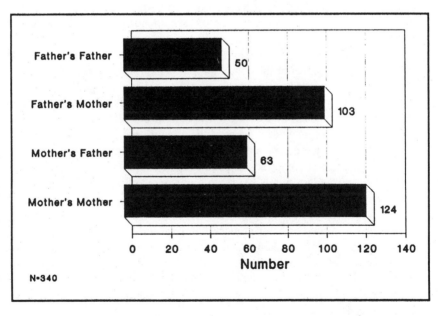

Figure 1. Distribution of grandparents by lineage and sex.

likely to be widowed than grandfathers. It is not surprising, then, that grandfathers were less likely to be living alone than were grandmothers and they were much more likely to be living with a spouse. Overall, the greatest percentage (half of the group) were living alone. Only a small proportion of grandparents resided with the respondents' parents, and all of these were with maternal kin. However, a sizable proportion of respondents report their grandparents lived with "other relatives."

The overwhelming majority of grandparents lived in independently owned homes. Most of the remaining grandparents lived in rental units in the wider community or senior citizen housing; fewer than 5 percent lived in nursing homes. How close did adult grandchildren live to their grandparents? Although almost none of our respondents lived in a household which included a grandparent, the majority of the respondents did live within an hour's drive of them. At the other extreme, a quarter of the grandchildren resided more than 500 miles away, or more than a day's drive from their grandparents.

RESULTS

Dimensions of Contact

The men and women reported ongoing relationships with their grandparents that often included high levels of association. However, there was variability in actual frequency of contact. Although few of the respondents had daily exchanges with their grandparents (5.4%), fewer still had no contact at all (1.5%). The majority were in touch at least several times a month; and 40 percent had weekly contact. On the other side of the continuum, though, 13.3 percent reported they interacted with their grandparents once a year or less. Even though these findings suggest a large proportion of engaged cross-generational relationships, there was a group of adult grandchildren who, even with their closest grandparent, lacked frequent contact. To gain a better sense of the dimensions of association, respondents were asked to identify when the last contact with their grandparent had taken place. Sixty-one percent reported they had been in contact within the last week; 84 percent within the last month. Less than four percent of the sample reported no contact between the generations during the prior year.

Closer examination of these findings reveals noteworthy differences in contact between certain groups of adult grandchildren and their grandparents. Table 3 presents a comparison of ranked means for frequency of contact among several groups. Because of the nonparametric nature of the data, the Mann-Whitney U (Wilcoxon Rank Sum W) method was used to determine differences among sample groups. This method produced a Z-score comparable to the t-test of compared means in parametric statistics.

The data show a strong relationship between physical proximity and frequency of contact; the closer the generations lived to each other, the more frequently they

Table 2. Demographic Characteristics of Closest Grandparents
($N = 208$)

Characteristic	Percent (N)	Characteristic	Percent (N)
Gender		Residence Type	
Male	24.5 (51)	Own home	69.8 (141)
Female	75.5 (157)	Rental	13.4 (27)
Household Status		Senior housing	8.4 (17)
Alone	49.5 (100)	Nursing home	4.5 (9)
Spouse	26.7 (54)	Other	4.0 (8)
With respondent's parents	2.0 (4)	Propinquity	
		Under 5 miles	20.9 (41)
Other relatives	19.3 (39)	6-25 miles	25.5 (50)
Friend	2.5 (5)	26-50 miles	8.2 (16)
		51-99 miles	6.1 (12)
		100-499 miles	13.8 (27)
		500 plus	25.5 (50)

interacted. Propinquity is also related to a number of other factors which may affect frequency of contact. For example, age of the respondent was significantly related to proximity. Younger men and women lived closer to their grandparents than did their older counterparts; many of them still lived in the homes of their parents who in turn lived close to the oldest generation. A comparison of the ranked means between the younger cohort and the older cohort of adult grandchildren, reveals that the younger respondents did interact more frequently than did their older counterparts. Female respondents also lived significantly closer to their grandparents than did the male respondents, although this did not result in a statistically significant difference between male and female contact patterns.

The data also show differences in ranked means of several non-demographic variables. Significant differences existed in reported frequency of contact between respondents who considered themselves emotionally close to their grandparents and those who did not. Those men and women who reported that they had a "very close" or a "quite close" relationship with their grandparents also had more frequent contact. Additionally, those respondents who perceived the relationship between their parent and grandparent as close, reported higher levels of contact. Level of contact between respondents and their parents was also significantly related to contact between the cross-generations; men and women who were in frequent contact with their own parent were more likely to be in frequent contact with their grandparent as well.

Table 3. Comparison of Groups on Frequency of Contact

Respondent's Characteristics	Mean Rank	Z-score
Age		-2.7673*
Younger	105.90	
Older	83.91	
Gender		-1.8254
Male	94.37	
Female	109.26	
Propinquity		-8.2591**
LE an hour's drive	128.66	
GT an hour's drive	62.24	
Emotional Closeness		-6.4199**
Close	118.67	
Not close	61.82	
Lineage		-.6944
Paternal	99.76	
Maternal	105.58	
Parental Contact		-3.0041*
Frequent	96.95	
Infrequent	58.45	
Emotional Closeness—		
Parent and Grandparent		-1.8899*
Close	96.36	
Not close	78.59	

*p < .05
**p < .001

Levels of association between adult grandchildren and their grandparents varied but, overall, could be accurately described as remarkably high. What form does that contact take? The largest proportion of the respondents (27%) reported that most of the time, they interacted with their grandparents in person. A fifth of the sample spoke with them primarily on the telephone. Another quarter reported that they did both equally. Writing letters was clearly not the method of choice for most of the sample, though in concert with other methods of communication, it was a reasonable option.

Respondents were often the recipients of their grandparent's attention. Sixty percent reported they received calls on a regular basis from their grandparents and almost as many (55%) said their grandparents came to visit them. Although in most of these visits the grandparent was accompanied by a spouse or a middle generation son or daughter, almost 40 percent of the visits were unaccompanied (i.e., a grandparent came to visit the adult grandchild alone, without the presence of the bridge generation).

Additionally, it was clear that certain traditions were preserved in many relationships. The exchange of birthday greetings among family members is used as a ritual measure of contact. A majority (60%) of the respondents were not only aware of the date of their grandparents' birthdays, 90 percent of those who knew the date, had contacted them in some way to acknowledge their most recent birthday either with a card, a phone call or a visit. Almost three quarters of the respondents reported that they had received cards from grandparents on their last birthday.

Dimensions of Closeness

Levels of association are just one indicator of the quality of bonds between adult grandchildren and their grandparents. The emotional strength of that bond is another measure of the relationship. When asked to rate the closeness of their relationships (1 = not close at all; 4 = very close), the mean response was 3.01 (*S.D.* = .94). By self-report, 37.9 percent of the grandchild/grandparent bonds were considered very close, while another 32 percent rated their relationship as quite close. Thus, 70 percent of the relationships were rated as unequivocally positive. The remaining relationships were judged to be somewhat close (23.6%) and not close (6.4%).

A number of characteristics of the respondents and the grandparents were associated with the closeness of the relationship. Table 4 presents a comparison of ranked means for subjective evaluation of closeness between grandchild and grandparent. Not surprisingly, the two variables where differences were strongest were frequency of contact and geographical proximity. These two variables have already been shown to be associated with each other and it is possible that they are working together to affect the emotional ties of the dyad.

The importance of the bridge generation to the grandchild/grandparent relationship that was evident in the earlier findings about frequency of contact was also important in the emotional dimension of the relationship. A comparison of the ranked means shows that the respondents' familial relationships are associated with the strength of cross-generational ties. When respondents perceived the bonds between their parent and grandparent to be positive, their own bonds were perceived as positive.

Gender did relate significantly to closeness in two ways: lineage and sex of the grandparent were factors in the selection of the closest grandparent. Table 5 expresses these results as the ratio of "likelihood to be picked as the closest grandparent" for each of the four relationships. When asked to choose the grandparent with whom they had the emotionally closest relationship, respondents were more likely to pick a maternal grandparent rather than a paternal grandparent. Regardless of their own sex, respondents were also more likely to

Table 4. Comparison of Groups on Emotional Closeness

Respondent's Characteristics	Mean Rank	Z-score
Age		−.2151
Younger	96.75	
Older	95.11	
Gender		−.0883
Male	101.64	
Female	102.33	
Propinquity		−2.4573*
LE an hour's drive	106.53	
GT an hour's drive	87.63	
Frequency of Contact		−6.3053**
Frequent	123.77	
Infrequent	74.34	
Lineage		−2.9647*
Paternal	87.33	
Maternal	111.16	
Parental Contact		−.4382
Frequent	94.63	
Infrequent	88.63	
Emotional Closeness— Parent and Grandparent		−2.0149*
Close	96.95	
Not close	78.69	

*$p < .05$
**$p < .001$

choose a grandmother over a grandfather. When both grandmothers were still living, respondents more frequently chose their maternal grandmothers than their paternal grandmothers.

Having made a judgement as to who among their living grandparents was the closest, respondents were asked to reflect on that choice. Rather than offering structured parameters, an open-ended question was used to allow respondents to describe in their own words their reasons for a particular choice. Qualitative data are useful here to discern themes which emerge around the topic. Although individual respondents made choices based on a variety of concerns, patterns clearly emerged from their answers.

One often repeated explanation for the choice of closest grandparent was that closeness derived from contact. For example, there was the forty-two-year-old woman who said, "I feel closest to (this particular grandmother) because she lives

Table 5. Likelihood To Be Picked as Emotionally Closest Grandparent[a]

Relationship	Ratio[b]	Percent
Father's father	7/38	18.4
Father's mother	23/65	35.4
Mother's father	17/49	34.7
Mother's mother	46/73	63.0

[a]Respondents with only one living grandparent were excluded.
[b]The denominator is equal to the number of respondents with more than one living grandparent, one of whom was of a specific lineage and sex (i.e., father's father); the numerator is equal to the number of that lineage and sex who were chosen as closest.

so much closer and I can see her all the time." A twenty-four-year-old man had much the same to say about his choice when he reasoned, "It makes sense that I'm closest to her; she's over here about every other day so she's pretty much a part of my life." Physical proximity and frequency of contact were the most frequently cited reasons for the designated choice of "closest" grandparent. In many ways, the two variables were indistinguishable in peoples' minds ("she lives near, so I see her").

Another theme that emerged to explain the choice of closest grandparent was whether the grandchild had been raised by or lived with that particular grandparent at some point earlier in life. One nineteen-year-old man offered the observation that "I was raised by her and she knows me so well." A twenty-four-year-old woman stated the relationship between the two variables very clearly, "My grandmother took me in for five years. You can get pretty close in five years of living together." In these and other cases, time spent in an extraordinary relationship (like that of a grandparent acting as surrogate parent for a grandchild) fixed a permanent attachment between the generations.

Personal characteristics of the closest grandparent often accounted for a grandchild's preference. The choice of grandparent depended on such traits as "She's a good listener," and "She really cares about me and my family." Many times the question was answered with a revelation about what mattered most to the respondent: "She's the one who always spoils me," and "I've always been Grandpa's little girl." Sometimes, respondents chose their closest grandparent by default because of negative feelings about the traits of other living grandparents. "My mother's mother is closest, I'd say, because she's not stuck up like my dad's mother," offered one twenty-five-year-old woman.

Asked, then, to reflect on reasons for their choice of closest grandparent, the respondents cited a variety of related factors. But relationships are dynamic and these respondents recognized some of the changes which had taken place within their own grandchild/grandparent dyad. When respondents were asked to evaluate changes in their relationships with their closest grandparent over the past few years, many in the sample said they had become closer over time. Men and women alike remarked that as they had grown to adulthood, they were more likely to appreciate their grandparents. "I think I got old enough to see her as a real person and I found out we had a lot in common," said one twenty-nine-year-old woman of her grandmother. Another young man of twenty-four offered his explanation for his increasingly close feelings towards his grandfather, "Now that I'm not a kid I'm taking the time to really get to know him."

Other explanations for increasing closeness indicated that a grandparent was growing older and this created a need to relate while there was still an opportunity to do so. "I know that he's not going to be around too much longer and I want to make sure I see him now," said one thirty-six-year-old woman of her seventy-two-year-old grandfather. That sentiment was also carried through slightly differently by respondents who felt they had become closer so that their own children could get to know their great-grandparents: "I want my two girls to see why I love her so much before she's gone."

Personal crises also prompted some respondents to seek a closer relationship with a grandparent. Although it was most often the crisis of the grandparental generation which set the stage, occasionally a grandchild would turn to a grandparent during times of great personal need. "When my husband died, she really helped me through it, and now we're very close." Health problems and death of a spouse in the older generation tended to provide reasons for many respondents to strengthen the bond. Pointing to instrumental needs, one eighteen-year-old man explained his relationship to his grandfather, "He needs a lot of help now, 'cause he got sick, so I help him out." A thirty-six-year-old woman, who was more concerned with the emotional side, said of her grandmother, "My grandfather died and so I make an effort for her, because she needs me to talk to."

Although there were many respondents who followed the pattern of growing closer to grandparents in adulthood, others saw no change in their relationships or reported that they felt more distant than they had in previous years. For those whose bonds had grown more tenuous, the overwhelming reason was an increase in physical distance. "I just live so far away now; I can't do much about it." Other reasons for drifting apart were health problems of the grandparent, institutionalization, or family disagreements which inhibited contact between cross-generations. Only two individuals argued that they had "no time" to maintain their bonds.

DISCUSSION

Although it is true that levels of association between adult grandchildren and their grandparents vary across the sample, there is strong evidence that the majority of adult grandchildren maintained a high degree of contact with their grandparents. Despite speculative assumptions to the contrary (e.g., [15]), these older grandchildren have not terminated their bonds with their grandparents, nor have they maintained these bonds only on an obligatory and ritualistic basis. They report reciprocal visiting and calling on a regular basis; contacts which are unconnected to any particular occasion or holiday. Many interact frequently and more often than not in person. This finding echoes the conclusions of several previous studies [25, 26, 28] which focus on young adult grandchildren and offers evidence of the continuing bonds which weave through the "beanpole" [14] family structure.

The data suggest that a large proportion of adult grandchildren maintain contact with their closest grandparent on a regular basis. The level of contact is associated with several factors. Physical proximity is one which relates significantly to frequency of contact between the generations. These findings support Hoffman's conclusions [25] regarding the robustness of the relationship between the two variables, a relationship which is also documented in the literature on grandparent/child contact [3, 31]. Perhaps propinquity provides the means for contact by providing access and availability.

For this sample, grandchild's age is another variable which is associated with contact. One possible explanation for that finding is the linkage formed by the middle generation. Many of the younger respondents are still living in the homes of their parents and, thus, are still part of the contact patterns established by them. But even when the adult grandchild is no longer living at home, the importance of the bridge generation is evident in the data. The importance of the bridge genera-tion for grandparent/grandchild relationships which is suggested in this study has been mentioned in earlier studies [32-34]. Parents who are actively involved with their own parents set the stage for involvement between the cross-generations. Two explanations for this finding are possible and not mutually exclusive. Middle-aged parents who interact on a regular basis with their aging parents provide role models for their own children. Spending time with the grandparental generation may establish family norms or strengthen linkages which are played out between the cross-generations. Another explanation may be that parents who interact with the oldest generation literally "bring along" the youngest generation. The notion of family obligation is operational here. That is, grandchildren interact with their grandparents because they are participating in family rituals, not in voluntary associations.

The reported strength of the affectual bonds between grandchild and grand-parent must be analyzed in light of the fact that the respondents had already designated these particular grandparents as their emotionally closest grandparent. The closeness of these relationships, therefore, is not necessarily representative of the strength of their bonds to all living grandparents. Nevertheless, strong ties exist and grandchildren, even as adults, maintain affectual bonds with the oldest generation.

Gender differences in emotional ties have been widely reported in the family literature [2, 35]. Women are more likely to report closeness to their extended family. In this study, granddaughters and grandsons showed no significant differences in their reported closeness to grandparents, however, gender differences were manifest in this way: maternal grandmothers were most likely to have been selected as the closest grandparent. This finding is not surprising given the traditional role of women as kinkeepers [32]. Generations of family literature have built a portrait of the dominant position of women in family affairs; and a generation of grandparent literature has shown how that dominance affects the relationships of maternal and paternal grandparents to their grandchildren [17].

CONCLUSIONS

Recognition of a demographically induced revolution in intergenerational relationships has focused attention on the bonds between grandparents and grandchildren. Within the normative constraints of family life, young children's relationships with grandparents are bound by the structures set up by their parents. Their contacts are limited by the contacts between their parents and their grandparents; the quality of their relationship is mediated by the quality of their parents' relationship with their grandparents. The connection is an obvious one, stemming from the dependent nature of childhood. But as the child grows to adulthood and reaches some degree of independence, parents do not necessarily have the same power to connect the cross-generations. Normative prescriptions do not yet exist. Adult grandchildren can rewrite the relationships that they share with their grandparents. This study has concentrated on several dimensions of those bonds as they exist between two generations of adults.

The findings reported here suggest that grandparents are more than mere symbols of past acquaintance for their adult grandchildren. The grandchild/grandparent bond continues with surprising strength into adulthood. Men and women alike report substantial contact with their grandparents, despite the time constraints posed by school, jobs, families of procreation, and distance. Interaction between the generations is high and so is affect. It is possible to maintain contact without any commensurate feelings of closeness, but these grandsons and granddaughters report that their emotional bonds are strong. Some questions concerning the grandchild/grandparent bond are raised by the findings. Knowing that the strength of bonds depends on age, lineage, geographical proximity, and parental involvement, we need to further assess each of these factors to determine their relative importance and how they interact with each other. Does the configuration change as the grandchild moves through adult life phases? Additionally, the importance of other factors such as race and social class need to be examined to determine if they affect the grandparent/grandchild relationship.

Growing to adulthood does not mean the abandonment of the role of grandchild. Despite predictions to the contrary, evidence is mounting which suggests lasting and fulfilling ties between the cross-generations. Exactly how several generations of adults will relate within the familial structure is yet to be determined, but surely, one of the consequences of the demographic revolution will be the ability to develop an adult relationship with a grandparent.

REFERENCES

1. E. Litwak, Geographic Mobility and Extended Family Cohesion, *American Socio-logical Review, 25*, pp. 385-394, 1960.
2. B. N. Adams, *Kinship in an Urban Setting*, Markham, Chicago, 1968.
3. G. R. Lee, Kinship in the Seventies: A Decade Review of Research and Theory, *Journal of Marriage and the Family, 42*, pp. 923-934, 1980.
4. W. E. Thompson and G. F. Streib, Meaningful Activity in a Family Context, in *Aging and Leisure: A Research Perspective into the Meaningful Use of Time*, R. Kleemeier (ed.), Oxford University Press, New York, 1961.
5. G. O. Hagestad, Problems and Promises in the Social Psychology of Intergenerational Relations, in *Aging: Stability and Change in the Family*, R. W. Fogel, E. Hatfield, S. B. Kiesler, and E. Shanas (eds.), Academic Press, New York, pp. 11-48, 1981.
6. E. Shanas, The Family as a Social Support System in Old Age, *The Gerontologist, 19*, pp. 169-174, 1979.
7. E. Shanas, Older People and Their Families: The New Pioneers, *Journal of Marriage and the Family, 42*, pp. 9-15, 1980.
8. E. Shanas and M. B. Sussman, The Family in Later Life: Social Structure and Social Policy, in *Aging: Stability and Change in the Family*, R. W. Fogel, E. Hatfield, S. B. Kiesler, and E. Shanas (eds.), Academic Press, New York, pp. 211-232, 1981.
9. C. P. M. Knipscheer, Temporal Embededness and Aging within the Multigenerational Family: The Case of Grandparenting, in *Emergent Theories of Aging*, J. E. Birren and V. L. Bengtson (eds.), Springer, New York, pp. 426-446, 1988.
10. V. L. Bengtson and D. Dannefer, Families, Work, and Aging: Implications of Dis-ordered Cohort Flow for the Twenty-First Century, in *Health in Aging: Sociological Issues and Policy Directions*, R. A. Ward and S. S. Tobin (eds.), pp. 256-289, 1987.
11. H. Q. Kivnick, Grandparents and Family Relations, in *Independent Aging: Family and Social Systems Perspectives*, Aspen Systems Corporation, Rockville, pp. 35-57, 1984.
12. E. Brody, Aged Parents and Aging Children, in *Aging Parents*, P. K. Ragan (ed.), University of Southern California Press, Los Angeles, pp. 267-287, 1979.
13. V. L. Bengtson, E. B. Olander, and A. Haddad, The Generation Gap and Aging Family Members: Toward a Conceptual Model, in *Time, Roles, and Self in Old Age*, J. F. Gubrium (ed.), Human Sciences Press, New York, pp. 237-263, 1976.
14. V. L. Bengtson, Diversity and Symbolism in Grandparental Roles, in *Grandparent-hood*, V.L. Bengtson and J.F. Robertson (eds.), Sage, Beverly Hills, pp. 11-29, 1985.
15. A. Cherlin and F. F. Furstenberg, Jr., *The New American Grandparent*, Basic Books, New York, 1986.
16. V. L. Bengtson and J. F. Robertson (eds.), *Grandparenthood*, Sage, Beverly Hills, 1985.
17. E. Kahana and B. Kahana, Grandparenthood from the Perspective of the Developing Grandchild, *Developmental Psychology, 3*, pp. 98-105, 1970.
18. A. Kornhaber and K. L. Woodward, *Grandparents/Grandchildren: The Vital Connec-tion*, Anchor Press, New York, 1981.

19. V. L. Bengtson, C. Rosenthal, and L. M. Burton, Families and Aging: Diversity and Heterogeneity, in *Handbook of Aging and the Social Sciences*, R. H. Binstock and L. K. George (eds.), Academic Press, San Diego, pp. 263-287, 1990.

20. V. Wood and J. F. Robertson, The Significance of Grandparenthood, in *Time, Roles, and Self in Old Age*, J. F. Gubrium (ed.), Human Sciences Press, New York, pp. 278-304, 1976.

21. G. O. Hagestad, Able Elderly in the Family Context: Changes, Chances, and Challenges, *The Gerontologist, 27*, pp. 417-422, 1987.

22. P. Uhlenberg, Death and the Family, *Journal of Family History, 5*, pp. 313-320, 1980.

23. C. C. Ramirez Barranti, The Grandparent/Grandchild Relationship: Family Resource in an Era of Voluntary Bonds, *Family Relations, 34*, pp. 343-352, 1985.

24. T. S. Hartshorne and G. J. Manaster, The Relationship with Grandparents: Contact, Importance, Role Conception, *International Journal of Aging and Human Development, 15*, pp. 233-245, 1982.

25. E. Hoffman, Young Adults' Relations with Grandparents, *International Journal of Aging and Human Development, 10*, pp. 299-309, 1979.

26. J. Robertson, Interactions in Three Generation Families, *International Journal of Aging and Development, 6*, pp. 103-109, 1975.

27. N. Langer, Grandparents and Adult Grandchildren: What Do They Do for One Another?, *International Journal of Aging and Human Development, 31*, pp. 101-110, 1990.

28. G. E. Kennedy, College Students' Expectations of Grandparent and Grandchild Role Behaviors, *The Gerontologist, 30*, pp. 43-48, 1990.

29. U.S. Bureau of the Census, *Current Population Reports: Population Profile of the United States Series P-23*, No. 159, United States Government Printing Office, Washington, D.C., 1989.

30. U.S. Senate Special Committee on Aging, *Developments in Aging: 1988*, Vol. 1, United States Government Printing Office, Washington, D.C., 1989.

31. L. E. Troll, S. Miller, and R. C. Atchley, *Families of Later Life*, Wadsworth, Belmont, 1979.

32. R. Hill, N. Foote, J. Aldous, R. Carlson, and R. MacDonald, *Family Development in Three Generations*, Schenkman, Cambridge, 1970.

33. V. R. Kivett, Grandfathers and Grandchildren: Patterns of Association, Helping, and Psychological Closeness, *Family Relations, 34*, pp. 565-571, 1985.

34. G. O. Hagestad and L. M. Burton, Grandparenthood, Life Context, and Family Development, *American Behavioral Scientist, 29*, pp. 471-484, 1986.

35. H. M. Bahr and F. I. Nye, The Kinship Role in a Contemporary Community: Perceptions of Obligations and Sanctions, *Journal of Comparative Family Studies, 5*, pp. 17-25, 1974.

Chapter 13

GRANDPARENTS AND ADULT GRANDCHILDREN: WHAT DO THEY DO FOR ONE ANOTHER?

Nieli Langer

Older people perceive kin to be the most appropriate source of support. Emphasis on the family arises from both the family's centrality in providing social care and its primacy in the lives of the elderly. Studies reveal that families have been steadfast in providing care for elderly members [1, 2]. Investigators, however, have not described the patterns of grandparents and adult grandchildren exchanging support. One major result of these bonds is that this kin relationship can theoretically function as a resource for the individuals and families as a whole by helping to absorb family pressures and provide assistance. Practically, the grandparent-adult grandchild dyad is a potential resource for the elderly in providing a wider circle of nurturance and support. Human-service workers need to strengthen this link by awareness of the level of exchange of services that exists between grandparents and adult grandchildren.

In a study by Brody [3], the majority of adult grandchildren believed that grandparents should depend upon them for assistance. Brody termed this bond "grandfilial responsibility." It is an outgrowth of the concept of adult offsprings' obligations to assume supportive or caretaking roles for their elderly parents. There is scant information about the extent to which adult grandchildren provide services for their grandparents. Nonetheless, the ideology of familial responsibility for elderly persons persists, even among younger family members [4].

The bond between grandparents and grandchildren is second in emotional power and influence only to the relationship between children and parents [5]. Kornhaber termed the ways in which the grandparent-grandchild relationship functions as resources for the family members, "Vital Connections." One conclusion drawn concerning studies that have been conducted is that there is a need to look more closely at the relationship between the grandparent and the adult grandchild over the age of eighteen.

Presently, 12 percent of the U.S. population is composed of men and women sixty-five years of age and older, 70 percent of whom are grandparents [3]. Adults are spending more of their lives in this role than adults in previous generations. Similarly, more persons have the opportunity to be grandchildren for a substantial period of their adult life. As a result of basic demographic changes, the contemporary American family is faced with new opportunities for long-term intergenerational connections across the life spans of individuals. The grandparent-adult grandchild bond may provlde an opportunity for studies of intergenerational ties based on warmth and intimacy.

Assistance within the family tends to be based on a system of mutual reciprocity stretching over the life cycle. Reciprocity of exact service assistance is secondary to each individual's opportunity to both give and receive support. Kahn and Antonucci employed the term *convoy* of social support to describe the dynamic concept of life-long social networks [6]. The presence alone of a support element, however, is not considered sufficient to assure meaningful assistance. In order for a support element to be considered "functional," there must be evidence of an ongoing relationship to guarantee meaningful support [7].

Older Americans exchange assistance and support with adult children [2, 8]; however, they differentiate between emotional (expressive) and physical and financial (instrumental) support. The tendency is for parents to expect more expressive than instrumental support from offspring [9].

"Functional solidarity" is a construct that measures the exchange of assistance and support between generations. The frequency of exchange of services as well as the perception of potential support between the dyad are measures of functional solidarity. Equivalent exchange in expressive and/or instrumental services is termed reciprocal support [10]; nonreciprocal support is characterized by excessive giving or receiving in the relationship (i.e., the grandparent receives more services than (s)he gives to the adult grandchild). This chapter reports finding from a study in which the functional exchange relationship between grandparents and the adult grandchild with whom they have the most frequent contact was examined [11]. Anticipating that the demographic trends will continue, we may strengthen the social-support network of the elderly with knowledge of the reciprocal and nonreciprocal, expressive and instrumental social support exchanged between these two generations.

METHOD

Procedure

A questionnaire consisting of several batteries of items measured both the objective and subjective aspects of kinship relationships between the grandparent and the adult grandchild. Interactional characteristics included size and distribution of family network, frequency and kinds of association, and services exchanged. The subjective elements included affectual closeness and norms of kinship relations.

Functional solidarity between the grandparent and the adult grandchild was determined by the frequency with which grandparents gave assistance and received assistance in twelve activity categories to/from the adult grandchild with whom they had the most frequent contact. The categories included expressive support: phoning, letter-writing, sending greetings cards, visiting, exchanging gifts, and giving advice; and instrumental support: help with transportation, bureaucratic red tape, personal care, shopping, meal preparation, and household chores. Four response categories measured frequency: very often, fairly often, occasionally, or never. The research focused on perceived rather than actual reciprocity as the data are based on self-reports from the principal respondents.

In order to measure the potential help given an adult grandchild by the grandparent, respondents reported if they wanted to do more, about the same, or less for the adult grandchild. Grandparent need was determined by responses to wanting more, about the same, or less from the adult grandchild.

Sample

The target for the study was the population of noninstitutionalized, Jewish, biological grandparents over sixty-five years of age with at least one adult grandchild over age eighteen. The geographic proximity of the adult grandchild of most frequent contact to the grandparent was measured as living in Miami Beach, within 50-100 miles, or out-of-state. The sample consisted of 118 senior citizens residing in a cooperative apartment house in Miami Beach, Florida. They constitute a middle-to-upper-middle class population of Jewish elderly ranging in age from sixty-five to ninety-one (see Table 1).

RESULTS

Indicators of both expressive exchange and instrumental exchange were summarized in expressive and instrumental exchange scores. The score was an indicator of a respondents' perception of reciprocity in each index. In the indices, if the calculation resulted in a score of 100, this indicated a reciprocal relationship between the dyad. A score >100 indicated more respondent support given than received, while a score of <100 indicated that respondents received more support than they gave.

Twenty-one percent of the respondents had a reciprocal relationship based on expressive exchange; 42 percent shared a reciprocal relationship based on instrumental support. However, the reciprocal instrumental exchange was based on respondent reports of never giving or receiving help in instrumental activities. For 43 percent of the respondents, the perception of reciprocity was that they received

Table 1. Profile of Grandparent Respondents

	Number	Percent
Male Respondents	34	29
Female Respondents	84	71
Place of Birth		
United States	73	62
Eastern Europe	45	38
Marital Status		
Married		
Male		
65-74	10	30
75-84	16	49
85+	1	3
Female		
65-74	24	29
75-84	13	16
85+	1	1
Widowed		
Male		
65-74	0	0
75-84	6	18
85+	0	0
Female		
65-74	14	16
75-84	26	31
85+	6	7
Annual Household Income		
<$5,000	5	4
$5,000-$14,999	5	4
$15,000-$24,999	27	24
$25,000-$39,999	35	30
>$40,000	45	38
Health Status		
good	68	58
fair	43	37
poor	6	5
Level of Education		
<high school	20	17
some high school	17	14
high school graduate	41	36
some college	20	16
college graduate	18	17

more expressive support from the adult grandchild; 36 percent perceived reciprocity as giving more expressive support to the adult grandchild. Adult grandchildren (31%) gave instrumental support to the 27 percent of the grandparents who gave instrumental support.

The majority of grandparent-adult grandchild relationships were not reciprocal in either expressive or instrumental support. The grandparents' perception of reciprocity was that they received more than they gave.

As shown in Table 2, the majority of respondents reported never helping their adult grandchild or being helped by the adult grandchild in instrumental helping activities. For those respondents with an adult grandchild living out-of-state, distance may have precluded exchange based on instrumental services, yet the levels reported for them generally did not differ from those who lived closer to their grandparent. This result suggests that exchange in these activities is somewhat rare. The findings also indicate, however, that adult grandchildren living in

Table 2. Grandparents/Adult Grandchild Provision of Service by Type of Instrumental Exchange

Activity	Grandparent		Adult Grandchild	
	Never Exchange (Percent)	Exchange (Percent)	Never Exchange (Percent)	Exchange (Percent)
Shopping				
Miami[a]	71	29	29	39
Out-of-State[b]	70	30	76	24
Meal Preparation				
Miami	68	32	87	13
Out-of-State	67	33	85	15
Chores				
Miami	94	7	87	13
Out-of-State	94	6	85	15
Transportation				
Miami	84	16	58	42
Out-of-State	90	10	66	35
Bureaucracy				
Miami	87	13	90	10
Out-of-State	91	9	95	5
Personal Care				
Miami	84	16	84	16
Out-of-State	87	13	94	6

[a] $n = 31$
[b] $n = 87$

Miami Beach did provide transportation and shopping services to grandparents, 42 percent and 39 percent, respectively (see Table 2).

Functional solidarity is also a measure of the perception of potential support between grandparent and adult grandchild. Forty-one percent of the grandparents wanted to do more for their adult grandchild, and 59 percent wanted to do the same as they were presently doing. Ninety-one percent wanted to receive the same as they were currently receiving, while 9 percent wanted more support from the adult grandchild than (s)he was presently receiving (Chi square 3.9, $df = 1$, $p = 0.05$).

The relationship between exchange of support and respondent characteristics of gender, health status, distance from the adult grandchild, and age were measured. No difference (Student's T-test) existed in the extent to which men and women respondents reported perceived expressive and instrumental exchange. The health status of the respondents and the scores on the two indices showed no significant difference. Additionally, no relationship was found between distance from the adult grandchild and expressive- or instrumental-exchange rates.

No difference in expressive-exchange scores was found between the younger grandparents (65-74) and the older grandparents (75-91). When the association between the age of the respondent and the expressive-exchange rates were examined, a positive correlation ($r = 0.21$, $p = 0.02$) was found indicating that the older respondents gave more expressive support than they received.

DISCUSSION

A major element in grandparent-adult grandchild relationships is functional support. Intergenerational family functioning generally involves feelings of satisfaction that one member gains from doing things for or caring for the other. This includes not only concrete instrumental assistance, but also emotional support. Exchange reflects the assistance provided and received by both the grandparent and the adult grandchild. It is not necessary that each provide and receive the same kinds of support, as some types of activities are not needed by both generations. Adult grandchildren give both more expressive and instrumental support than they receive from the grandparent. The adult grandchild also gives more expressive than instrumental support. The majority of relationships are nonreciprocal, and the grandparents perceive reciprocity as receiving more than they give. Additionally, the majority of grandparents want to continue the same exchange pattern with the adult grandchild.

The results of the measure of the levels of grandparent expectations of support from the original study [11] revealed that the grandparent respondents have expressive expectations of social support from their adult grandchild (mean = 65 ± 2.5) and low levels of instrumental expectation (mean = 19 ± 3.1). These expressive expectations are gratified by the adult grandchild. The high degree of congruence between the level of expressive expectation of support and the behavioral reality of grandparent-adult grandchild expressive-exchange relations suggests that the adult grandchild is a "functional" member of the grandparents' social-support system. There is evidence of an ongoing relationship based on meaningful expressive support. It is interesting that these findings are similar to the well-established body of literature on the relations between adult children and their aging parents [9]. The grandparent-adult grandchild dyad is providing a wider circle of social and emotional support.

Kastenbaum [15] studied interdependent relationships among three adult generations drawn from the same families. Attention was given to assessment of the cognitive and emotional aspects of dependency. Lack of knowledge of what to do and inadequate emotional support will affect the probability of the failure of individuals to initiate activities that are in their own interests thereby contributing to their dependency.

The study indicated that the elders constituted the least dependent generation in the study. They, however, were much more affected by reduction in emotional support than were the other two generations. Functional solidarity in the present study was based mainly on the exchange of expressive support. The participants in the study also indicated that they expected emotional support from adult grandchildren and in most cases reported receiving this support.

The adult grandchild, by the fact of just being, plus the contact (s)he keeps with his/her grandparent, bolsters the sense of self-worth of the grandparent. By maintaining strong affectual ties and mutually acceptable levels of association and reciprocity, the older generation can evaluate and balance their priorities (i.e., the need for emotional contact with the need to preserve independence and individuality).

Kahn and Antonucci [6] identified the term *convoy* of social support to describe the ever-changing social networks over the life course that are founded on patterns of exchange, which may not be reciprocal. As a result of demographic changes, the adult grandchild is now a member of the convoy of social support. Life-long patterns of interaction with the grandparent are present, and these patterns become more evident over time. Thus, persons may only be receiving support at this time while having provided it at an earlier time and, therefore, feel they are drawing from a "support bank" [12]. Private transfers of money and assets are common forms of support from the grandparent to grandchildren [13]. To what extent is giving financial gifts "with a warm hand" an expression of "deposit" to the adult grandchild with a silent hope for future "withdrawals" in the form of expressive or tangible support? The concept of a "support bank" into which one makes deposits and withdrawals needs to be explored for this dyad in future studies in light of the greater length of time that grandchildren are able to share their grandparents' lives.

Antonucci also suggested that the norm of reciprocity varies within the context of different relationships over time [10]. The elderly are more likely to receive support from their children while maintaining reciprocal relationships with their spouses and friends.

Wentowski described three types of reciprocity: immediate, deferred, and generalized [14]. Immediate reciprocity is founded on distance and minimal obligations; deferred reciprocity repayment of a gift or service is postponed, encouraging greater trust. These two kinds of exchange are based on balanced reciprocity, i.e., exact repayment. Generalized reciprocity emerges after the first two forms have occurred for some time, and exact repayment is not expected. The assumption is that persons will contribute to others' well-being and will eventually be compensated themselves. Generalized reciprocity probably is characteristic of the relationship between the elderly and their families. The present study suggests that grandparent-adult grandchild bonds are based on generalized reciprocity of meaningful expressive support. Generalized reciprocity takes into account previous life periods when older persons provided family members with more support than they received. This perspective makes it less difficult today to maintain a relationship in which the respondent receives more than (s)he provides (i.e., the grandparent receives more expressive and instrumental support than (s)he is presently giving).

One must be cognizant of the fact that culture provides different attitudes toward behaviors in different ethnic groups. The grandparents in this sample have few expectations of instrumental support from adult grandchildren. The attitude reflected here is that children should not be unduly burdened with responsibilities for caring for parents. This outlook is consistent with the middle-class background and Jewish cultural norms of the sample population. Jewish parents have traditionally seen themselves as givers as opposed to receivers of service.

The homogeneity of the study sample in terms of health and socio-economic level restricts the generalizability of the findings. This lack of generalizability is not necessarily a problem; the goal of this study was not to test causal relationships, which requires representative samples, but to generate hypotheses on the service expectations of grandparents. The findings provide insight into an under-researched category of the elderly. These findings should be viewed as hypotheses that await systematic testing on a representative sample.

CONCLUSION

Assistance within the family has consistently been based on a system of mutual reciprocity stretching over the life cycle. The role of informal supports in providing affective, emotional support is crucial and can be as important as the provision of instrumental support. Implications for social-work policy practice suggests that adult grandchildren are an integral part of the informal support system; they voluntarily provide expressive assistance. The adult grandchild, hopefully, will continue to provide such support even when there is physical or mental decline in a grandparents' health. The extent of this support will depend upon the grandparent-adult grandchild history of assistance, individual characteristics, and the emotional ties shared by the pair. Adult grandchildren are a natural link in the social-support system of the grandparents.

REFERENCES

1. E. Shanas, Older People and Their Families: The New Pioneers, *Journal of Marriage and the Family, 42,* pp. 9-15, 1980.
2. V. G. Cicirelli, *Helping Elderly Parents: The Role of Adult Children,* Auburn House, Boston, 1981.
3. E. Brody, Women's Changing Roles and Help to Elderly Parents: Attitudes of Three Generations of Women, *Journal of Gerontology, 38:5,* pp. 597-607, 1983.
4. M. Sussman,The Family Life of Old People, in *Handbook of Aging and the Social Sciences,* R. Binstock and E. Shanas (eds.), Van Nostrand Reinhold, New York, 1976.
5. A. Kornhaber and K. L. Woodward, *Grandparents/Grandchildren: The Vital Connection,* Anchor Press Doubleday, New York, 1981.
6. R. L. Kahn and T. Antonucci, Convoys Over the Life Course: Attachment Roles and Social Support, in *Lifespan Development and Behavior,* P. Baltes and O. G. Brim (eds.), Academic Press, New York, 1980.
7. M. Cantor, Life Space and the Social Support System of the Inner-city Elderly of New York, *The Gerontologist, 15,* pp. 23-27, 1975.
8. M. Sussman, Relationships of Adult Children with Their Parents in the U.S., in *Social Structure and The Family,* E. Shanas and G. Streib (eds.), Prentice Hall, Inc., Englewood Cliffs, New Jersey, 1965.
9. W. C. Seelbach, Correlates of Aged Parents: Filial Responsibility Expectations and Realizations, *The Family Coordinator,* pp. 341-350, 1978.
10. T. Antonucci, Reciprocal and Nonreciprocal Social Support: Contrasting Sides of Intimate Relationships, *Journal of Gerontology, 43:3,* pp. S65-73, 1988.
11. N. Langer, *Grandparent Expectations of Adult Grandchildren,* doctoral dissertation, Fordham University, New York, 1988.
12. T. Antonucci, Personal Characteristics, Social Support, and Social Behavior, in *Handbook of Aging and the Social Sciences* (2nd. Edition), R. Binstock and E. Shanas (eds.), Van Nostrand Reinhold, New York, 1985.
13. R. C. Crandall, *Gerontology,* Addison Wesley, Massachusetts, 1980.
14. G. J. Wentowski, Reciprocity and the Coping Strategies of Older People: Cultural Dimensions of Network Building, *The Gerontologist, 21,* pp. 600-609, 1981.
15. R. Kastenbaum, in *The Dependencies of Old People,* R. A. Kalish (ed.), University of Michigan-Wayne State University, August 1969, (monograph).

Chapter 14

GENDER AND PERCEPTIONS OF GRANDPARENTHOOD

Jeanne L. Thomas

Grandparenthood is increasingly recognized as a normative family experience offering psychological benefits to both grandparents and grandchildren [1-5]. Grandparents' involvement with grandchildren is likely to reflect their satisfaction with these relationships, their responsibilities in grandchildren's upbringing, and the personal meaning of relationships with grandchildren. Furthermore, the extent to which potential psychological benefits of grandparenthood are realized is likely to depend upon the depth of relationships with grandchildren. As grandparenthood now spans most of middle and later adulthood, understanding the experience could provide insight into mental health during this period of life.

In this study, associations between gender and perceptions of grandparenting were examined. Two research questions were addressed. First, do views of grandparenthood vary according to grandparent gender, grandchild gender, or maternal/paternal grandparent status? Second, are there additive or interactive effects of grandparent gender, grandchild gender, and maternal/paternal grandparent status? Research informs us that gender differences in family experience, in interpersonal bonds, and in social networks exist throughout the life cycle. Identifying associations between gender and relationships with grandchildren could clarify some of the life-span consequences of these gender differences in roles and relationships.

Gender can potentially be related to grandparenthood through at least three routes: grandparents' gender, grandchildren's gender, and maternal/paternal grandparent status. Researchers have given more consideration to correlates of grandparent gender than to those of grandchild gender or of maternal/paternal grandparent status. Correlates of grandparent gender include caretaking involvement, influence patterns, and the personal meaning of grandparenthood. Early work showed that grandmothers took care of grandchildren more often than did grandfathers [6, 7]. However, in recent research grandfathers expressed more responsibility for grandchildren's care and for offering advice, but less grandparenting satisfaction than did grandmothers [8]. Hagestad found that grandfathers in three-generation families attempted to influence young adult grandchildren only in instrumental matters (e.g., jobs, finances), whereas grandmothers attempted to influence grandchildren's interpersonal and instrumental activities [9].

In a classic study that included examinations of grandparenthood meaning, grandmothers often found a sense of biological renewal in grandparenting; grandfathers most often viewed grandparenting as an opportunity for emotional fulfillment [7]. More recently, Kivnick found that grandparenthood meaning had distinct relationships to mental health for women and for men [2-4]. For grandmothers, the extent to which grandparenthood became a central component of life and permitted reinvolvement with the past increased with deprivations of later life; these functions of grandparenthood compensated for deprivations in their relationship to life satisfaction and morale. For grandfathers, emphasis upon indulgence and a sense of immortality through grandparenting increased as deprivations decreased; these components of grandparenthood meaning were positively related to life satisfaction and morale.

Grandparent gender, then, is associated with perceptions of grandparenthood. Although researchers of parent-child relationships have shown that children's gender has powerful influence upon parents' behaviors [e.g., 10], scholars have given little attention to ways in which grandchildren's gender is related to the character of grandparenthood. In a recent qualitative study, however, grandparents described relationships with grandsons and granddaughters differently. These grandparents conformed to traditional views of male and female roles in their gifts for and activities with grandchildren [11]. In Hagestad's study of grandparents in three-generation families, grandparents' efforts to influence grandchildren were most pronounced within same-sex grandparent-grandchild dyads [9].

Finally, the gender of the parental "link" between grandparent and grandchild may be associated with the nature of grandparenting. Scholars assert that parents play a critical mediating role in grandparent-grandchild relationships [e.g., 12]. Data support this assertion, as young adults have reported that their parents' attitudes and behavior toward grandparents affected their own relationships with grandparents [13, 14]. Gender may be associated with parents' mediation of grandparent-grandchild relationships. Discussions of women as kin-keepers imply that more intensive mediation efforts are directed toward grandmothers and/or toward maternal grandparents [15]. And in fact, grandchildren do evidence closer bonds to maternal grandparents, particularly the maternal grandmother, than to paternal grandparents [16].

Earlier work has documented associations between views of grandparenting and the grandparent's gender. Previous research has also, to a lesser extent, specified differences between relationships with grandsons and granddaughters and ways in which grandparent-grandchild relationships reflect bonds with parents.

At this point, more integrative research is needed. In particular, consideration of possible interactions among the effects of grandparent gender, grandchild gender, and maternal/paternal grandparent status could permit more comprehensive conclusions regarding associations between gender and grandparenthood.

Such an integrative approach might also provide more general insight into ties between gender and aging. Gender differentiation in family roles has been the norm for contemporary cohorts of middle-aged and older adults [e.g., 17]. The notion of women as kin-keepers suggests that men's and women's family experiences continue to differ in later life, with women having more intensive family bonds [15]. On the other hand, discussions of the "normal unisex" of later life [e.g.,18] suggest that men and women experience post-parental family ties in similar ways. Considering gender correlates of grandparenthood may provide a vantage point for synthesizing these perspectives.

The study examined differences in Thomas's [8] measures of *grandparenting satisfaction* and *perceived grandparenting responsibilities* and in Kivnick's [2-4] dimensions of *grandparenthood meaning* that were associated with grandparent gender, grandchild gender, and maternal/paternal grandparent status. In structured interviews, grandparents described their relationship with one grandchild. The grandchild discussed was the oldest grandchild in the two-parent household geographically closest to the grandparent.

This grandchild was selected as the focus for interviews in the belief that grandparents would have had more opportunities for contact with older grandchildren and with grandchildren living nearby, as compared to younger and more geographically distant grandchildren. With more opportunities for contact, grandparents would potentially have a rich basis for responding to interview questions. Specified grandchildren were selected from those in two-parent households because research reveals that divorce has profound effects on grandparent-grandchild relationships [e.g., 19, 20]. Although these impacts are important, they were beyond the scope of this research.

An interviewing focus upon the grandparent's relationship with one grandchild (rather a discussion of grandparenthood in general, or of relationships with all grandchildren) was chosen to provide a relatively uniform response basis for the total sample of grandparents, who varied in numbers of grandchildren. This approach to interviewing insured that not only comparisons between grandmothers and grandfathers, but also comparisons between maternal and paternal relationships and between relationships with grandsons and granddaughters, could be made. Such comparisons were not possible in earlier research on grandparenting, which described grandparenthood in general.

On the basis of Thomas's earlier work [8], it was hypothesized that grandmothers would express greater grandparenting satisfaction and less responsibility for grandchildren's care and for offering childrearing advice than would grandfathers. Kivnick's earlier work suggested that grandmothers would stress the importance of immortality through clan to a lesser extent than would grandfathers

[3]. Discussions of women as kin-keepers suggested that maternal grandparents would express greater grandparenting satisfaction and responsibility toward grandchildren than would paternal grandparents. On the basis of Hagestad's finding that influence patterns were particularly pronounced within same-sex grandparent-grandchild dyads [9], it was hypothesized that grandmothers with granddaughters and grandfathers with grandsons would express higher levels of perceived responsibilities for discipline and advising and would stress the importance of sharing wisdom with grandchildren more than would other grandparents. Thus, this study sought to confirm previously identified gender differences in grandparents' perceptions and to identify further ways in which gender is related to bonds with grandchildren.

METHOD

Participants

Participants were 115 grandfathers and 186 grandmothers aged forty-three to eighty-six. One member of married couples participated; thus, none of the grandmother participants was married to any of the grandfather participants. All were volunteers recruited through newspaper articles describing the research, requests made at meetings of church and civic organizations, and chain sampling. Each grandparent received a single payment of $25.00.

All participants were noninstitutionalized residents of southeastern Wisconsin. All were Caucasian, none were stepgrandparents of their target grandchild, and none shared a household with grandchildren. Great-grandparents were excluded from the sample. The transition to great-grandparenthood may affect perceptions of grandparenting in significant but as yet unknown ways [15]; although these effects are important, their examination was beyond the scope of this study.

As noted earlier, each grandparent described their experiences with one "target" grandchild. Approximately half of the target grandchildren (52.8%) were grandsons. Target grandchildren's ages ranged from one to twenty-four years; the mean age was 7.8 years. Nearly half of the participants (42.5%) were paternal grandparents of their target grandchild; there were sixty-four grandfathers with grandsons, and ninety grandmothers with granddaughters.

There were gender differences in several aspects of demographic background. Grandmothers were significantly younger than grandfathers, $t(298) = 4.14, p < .0001$ (Mean ages: grandmothers = 59.5, grandfathers = 63.2); number of grandchildren and age of the target grandchild did not differ significantly for grandmothers and grandfathers, p's > .05. Grandmothers were more likely to be widowed or divorced than were grandfathers, chi-square (2) = 20.21, $p < .00001$. The sample represented a wide range of occupations or former occupations, incomes, and educational backgrounds. Grandmothers were more likely than grandfathers to be employed part-time or not to be working outside of the home than were grandfathers, chi-square (3) = 10.34, $p < .02$. Finally, grandmothers were less likely than grandfathers to have received post-secondary education, chi-square (8) = 29.28, $p < .0003$. Grandmothers and grandfathers did not differ in annual household income, $p > .05$.

Maternal and paternal grandparents did not differ significantly in age, number of grandchildren, or age of the target grandchild, p's > .05; similarly, grandparents with grandsons and those with granddaughters did not differ significantly in age, number of grandchildren, or age of the target grandchild, p's > .05. Target grandchild gender and maternal/paternal grandparent status were not significantly associated with grandparents' marital status, occupational or educational background, or income, p's > .05. Geographic proximity of the target grandchild was not significantly associated with grandparent gender, with target grandchild gender, or with maternal/paternal grandparent status, p's > .05.

Table 1 summarizes grandparents' demographic background.

Procedures

The author or a research assistant conducted all interviews; interviews lasted sixty to ninety minutes. Interview topics included demographic characteristics, family characteristics, and perceptions of the relationship with the target grandchild. For the latter topic, Likert scales assessed perceptions of:

1. *Satisfaction* (Cronbach's alpha = .79),
2. *Perceived caretaking responsibility* (Cronbach's alpha = .55),
3. *Perceived discipline responsibility* (Cronbach's alpha = .84),
4. *Perceived helping responsibility* (Cronbach's alpha = .70),
5. *Perceived responsibility for offering childrearing advice* (Cronbach's alpha = .90),
6. *Centrality of the relationship in the grandparent's life* (Cronbach's alpha = .90),
7. *Valued elder* (Cronbach's alpha = .83),
8. *Indulgence* (Cronbach's alpha = .69),
9. *Reexperiencing the past through the relationship* (Cronbach's alpha = .82), and
10. *Immortality through clan* (Cronbach's alpha = .86).

These scales were modifications of measures used in previous research [2-4, 8]. All items presented statements describing the relationship with the target grandchild; Table 2 presents the sample items from each scale. Grandparents used a seven-point response scale (very strongly agree to very strongly disagree) to report the extent to which each statement corresponded to their experience; all scales included both positively and negatively worded items. Numerical values corresponding to item responses were added to produce scale scores.

Table 1. Grandparent Demographic Characteristics

	Percent	
Age	60.91	(7.67)
Target Grandchild Age	7.76	(5.10)
Number of Grandchildren	4.64	(3.38)
Marital Status		
Married	81	
Widowed	14	
Divorced	5	
Employment Status[a]		
Full-time	25	
Part-time	19	
Not Employed	28	
Retired	40	
Occupation of Employed Grandparents		
White Collar/Professional	13	
Clerical	13	
Blue Collar	6	
Service	9	
Agricultural	.3	
Other	1.3	
Former Occupations of Retired Grandparents		
White Collar/Professional	30	
Clerical	27	
Blue Collar	28	
Service	10	
Other	2	
Highest Level of Education Completed		
Less than High School Degree	17	
High School Degree	44	
Some College or Post-Secondary Schooling	25	
College Degree	9	
Graduate Degree	5	
Annual Household Income		
Less than $20,000	29	
$20,001 to $40,000	46	
More than $40,001	23	
Geographic Proximity of Target Grandchild's Family		
Within 15 minutes' drive	66	
Within 15-30 minutes' drive	8	
Within 30-60 minute drive	5	
Within 1-2 hour drive	8	
Farther than 2 hour drive	14	

Note: Standard Deviations appear in parentheses.
[a] Percentages do not sum to 100 as some retired grandparents were employed part-time.

Table 2. Sample Items for Grandparenting Scales

Satisfaction:
I'm enjoying [Target Grandchild Name] more than I did my own children.

Perceived Advising Responsibility:
I've steered clear of advising my children about [Target Grandchild Name].

Perceived Caretaking Responsibility:
I wouldn't want to be responsible for taking care of [Target Grandchild Name] everyday.

Perceived Discipline Responsibility:
I take lots of opportunities to point [Target Grandchild Name] in the right direction.

Perceived Helping Responsibility:
I want [Target Grandchild Name] to know that s/he can depend on me.

Centrality:
[Target Grandchild Name] influences how I think about myself. Other things in my life are more satisfying than being a grandparent.

Valued Elder:
I don't have any thoughts about how I want [Target Grandchild Name] to remember me.

Immortality Through Clan:
[Target Grandchild Name] is important because s/he's the one who will carry on the family line.

Reinvolvement in Past:
Being a grandparent has made me think about my own grandparents.

Indulgence:
A big part of being a grandparent is providing [Target Grandchild Name] with all kinds of treats.

RESULTS

Two 2 (grandparent gender) by 2 (grandchild gender) by 2 (maternal/paternal status) multivariate analyses of variance were performed. The perceptions of grandparenting scale scores were dependent variables. Cell sizes ranged from twenty to fifty-six; in order to maintain reasonable ratios between cell sizes and the number of dependent variables, five grandparenting scale scores were dependent variables in each analysis. Means for all dependent variables appear in Table 3.

In the first analysis, scores for grandparenting satisfaction, perceived caretaking responsibility, perceived discipline responsibility, perceived helping responsibility,

Table 3. Perceptions of Grandparenting Scale Scores

| | Grandmothers | | | | Grandfathers | | | |
| | Maternal | | Paternal | | Maternal | | Paternal | |
Scale	Grandson $n=52$	Granddaughter $n=56$	Grandson $n=43$	Granddaughter $n=34$	Grandson $n=34$	Granddaughter $n=31$	Grandson $n=30$	Granddaughter $n=20$
Satisfaction[a]	79.90 (9.70)	79.07 (11.21)	74.93 (10.62)	79.77 (9.77)	73.47 (9.91)	74.68 (10.73)	72.80 (11.16)	78.65 (10.69)
Discipline Responsibility	67.90 (9.93)	63.41 (12.03)	63.70 (8.73)	65.71 (11.92)	65.91 (11.29)	63.19 (10.39)	64.97 (10.72)	64.40 (7.97)
Caretaking Responsibility	9.96 (2.69)	10.18 (2.18)	9.88 (2.32)	9.53 (2.31)	9.88 (2.58)	10.52 (2.10)	9.43 (1.70)	10.60 (3.07)
Advising Responsibility	54.96 (8.40)	54.18 (9.62)	50.05 (8.79)	51.65 (10.78)	53.74 (10.49)	55.36 (9.24)	53.67 (7.89)	55.20 (8.84)
Helping Responsibility	21.65 (2.86)	20.77 (3.34)	20.47 (3.28)	20.91 (3.09)	20.85 (2.77)	20.74 (4.22)	19.93 (3.50)	21.70 (3.40)
Centrality of Relationship	67.21 (10.20)	63.57 (11.85)	63.77 (12.36)	65.62 (11.60)	64.06 (10.21)	63.61 (10.93)	63.17 (9.30)	66.95 (11.39)
Sharing Wisdom	65.02 (10.81)	61.64 (11.57)	63.49 (8.76)	64.68 (8.76)	63.94 (6.74)	61.29 (9.50)	61.97 (8.72)	63.15 (12.49)
Indulging Grandchild[a]	16.56 (3.08)	16.63 (2.67)	16.98 (3.09)	16.65 (2.27)	16.88 (2.43)	17.32 (2.86)	16.87 (1.93)	18.60 (3.50)
Reexperience the Past	33.79 (8.02)	29.36 (7.47)	31.77 (8.94)	33.82 (7.90)	33.00 (7.44)	32.97 (8.35)	32.67 (8.89)	33.25 (9.48)
Extension of Family[a]	61.08 (11.30)	57.41 (10.56)	60.72 (12.27)	62.09 (9.46)	63.65 (9.63)	61.00 (8.45)	61.47 (10.52)	66.20 (11.11)

Note: Standard deviations are in parentheses.
[a] Grandmothers' and grandfathers' mean scores differ, $p < .05$.

and perceived responsibility for offering childrearing advice were dependent variables. There were no interaction effects or main effects for grandchild gender or maternal/paternal grandparent status, p's < .08. There was a significant main effect for grandparent gender, multivariate $F(5,288) = 2.87$, Wilk's lambda = .953, $p < .015$. Grandmothers expressed greater grandparenting satisfaction than did grandfathers, $F(1, 292) = 7.68$, $p < .006$ (Means: grandmothers = 78.51, $s.d.$ = 10.49; grandfathers = 74.52, $s.d.$ = 10.66).

In the second analysis, scores for centrality of the relationship, valued elder, indulgence, reexperiencing the past through the relationship, and immortality through clan were dependent variables. There were no interaction effects or main effects for grandchild gender or maternal/paternal status, p's < .16. There was a significant main effect for grandparent gender, multivariate $F(5, 288) = 4.94$, Wilk's lambda = .921, $p < .0001$. Grandfathers stressed immortality through clan, $F(1, 292) = 4.62$, p < .03 (Means: grandmothers = 60.11, $s.d.$ = 11.05; grandfather = 62.81, $s.d.$ = 9.90), and indulgence, $F(1, 292) = 4.50$, $p < .03$ (Means: grandmothers = 16.70, $s.d.$ = 2.81; grandfathers = 17.30, $s.d.$ = 2.69), to a greater extent than did grandmothers.

As noted earlier, grandmothers and grandfathers differed in several demographic characteristics, including age. Because earlier work has identified age as well as gender difference in perceptions of grandparenthood [7, 8], one might question whether the gender differences identified here reflected the gender difference in grandparents' ages. However, grandparent age was not significantly associated with grandparenting satisfaction, immortality through clan, or indulgence (r's < .09, p's > .05). It did not appear, then, that these gender differences in perceptions reflected gender differences in age.

Similarly, there was no evidence that the gender differences reflected effects of target grandchildren's ages. In one earlier study [8], some gender differences in views of grandparenthood apparently stemmed from gender differences in grandchildren's ages. In the present study, target grandchildren's ages were not significantly associated with grandparent gender. Nor was target grandchild age significantly associated with grandparenting satisfaction, immortality through clan, or indulgence (r's < .05, p's > .05), although target grandchild age was negatively associated with perceived responsibilities for discipline and advising and positively associated with the importance of sharing wisdom with the grandchild (r's > .16, p's < .01). Target grandchild age was not significantly associated with perceived responsibilities for caretaking and helping, with the centrality of the relationship, or with the extent to which the relationship permitted reexperiencing the past (r's < .13, p's > .05).

DISCUSSION

This study has identified differences between grandmothers' and grandfathers' relationships with a grandchild. Grandmothers reported greater satisfaction with these relationships than did grandfathers; grandfathers placed greater stress upon generational extension of the family and upon indulging grandchildren than did grandmothers. There was no evidence that these associations reflected effects of grandparents' or grandchildren's ages.

In many respects, men and women viewed their relationships with the grandchild similarly. Grandmothers and grandfathers did not differ in levels of perceived responsibilities toward the grandchild. Nor did they differ in the extent to which they stressed the centrality of the relationship in their own lives, in the extent to which the relationship permitted reinvolvement with their past, or in the extent to which they valued sharing wisdom with the grandchild.

The hypothesis that grandmothers and grandfathers would differ in their views of the relationship with the grandchild was only partially supported. In particular, an earlier finding that grandfathers expressed greater responsibility for offering advice and for taking care of grandchildren was not confirmed [8] . Failure of the present study to support this hypothesis apparently reflects measurement differences between the two studies.

In this study, grandparents were interviewed about their relationship with one grandchild; in the earlier study, grandparents discussed grandparenthood in general. Questions concerning involvement in caretaking and advising thus elicited different reactions in the abstract context of grandparenthood in general as opposed to the more concrete context of a specific relationship. On an abstract level, grandparents view these functions as expressions of nurturance, whereas they may consider the same functions servile or actions representing interference in the framework of a particular relationship.

The hypothesis that maternal grandparents would express greater satisfaction and responsibility was not supported. Perhaps the affective quality of the grandparent-parent relationship (rather than maternal/paternal grandparent status) is the decisive element in parents' mediation of grandparent-grandchild bonds. If so, warm relationships between grandparents and parents should facilitate warm grandparent-grandchild relationships, in which grandparents express high levels of satisfaction and responsibility, whether the grandparent-parent relationship is maternal or paternal. Conversely, an antagonistic grandparent-parent relationship (again, whether maternal or paternal) would impede development of close grandparent-grandchild bonds.

The hypothesis that grandmothers with granddaughters, and grandfathers with grandsons, would express relatively high levels of perceived responsibilities and grandparenthood meaning also was not supported. This hypothesis was based upon Hagestad's study of influence between grandparents and grandchildren in three-generation families [9]. Failure to support this hypothesis could stem from differences between the samples or the measurement approaches of the two studies. Most grandparents (77%) in this study described relationships with preadolescent grandchildren; the grandparents in Hagestad's research discussed young adult grandchildren. The significance of same-sex grandparent-grandchild dyads may emerge when grandchildren reach adolescence or adulthood and assume more mature social roles. It is also possible that none of the measures of influence (e.g., responsibility for discipline, responsibility for advising, importance of sharing wisdom with the grandchild) corresponded to Hagestad's measures of grandparental influence.

Current notions regarding gender and aging (e.g., cohort history of gender-specific family roles as opposed to the "normal unisex" of later life) imply somewhat different profiles of older men's and women's family experience. It was hoped that this consideration of grandparenthood would provide a basis for synthesizing these perspectives. The gender differences in grandparenthood meaning and satisfaction identified in this study reflect individual growth, cultural context, and earlier family experience. Like Thomas's previous findings of grandfathers' greater stress upon caretaking and advising [8], these grandfathers' stress upon indulging grandchildren may reflect male nurturance and expressivity of middle and later adulthood, an aspect of the "normal unisex" of later life [18]. Grandfathers' endorsement of family extension through grandchildren is consistent with cultural traditions of patrilineal descent. For grandfathers, therefore, relationships with grandchildren have both developmental and cultural importance.

Nonetheless, these grandfathers expressed less satisfaction with the relationships than did the grandmothers. Grandmothers' higher satisfaction scores could reveal continuity of earlier and current family experiences. For contemporary grandmothers, childrearing has been a culturally encouraged area of competence throughout the life course. Exercising these familiar functions would be satisfying as opportunities draw upon this expertise. The findings of this study suggest that relationships with grandchildren reflect consequences of both sex-role differentiation earlier in the life course and movement toward androgyny in middle and later adulthood.

Future researchers should continue to examine relationships between experiences with grandchildren and grandparents' mental health, a research approach that Kivnick has begun [2-5]. The gender differences reported here suggest that grandparenting may have unique developmental significance for grandfathers and grandmothers. In fact, Kivnick's research to date has revealed distinct compensatory functions of grandparenthood meaning for women and men [2-4]. Identifying additional associations among gender, perceptions of grandparenthood, and mental health would further clarify the clinical significance of relationships with grandchildren.

In addition, the nature of the parental "link" between grandparent and grandchild should be examined in greater detail. The affective quality, if not the lineage, of the relationship with the parental generation may influence relationships with grandchildren. Furthermore, grandparent-parent affect could moderate any mental health benefits that grandparenthood provides.

This study, like most grandparenthood research, followed a quasi-experimental design and reflected the experiences of a relatively homogenous, self-selected sample of grandparents. The findings therefore could be usefully extended through research with more diverse samples. Examining racial variation in the functions of grandparenthood would be especially valuable. With these data, scholars would be better prepared to offer insight into the nature and importance of grandparenthood to researchers, to practitioners, and to grandparents and their families.

REFERENCES

1. V. L. Bengtson and J. F. Robertson (eds.), *Grandparenthood*, Sage Publications, Beverly Hills, 1985.
2. H. Q. Kivnick, Grandparenthood: An Overview of Meaning and Mental Health, *The Gerontologist, 22,* pp. 59-66, 1982.
3. H. Q. Kivnick, *The Meaning of Grandparenthood*, UMI Research Press, Ann Arbor, 1982.
4. H. Q. Kivnick, Grandparenthood and Mental Health: Meaning, Behavior, and Satisfaction, in *Grandparenthood,* V. L. Bengtson and J. F. Robertson (eds.), Sage Publications, Beverly Hills, 1985.
5. E. H. Erikson, J. M. Erikson, and H. Q. Kivnick, *Vital Involvement in Old Age,* W. W. Norton, New York, 1986.
6. P. Albrecht, The Parental Responsibilities of Grandparents, *Marriage and Family Living, 16,* pp. 201-204, 1954.
7. B. L. Neugarten and K. Weinstein, The Changing American Grandparent, *Journal of Marriage and the Family, 26,* pp. 199-204, 1964.
8. J. L. Thomas, Age and Sex Differences in Perceptions of Grandparenting, *Journal of Gerontology, 41,* pp. 417-423, 1986.
9. G. O. Hagestad, Continuity and Connectedness, in *Grandparenthood,* V. L. Bengtson and J. F. Robertson (eds.), Sage Publications, Beverly Hills, 1985.
10. B. Birns, The Emergence and Socialization of Sex Differences in the Earliest Years, *Merrill-Palmer Quarterly, 22,* pp. 229-254, 1976.
11. J. L. Thomas, The Development of Grandparents' Relationships with Their Grandchildren: A Qualitative Study, Doctoral dissertation, West Virginia University, *Dissertation Abstracts International, 43,* pp. 4211-4205B, 1982.
12. J. F. Robertson, Interaction in Three Generation Families, Parents as Mediators: Toward a Theoretical Perspective, *International Journal of Aging and Human Development, 6,* pp. 103-110, 1975.
13. R. Gilford and K. D. Black, *The Grandparent-Grandchild Dyad: Ritual or Relationship?,* paper presented at the annual meeting of the Gerontological Society of America, San Juan, Puerto Rico, December 1972.
14. J. F. Robertson, The Significance of Grandparents: Perceptions of Young Adult Grandchildren, *The Gerontologist, 15,* pp. 137-140, 1976.
15. L. E. Troll, S. J. Miller, and R. C. Atchley, *Families in Later Life,* Wadsworth Publishing Company, Belmont, California, 1979.
16. B. Kahana and E. Kahana, Grandparenthood from the Perspective of the Developing Grandchild, *Developmental Psychology, 3,* pp. 99-105, 1970.

17. A. S. Rossi, Aging and Parenthood in the Middle Years, in *Life-Span Development and Behavior,* Vol. 3, P. B. Baltes and O. G. Brim (eds.), Academic Press, New York, 1980.
18. D. L. Gutmann, Parenthood: Key to Comparative Study of the Life Cycle, in *Life-Span Developmental Psychology: Normative Life Crises,* N. Datan and L. Ginsburg (eds.), Academic Press, New York, 1975.
19. A. J. Cherlin and F. F. Furstenberg, *The New American Grandparent,* Basic Books, New York, 1985.
20. C. L. Johnson, Active and Latent Functions of Grandparenting during the Divorce Process, *The Gerontologist, 28,* pp. 185-191, 1988.

Chapter 15

STRENGTHS AND NEEDS OF BLACK GRANDPARENTS

Robert Strom
Pat Collinsworth
Shirley Strom
and
Dianne Griswold

Black Americans are confronted by a higher proportion of difficulties throughout life. The obstacles begin at birth when Black infants die at more than double the rate of Anglos. Growing up in poverty is more prevalent among Black youngsters (45%) than Anglos (15%) [1]. Living with a single parent has become the norm for Blacks (60%) but not for Anglos (22%) [2]. Black children encounter greater risks that jeopardize health and safety such as inadequate medical care, improper nutrition, environmental hazards, exposure to violent behavior, and unwanted pregnancies [3-5].

There is general agreement that education offers Black children the best possibility for escape from poverty. Nevertheless, going to school is viewed by many Black students as a disappointing ordeal. When children conclude academic success cannot be attained, they withdraw before earning a high school diploma. Graduation rates are lower for Blacks (75%) than for Anglo (82%) teenagers [6]. Even when they attend college, a smaller proportion of Blacks (41%) earn degrees than Anglos (61%) [7]. Moreover, Black university graduates often earn lower incomes than Anglos with comparable education [8].

Aging is also more difficult for Black men and women. More than half of the older Black population did not attend school beyond eighth grade [9]. Their life on the job has been characterized by low salaries and lengthy layoffs so they have little in the way of retirement assets such as pensions and health insurance. They often leave the work force early, more frequently depend on social security, and live in poverty at twice the rate of other older adults [10]. Elderly Blacks commonly suffer from a lack of education, not enough income, substandard housing, poor health, and fewer years of life. And, because they grew up before civil rights legislation created opportunities, these men and women have been victims of greater prejudice than younger relatives [11].

INTERGENERATIONAL SUPPORT IN BLACK FAMILIES

There is a positive side to life in Black families. They have more in common than a need to overcome adversity. There is a shared commitment to support family members whenever help is needed, a willingness to honor and maintain close intergenerational ties, and a desire to preserve differences from other sub-populations, particularly those valued aspects of lifestyle that reflect ethnic heritage [12, 13]. These favorable qualities appear to be passed on from one generation to the next. To illustrate, the National Council on Aging polled public attitudes toward older adults [14]. One aspect of the poll explored helping relationships across generations. It was found that, when compared to Anglos, Black parents were more likely to give money to grandparents, take them places, shop and run errands, repair things, and provide care during times of illness. In a reciprocal way, Black grandparents were more likely than Anglo grandparents to assist sons and daughters by taking grandchildren into their homes and caring for them.

Data from the most recent national census confirms that grandparent initiative to support parents is still in place [15]. About 13 percent of Black children live in the home of a grandparent compared to 3 percent of Anglo children. Black grandparents are also more involved in raising grandchildren. The pattern of reciprocal intergenerational assistance remains a priority in Black families [16, 17].

BENEFITS OF EDUCATION FOR GRANDPARENTS

We began to work with grandparents by offering a free class for them at churches and senior centers in Phoenix, Arizona. The 400 mostly Anglo middle-class grandparents attending the weekly semester-length classes understood our purposes were to 1) acquaint them with the goals that parents now have for raising children, 2) discover what it is like to be growing up at the present time, and 3) recognize how these changes call for corresponding shifts in the grandparent role. In return, participants agreed to share their grandparent experiences by letting us know the things that pleased and concerned them about their family. This sharing format was considered necessary because an extensive search of the literature on intergenerational relationships failed to reveal programs to help grandparents grow. In order to obtain baseline data, our discussions with grandparents were recorded [18].

The resulting observations enabled us to formulate the nation's first educational program for grandparents. A field test of the curriculum was conducted in cooperation with the American Association of Retired Persons Andrus Foundation [19]. Three generations were asked to evaluate the attitudes and behavior of 210 grandparents before and after they took the twelve-week course on *Becoming A Better Grandparent*. All of the participants, and the relatives they selected, were administered the *Grandparent Strengths and Needs Inventory* [20]. At the end of the intervention program grandparent score changes revealed they had made significant improvements. This progress was corroborated by their sons, daughters, and grandchildren [21]. Subsequently, the course on *Becoming A Better Grandparent* [22, 23] and its sequel entitled *Achieving Grandparent Potential* [24, 25] have been made commercially available. There is also a guide for leaders [26].

ADAPTING GRANDPARENT EDUCATION

Scholars believe that most grandparents are capable of making a greater contribution to families and urge that programs be designed to help them achieve their potential [27]. Clinton Wharton, Chairman of the Rockefeller Foundation, contends that society must find new ways to strengthen Black families or the institutional reforms for them will be less effective [28]. Black columnist William Raspberry shares this concern and recommends the same focus: "If I could offer a single prescription for the survival of America, and particularly of Black America, it would be to restore the family" [29].

The purpose of the present investigation was to identify differences in performance and effectiveness of Black grandparents from different regions of the United States in comparison to Anglo families. Perceptions regarding Black grandparents from Arizona were compared to perceptions about Anglo grandparents in the same locale and with Black grandparents from Alabama. We sought to discover ways in which the *Becoming A Better Grandparent* course focus should alter to maximize relevance for Black grandmothers and grandfathers.

METHOD

Two Generational Assessment

The self-selected sample of 408 grandparents drawn from churches and senior centers included 204 Anglos and 100 Blacks from Arizona and 104 Blacks from Alabama. Anglo grandparents (74%) and grandfathers (26%) were mostly from middle-class backgrounds, whereas the Black grandmothers (79%) and grandfathers (21%) reported considerably lower annual incomes.

A sample of 470 grandchildren consisted of 175 Anglos and 104 Blacks from Arizona, and 191 Blacks from Alabama. These seven- to eighteen-year-old girls (55%) and boys (45%) were not relatives of the grandparent sample but came from families of similar income. A greater proportion of the Anglo children lived with married parents (73%) than did the Black children from Arizona (39%) or Alabama (43%).

Black grandparents were asked to choose one grandchild to think about while completing a questionnaire which revealed personal views about their family role. They were told the results of the investigation would be used to develop a free course on grandparenting for them. The Black grandchildren were asked to describe how they thought a particular grandparent of their choice performed his or her role. Boys and girls were assured that their responses would not be shown to the grandparents. A comparison group of Anglo grandparents and grandchildren completed the same questionnaire as part of a program designed for them [30].

The 60 Likert-type items of the *Grandparent Strengths and Needs Inventory* are divided equally into six subscales emphasizing separate aspects of grandparent development [20]. Respectively, these subscales emphasize:

- Satisfaction—aspects of being a grandparent that are pleasing;
- Success—ways in which grandparents successfully perform their role;
- Teaching—the kinds of lessons grandparents are expected to provide;
- Difficulty—problems encountered with grandparenting obligations;
- Frustration—behaviors of grandchildren that upset grandparents; and
- Information needs—things grandparents need to know about grandchildren.

Women and men who completed the grandparent version reported about their self-impression. Another version of the inventory allowed grandchildren to report their views regarding a particular grandparent. Certainly grandmothers and grandfathers are the most qualified persons to identify the demands placed upon them. However, if they serve as the only source of perception about their competence, some pivotal issues might be overlooked. Grandparents are not alone in defining their role and judging their success. Grandchildren have expectations that deserve consideration too. A broader perspective about family interaction offers a more complete picture of grandparent strengths and needs, the attitudes and behaviors they should continue and those they ought to reconsider.

Data Analyses

Comparisons were made between the Black and Anglo groups and regional differences were calculated between the two Black populations. Multivariate analysis of variance procedures were performed using the six subscales of the inventory as dependent variables. The independent variables, drawn from a review of the literature on intergenerational relationships, included ethnicity, location, grandparent age, grandparent gender, grandchild age, time with grandchild, and geographical proximity. To further confirm results, MANOVA procedures with only a single independent variable were used to determine effects on the subscales. Univariate and Scheffé measures were also performed in order to locate specific sources of significance. Within-group differences were determined by t-tests. Homogeneity of response was calculated by analyzing standard deviation scores for each item on the inventory.

RESULTS

Table 1 presents a summary of the MANOVA results for Anglo and Black grandparent responses. The multivariate F-statistic, evaluating the main effect of ethnicity was significant ($p < .001$). Two other significant main effects were age of grandchild ($p < .05$), and amount of time per month spent with grandchild ($p < .001$). The measurement model contained testing for interaction effects which included ethnicity paired with each of the other independent variables. These calculations yielded three significant F-outcomes: ethnicity by age of grandparent ($p < .01$), ethnicity by age of grandchild ($p < .05$), and ethnicity by distance ($p < .05$). Table 2 shows MANOVA procedures performed on test results of Anglo and Black grandchildren also yielded significant main effects for ethnicity ($p < .001$) and age of grandchild ($p < .001$). One significant interaction effect emerged, ethnicity by age of grandchild ($p < .05$).

Ethnicity and Grandparent Performance

Both ethnic groups of grandparents demonstrated overall favorable self-perceptions. However, the scores of Blacks were significantly higher than Anglos on all six subscales and for the majority of items. Black grandparents believe their greatest strength is teaching. This conclusion is shared by Black grandchildren. Mean scores for items on the inventory further define the dimensions of successful teaching. The highest scores of Blacks were for teaching grandchildren to care about the feelings of others, teaching good manners, teaching a sense of right and wrong, and teaching the need for learning throughout life. Black grandchildren reported that their grandparents were consistently willing to listen to them.

Black grandparents were also seen by grandchildren as needing improvement. In particular, they gave grandparents less favorable scores than grandparents assigned themselves for the way they handle difficulties, cope with frustrations, and understand what it is like to be growing up today. For each of these three subscales Anglo grandchildren gave their grandparents significantly more favorable scores. The degree of variability on item responses was greater among

Table 1. Analysis of Variance of GSNI Subscales and Independent Variables for Anglo and Black Grandparents

| | | Test Statistics | | | | | | |
| | | Multivariate | | Univariate F | | | | |
Source of Variation	df	F	Satisfaction	Success	Teaching	Difficulty	Frustration	Information
Grand Mean	1	—	—	—	—	—	—	—
Ethnicity	1	11.158***	3.075	11.234***	47.875***	9.168**	.487	11.346**
Age of GP	1	.264	.096	.132	.100	.254	.188	.300
Sex of GP	1	.975	.756	1.886	2.411	.270	.869	.261
Age of GC	1	2.662*	6.757**	6.736**	.355	9.994**	7.045**	7.267**
Time	1	5.490***	18.931***	17.968***	19.420***	11.447***	3.628	6.451*
Distance	1	1.676	4.129*	.117	.046	.182	.671	5.283*
Ethnicity x GP Age	1	3.172**	4.405*	8.717**	.000	4.390*	2.296	6.441*
Ethnicity x GP Sex	1	.343	.655	.019	.023	.510	1.332	1.278
Ethnicity x GC Age	1	2.239*	.360	1.414	3.018	.026	1.586	.142
Ethnicity x Time	1	1.542	2.798	.057	1.637	1.270	2.342	3.578
Ethnicity x Distance	1	2.785*	5.577*	.399	.000	7.345**	3.019	8.606**

* .05 significance level
** .01 significance level
*** .001 significance level

Table 2. Analysis of Variance of GSNI Subscales and Independent Variables for Anglo and Black Grandchildren

| | | Multivariate | Univariate F | | | | | |
| | | | Test Statistics | | | | | |
Source of Variation	df	F	Satisfaction	Success	Teaching	Difficulty	Frustration	Information
Grand Mean	1	—	—	—	—	—	—	—
Ethnicity	1	6.769***	.049	.538	17.970***	11.689***	8.452**	8.338**
Age of GP	1	.492	.644	.618	.005	.604	.185	.000
Sex of GP	1	.929	.465	.038	.001	.656	4.638*	.226
Age of GC	1	5.590***	19.455***	4.910*	.437	4.432*	.287	1.448
Time	1	1.553	.409	.902	1.421	2.796	7.90	.233
Distance	1	1.016	.084	.109	.268	1.567	1.785	5.073*
Ethnicity x GP Age	1	.958	2.807	3.706	.748	1.751	1.436	1.161
Ethnicity x GP Sex	1	.410	.726	.001	.370	.103	.411	.988
Ethnicity x GC Age	1	2.284*	.363	1.332	.000	10.630***	5.310*	6.494**
Ethnicity x Time	1	1.292	6.711**	1.957	1.753	1.387	1.238	.036
Ethnicity x Distance	1	.469	2.415	1.246	1.205	.280	.001	.022

*.05 significance level
**.01 significance level
***.001 significance level

Blacks than Anglos, indicating a wider range of experience within the Black population.

Amount of Time Spent with Grandchild

The amount of time grandparents spend with grandchildren has an influence on how grandparents perceive their effectiveness and on the way grandchildren evaluate them. Regardless of ethnicity, grandparents who spent the most time interacting with grandchildren considered themselves significantly more effective in their role on all the subscales. Grandchildren in both racial groups also reported more favorable views of grandparents' level of satisfaction, degree of success, and quality of teaching when they spent more time with them. The proportion of Black grandparents (72%) indicating they devote five or more hours monthly to grandchildren was greater than expressed by Anglo grandparents (30%). This disparity is corroborated by the proportion of Black (65%) and Anglo (27%) grandchildren who reported that grandparents spend five or more hours a month with them.

Distance from Grandchild

The distance grandparents live from grandchildren is viewed differently by Anglos as compared to Blacks. Anglo grandparents who live less than 200 miles away consider themselves more successful, more effective teachers, and better able to manage difficulties. Anglo children who live close to grandparents also regard them as more influential teachers than those who live farther than 200 miles away. But distance is not a factor for Black grandparents. Those who live far from their grandchildren and those who live close are similar in what they expect of themselves and the effectiveness they assign to their efforts. The impressions Black grandchildren have of grandparents are not influenced by distance either. These boys and girls believe they can count on grandparents whether they live nearby or in a distant place.

Age of Grandparent

There were significant interaction effects for ethnicity and grandparent age. Older Black grandparents (age sixty and over) and younger Anglo grandparents (under age sixty) regard themselves as more effective in their role. Differences were found for level of satisfaction, degree of success, scope of teaching, ability to manage problems, and having needed information on grandchildren. Black grandchildren also consider their older grandparents as more successful and having greater influence on them. Conversely, Anglo grandchildren feel that younger grandparents offer more effective support and are a better resource to rely on.

Differences were found in the amount of time that older and younger grandparents devote to grandchildren. Within the Anglo sample, 30 percent of older grandparents and 33 percent of younger ones spent five or more hours per month with grandchildren. In contrast, 65 percent of older and 69 percent of younger Black grandparents from Arizona spent more than five hours a month with grandchildren. In Alabama, 68 percent of older Black grandparents and 80 percent of younger grandparents spent more than five hours per month with grandchildren.

Age of Grandchild

There were no significant differences between Anglo and Black grandparents according to age of the grandchild they were reporting on. Both groups assigned more desirable scores when evaluating themselves with younger grandchildren. Anglo grandparents considered themselves more successful in all aspects of grandparenting when they have younger grandchildren (under age twelve). Anglo grandchildren shared this point of view. Black grandparents with younger grandchildren also believe they can handle difficulties and frustrations better than peers with older grandchildren. However, Black grandchildren present a different point of view. Older Black grandchildren (age 12 to 18) scored their older grandparents more favorably than did younger grandchildren on the difficulty, frustration, and information needs subscales.

A related outcome is the differences observed in the amount of time that grandparents spend with grandchildren based on the grandchild's age. More Anglo grandparents spent five hours a month with younger grandchildren (39%) than older grandchildren (19%). The Anglo grandchildren agreed with these reports. Black grandparents and grandchildren felt that the age of the grandchild did not affect the amount of time they spent together. A slightly higher proportion of twelve- to eighteen-year-old Black grandchildren (70% in Arizona and 65% in Alabama) reported that grandparents spend five hours or more per month with them as compared with seven- to eleven-year-old grandchildren (68% in Arizona and 60% in Alabama). The willingness of Black grandparents to give as much time to older grandchildren as the younger ones extends the duration of their influence.

Gender of Grandparent

Only one of the statistics generated by univariate analysis was significant for grandparent gender. With the responses of Anglo and Black grandparents combined, the teaching variable indicated a significant discrepancy between mean scores in favor of the grandmothers ($p < .02$). Scheffé contrasts revealed similar results. Grandchildren offered corresponding evaluations of grandmothers and grandfathers, except for coping with frustration where they feel grandfathers perform better ($p < .05$).

PROGRAM IMPLICATIONS

Black grandparents are often seen by parents as a valuable source of help in raising children. By improving the readiness of grandparents to support child development, everyone in the family can benefit. A new method to better prepare grandparents involves an educational program that honors their strengths and offers effective ways to overcome personal limitations. Adaptation of grandparent courses to fit the needs of ethnic groups should be based on information about the target population that is accurate and culturally sensitive. As a result of this study, the following recommendations have been incorporated into the *Becoming A Better Grandparent* program currently offered to Black families.

Educators should appeal to the Black grandparents' appreciation of teaching as motivation for them to learn more about the attitudes, opinions, and behaviors that prevail in their grandchildren's peer groups. Black grandparents, compared to Anglos, received more favorable scores on the potentials index. This index, which is drawn from three subscales, reveals grandparent devotion of time and attention, amount of encouragement, emotional support, and willingness to teach the nonacademic lessons children need to know. Even though they have less formal education, Black grandparents are considered more active teachers than Anglo grandparents. They are seen as more influential in providing children a sense of direction through lessons on respecting other people's feelings, demonstrating the worth of religious faith, using good manners, reinforcing a sense of right and wrong, giving advice, and teaching the importance of learning throughout life.

Grandparents can become better informed by devoting more conversations to topics that interest grandchildren. Priority should be given to conversations about making and keeping friends, overcoming the forces of an adverse environment, handling problems with teachers or fellow students, and sharing feelings about personal choices that have to be made. Black grandparents communicate easily with grandchildren. But the scores grandchildren assign them on the information needs subscale shows they are not doing as well as they could in understanding younger family members. According to both generations, grandparents need more understanding about the problems grandchildren encounter at school and in the neighborhood, the things they worry about, their goals for the future, daily episodes of stress, and conflicts with peers. Grandparents who lack knowledge about grandchildren's abilities are more likely to set unreasonable expectations for achievement. Because the older generation did not experience some of the current opportunities and related pressures, there is a danger in pushing children more than guiding them.

The curriculum for Black grandparents should emphasize problem solving, ways to help adolescents avoid and overcome obstacles to a successful future. Black teenagers have high rates of pregnancy, school dropout, and criminal activity. Adolescents need to set goals for a sense of personal direction, to gain confidence to reject peer pressure to behave in ways that are not in their best interest, and to develop constructive methods for responding to the demands of school. These healthy characteristics can best be supported by grandparents who, in addition to nurturing strengths, also possess problem solving and guidance skills.

Black grandparents should get to know more about grandchildren as individuals. They ought to participate more in activities grandchildren enjoy, accept the values of young people, admit when they do not know about something, look at social change in new ways, respect the televiewing habits of grandchildren, and learn about their personal worries, choices, and conflicts. Racial prejudice deserves special attention because it implicates self-esteem and personal identity. Older adults and children need to talk about how they deal with unfair treatment from people of other backgrounds.

Curriculum for Black grandparents with young grandchildren should feature the role of play in the development of creative thinking. Using play as a method of teaching can encourage boys and girls to value their imagination as a powerful resource. Black grandparents tend to discourage play because they feel it will not prepare children for the harsh realities of growing up in a hostile environment. On the contrary, fantasy is a valuable defense for living with adversity. Play offers choices, enables a sense of what is possible, and motivates the persistence needed to succeed in the real world.

Black grandparents need to know how to support the educational opportunities of grandchildren. Confidence is needed in talking with a grandchild's teachers. It is also important to understand changes in the educational system, difficulties that grandchildren experience in school, and ways to cooperate with teachers. Knowing how to help a grandchild find out about college and acquire financial assistance can be the motivating force needed by youngsters who might otherwise give up in pursuing their dreams.

Grandparent curriculum ought to clarify the worries and concerns of single parents, identify the risks these families commonly encounter, and illustrate ways in which the grandparents can be supportive. The majority of Black children live in single-parent households. Black women and men are usually grandparents at an earlier age than Anglos and they obligate themselves to greater involvement in helping raise grandchildren. Relationships between grandparents and sons or daughters who are single parents can improve when education provides practical and creative alternatives for the extended family to share its load and recognize everyone's needs.

Educators should make a concerted effort to recruit elderly grandmothers and grandfathers and emphasize their potential for continued influence. Older Black grandparents (age 60 and older) are seen more favorably than younger grandparents (under age 60) in terms of self-impression and in the estimate of grandchildren. This broader base of support can benefit grandchildren and their parents as well as bolster the self-esteem of grandparents.

Indigenous volunteers in the Black community should be identified and urged to lead a grandparent course. They can offer the *Becoming A Better Grandparent* and *Achieving Grandparent Potential* courses at schools, churches, and senior centers on a continuing basis. The choice to make a substantial contribution to the life of grandchildren already has been made by many Black grandmothers and grandfathers. They are more likely to reach this goal when indigenous leaders offer them easy access to an appropriate curriculum.

CONCLUSION

This comparative study of grandparent performance reinforces the need to consider ethnic differences in planning educational programs for families. Black grandparents have notable strengths in teaching effectiveness and breadth of instruction, willingness to spend time with grandchildren, acceptance of family obligations regardless of distance from loved ones, offering continuity of support even during old age, and making an effort to guide grandchildren as they become adolescents. In combination, these strengths make Black grandparents a powerful influence in the lives of grandchildren.

We have determined that grandparent effectiveness can be improved by more conversations on topics that are of concern to grandchildren, getting to know them as individuals and adjusting expectations accordingly, helping with goal setting and problem solving, sharing constructive ways to cope with unfair treatment by others, recognizing the value of imagination and creative thinking, understanding the schooling process, recognizing ways to get help with academic problems, and identifying opportunities for further education of grandchildren.

REFERENCES

1. Children's Defense Fund, *The State of Children, 1991,* M. Edelman, Washington, D.C., 1991.
2. S. Bianchi, *The New World of Children,* Population Reference Bureau, Washington, D.C., 1990.
3. D. Besharov, *Recognizing Child Abuse: A Guide for the Concerned,* Macmillan, New York, 1990.
4. S. Hewlett, *When the Bough Breaks: The Cost of Neglecting our Children,* Basic Books, New York, 1991.
5. K. Zinsmeister, Growing Up Scared, *The Atlantic,* pp. 49-66, June 1990.
6. R. Louv, *Childhood's Future,* Houghton Mifflin, Boston, Massachusetts, 1990.
7. E. Boyer, A close look at college, in *America's Best Colleges,* B. Baver (ed.), U.S. News & World Report, Washington, D.C., pp. 40-43, 1990.
8. J. Meisenheimer, Black College Graduates in the Labor Market, 1979-1989, *Monthly Labor Review,* U.S. Department of Labor, Bureau of Labor Statistics, *113:*11, 1990.
9. J. Dizard and H. Gadlin, *The Minimal Family,* University of Massachusetts Press, Amherst, Massachusetts, 1990.

10. E. McKinney and Z. Harel, *Black Aged,* Sage Publications, Beverly Hills, California, 1989.
11. C. Lincoln and L. Mamiya, *The Black Church in the African American Experience,* Duke University Press, Durham, North Carolina, 1990.
12. R. Hill, The Black Family: Building on Strengths, in *On the Road to Economic Freedom: An Agenda for Black Progress,* R. Woodson (ed.), Regnery Books, Washington, D.C., pp. 82-86, 1987.
13. J. Jackson, *Life in Black America,* Sage Publications, Newbury Park, California, 1991.
14. M. Jackson and J. Wood, *Aging in America: Implications for the Black Aged,* National Council on Aging, Washington, D.C., 1976.
15. Bureau of the Census, *1990 Census of Population and Housing,* Bureau of the Census, Data User Service Division, Washington, D.C., February 1991.
16. F. Furstenberg and A. Cherlin, *Divided Families,* Harvard University Press, Cambridge, Massachusetts, 1991.
17. J. Stacey, *Brave New Families: Domestic Upheaval,* Harper Collins, New York, 1990.
18. R. Strom and S. Strom, Preparing Grandparents for a New Role, *Journal of Applied Gerontology, 6*:4, pp. 476-486, 1987.
19. R. Strom and S. Strom, *Grandparent Development,* American Association of Retired Persons Andrus Foundation, Washington, D.C., 1989.
20. R. Strom and S. Strom, *Grandparent Strength and Needs Inventory,* Scholastic Testing Service, Chicago, Illinois, 1993.
21. R. Strom, S. Strom, and P. Collinsworth, Improving Grandparent Success, *Journal of Applied Gerontology, 9*:4, pp. 480-491, 1990.
22. R. Strom and S. Strom, *Becoming A Better Grandparent: A Guidebook for Strengthening the Family,* Sage Publications, Newbury Park, California, 1991.
23. R. Strom and S. Strom, *Becoming A Better Grandparent: Viewpoints on Strengthening the Family,* Sage Publications, Newbury Park, California, 1991.
24. R. Strom and S. Strom, *Achieving Grandparent Potential: A Guidebook for Building Intergenerational Relationships,* Sage Publications, Newbury Park, California, 1992.
25. R. Strom and S. Strom, *Achieving Grandparent Potential: Viewpoints on Building Intergenerational Relationships,* Sage Publications, Newbury Park, California, 1992.
26. R. Strom and S. Strom, *Grandparent Education: A Guide for Leaders,* Sage Publications, Newbury Park, California, 1991.
27. A. Cherlin and F. Furstenberg, *The New American Grandparent,* Basic Books, New York, 1986.
28. C. Wharton, *A Ten-year Plan for the 21st Century,* Endowment for Community Leadership, Arlington, Virginia, 1989.
29. W. Raspberry, Bring Back the Family, *The Washington Post,* p. A19, July 18, 1989.
30. R. Strom, P. Collinsworth, S. Strom, and D. Griswold, Perceptions of Parent Success by Black Mothers and their Preadolescent Children, *The Journal of Negro Education, 59*:4, pp. 611-622, 1990.

Chapter 16

THE SIGNIFICANCE OF STEPGRANDPARENTS

Debra W. Trygstad
and
Gregory F. Sanders

The major purpose of this research was to examine the relationship that young adult stepgrandchildren have with their stepgrandparents. Current information on stepfamilies focuses almost exclusively on the stepparent-stepchild relationship and disregards the relationship between stepgrandchildren and stepgrandparents.

Approximately 60 percent of remarriages involve an adult with physical custody of one or more children [1]. Glick estimated that 6.5 million children under the age of eighteen were living with a stepparent in 1978, and predicted that by 1990, this number would increase to over 7 million and represent about 11 percent of all children [2]. Remarriage of parent(s) involves the addition of one or more new stepparents to the child's life and can mean as many as four stepgrandparents.

Several researchers have suggested that the stepgrandparent can be a support to the reconstituted family [3-5]. Furstenberg noted that ties existing through the remarriage chain create a support system for the child, even when kinship is not directly elicited [5]. The value of a grandparent type relationship has even been demonstrated outside the family system through a foster grandparent program, in which unrelated emotionally deprived children were paired with surrogate grandparents [6].

Although most of the previous work on stepgrandparents involved very exploratory methods or simply suggestions as to what the stepgrandparent-stepgrandchild relationship would be like, a review of that literature, along with grandparenting research, set the stage for the current study. As in the grandparent relationship, stepgrandparents are usually not consulted about becoming a stepgrandparent. In addition, there may be active pressure on stepgrandparents to treat the new children like grandchildren [3, 7]. Several writers suggest that stepgrandparents often view the relationship with their new stepgrandchildren in almost the same way that stepparents view their new stepchildren [7, 8]. "Most of the difficulties encountered by stepparents are also encountered by stepgrandparents, although usually at a diminished level" [p. 8; 132]. The stepgrandparent may be unclear about how to relate to the new stepgrandchildren, what title to use, how to treat the stepgrandchild, inheritance matters, and so forth.

In Cherlin and Furstenberg's longitudinal study on grandparenting, it was found that one-third of all grandparents in this group were also stepgrandparents [7]. In interviews of twelve of these stepgrandparents, two factors emerged as important. Regarding the first factor, age of the child at the time he or she became a member of the stepgrandparent's extended family, the older the children were at the time of remarriage, the less likely it was for the stepgrandparent role to be regarded as important as the biological grandparent role. The second important factor was whether or not the stepgrandchild lived full time with the grandparent's adult child. A remarriage in which stepchildren do not reside with the reconstituted family may have more clear cut boundaries between the stepgrandparent and the stepgrandchild. The tension may be reduced for these grandparents because they are able to visit their grandchildren without having to deal with their stepgrandchildren at the same time [18].

Visher and Visher [3] and Chilman [4] hypothesized that when stepgrandchildren reside with the reconstituted family, the way grandparents accept the remarriage has an effect on how they accept their new stepgrandchildren. They observed that some stepgrandparents could not accept their stepgrandchildren because they did not approve of their child's divorce or their new son-in-law or daughter-in-law.

Furstenberg and Spanier interviewed twenty-five newly remarried persons and asked them about the relationship between their children and their new partner's parents (children's stepgrandparents) [9]. They reported that three out of ten stepchildren saw their stepgrandparents at least once per week. Their children's experience in meeting the new partner's family was described as comfortable and pleasant.

Although there can be difficulty in this new family system, stepgrandparents can become an additional support for the reconstituted family [3-5]. Furstenberg believed that the social structure generated by extensive remarriage has the consequence of increasing the kinship ties and creating a large support network [5].

The purpose of the present investigation was to determine the significance of the stepgrandparent-stepgrandchild relationship from the perspective of the young adult stepgrandchild. By exploring the quantity and quality of interaction, evaluating the amount and importance of contact in the relationship, examining the factors involved in the remarriage, and further delineating the influences of age, social class, marital status, side of family, custody status, health, geographic proximity, and parental mediation between the stepgrandchild and the stepgrandparent, it was expected that a clearer understanding of the relationship between the stepgrandparent and the stepgrandchild could be developed.

METHODS

Procedures

The information for this study was collected at a Midwestern university from fifty-four young adult college students who were stepgrandchildren. Several large university courses were surveyed including: Child Development Family Science, Home Economics, Psychology, Textiles and Clothing, and Speech. The stepfamily situation the students were involved in had to be a result of their parent's remarriage. The spouse of a grandparent who remarries is also considered a stepgrandparent but, in the current study, stepgrandchildren from this type of situation were not used.

The participants were asked to select one stepgrandparent they saw most often. Both written and oral instructions were given. Some students completed the questionnaire in class, others took the questionnaire home and returned it the following class period. A total of eighty-five questionnaires were handed out, and sixty-five were returned, a return rate of 76 percent. Eleven of these questionnaires were not usable because some had been inadequately completed, and others were filled out by respondents who were stepgrandchildren because their grandparent remarried.

Instrumentation

Requested demographic characteristics of the young adult students consisted of: their age, gender, and race; the occupational prestige of their biological parents and stepparents; the geographic proximity to the stepgrandparent; the age respondents became stepgrandchildren; how they became stepgrandchildren (through death or divorce); if the stepgrandparent they evaluated was from the maternal side or the paternal side; and whether the stepgrandparent was connected through the custodial or noncustodial parent. Additional demographic characteristics collected about the stepgrandparents included age, gender, race, occupational prestige, marital status, and health status. Occupational prestige was evaluated by the National Data Program for the Social Sciences job prestige score listing [10]. The higher the score (18 to 78) on this listing, the higher the job prestige of an occupation. Job prestige was defined by the amount of respect earned by one's occupation.

Amount of Contact

The amount of contact was measured on a seven-point scale developed originally in reference to grandparents [11]. This scale was used to examine the amount of contact (*just about every day* to *almost never*) the respondents had with their stepgrandparents in person, by letter, and by telephone, for three time periods: currently, during high school, and during grade school. The *not applicable* category was added for purposes of this study because some of the respondents may not have had a stepgrandparent during high school or grade school.

Evaluation of Contact

The satisfaction with the amount of contact was assessed on a five-point scale from "much less than you could wish" to "much more than you could wish" [11].

Importance of the Relationship

The stepgrandchild's perception of the importance of the relationship with the stepgrandparent was measured using a five-point rating scale ("extremely important" to "extremely unimportant") [11].

Role Conception

Hartshorne and Manaster [11] adapted a scale for grandchildren's role conception from a scale developed by Robertson which measured grandparent's role meaning [12]. The purpose of this scale was to measure role conception along two dimensions—"social" (I feel I should do what is proper around my stepgrandparent so that he/she will not think less of me), and "personal" (There is so much I can learn from my stepgrandparent as an individual). Ten questions with responses ranging from strongly agree to strongly disagree were used, five measured social role, and five measured personal role. Coefficient alphas for this scale were: social scale = .68, personal scale = .83, and total scale = .86 [11].

Behaviors Expected

Perceptions of appropriate and/or expected stepgrandparent behavior was measured using a scale developed by Robertson [13]. This scale requires a *yes* or *no* response to questions about excessive and instrumental behaviors (step)grandchildren expect of (step)grandparents, for example, "Is your stepgrandparent somebody who gives you gifts of money?"

Relationship Strengths

An abbreviated form of the Family Strengths Scale was constructed to evaluate families in terms of their perceived behavioral characteristics [14]. The original thirty Likert-type items were previously condensed to fifteen Likert-type items through the use of a factor analysis. The response category ranged from "Very Frequently" to "Never." Items included positive behaviors "Is a good listener" or negative behaviors "Tries to control my behavior." Negative behaviors were reverse coded. For the original thirty-item scale, a Spearman-Brown split-half coefficient reliability of .86 was obtained.

Relationship with Stepparents

The respondents were asked to rate the satisfaction with the remarriage of their parents from "very satisfied" to "very dissatisfied" and the importance of the relationship to the stepparent from "extremely important" to "extremely unimportant."

Respondents

The respondents were fifty-four young adult college students (19 to 35, mean = 21) who were members of a stepfamily. Seven percent of both the sample and stepgrandparent targets were female. The stepgrandparents the students chose ranged in age from fifty-seven to ninety-eight, with a mean age of seventy-two. A total of 68 percent of the stepgrandparents were currently married, and 58 percent were in good or excellent health.

The majority (75%) of stepgrandchildren were involved in a reconstituted family as a result of the parents divorce. Sixty percent became stepgrandchildren after age ten, and more than half (64%) of the stepgrandparents chosen were parents of the stepfather and were connected through the custodial stepparent (66%).

Design and Data Analysis

As in Hartshorne and Manaster's grandparent research, measures of central tendency were used to describe the amount of contact between the stepgrandchild and the stepgrandparent, how satisfied the respondents were with that contact, how important the relationship was to them, perceptions of the relationship as personal role and social role, the behaviors expected, and the family strenghts of the relationship between the stepgrandchild and the stepgrandparent using the individual items as well as the total family strengths score [11].

A simple zero order Pearson-Product-Moment correlational design was used to determine the relation between several relationship variables and demographics.

A *t*-test analysis was used to determine the relation between the relationship variables and the gender of the student and the stepgrandparent; how the stepgrandchild acquired the stepgrandparent (divorce or a death of the biological parent); side of the family the stepgrandparent is from (stepmother or stepfather); and the stepgrandparent's connection to the family (through the custodial or noncustodial parent). Analysis of variance was used to test the relation between relationship variables and the marital status of the stepgrandparent. Pearson correlations were also utilized to test the relations between the various measures of stepgrandparent/stepgrandchild interaction.

RESULTS

Contact

Because of the way the scoring was done, a low score indicated greater contact. Differences in number of responses were due to the fact that some of the respondents did not have a stepgrandparent at that time period. There was more contact *in person* at all time periods than by *letter* or by *telephone*. As seen in Table 1, the most frequent personal contact between the stepgrandchild and the stepgrandparent occurred during high school (mean = 3.37). The majority of respondents reported that they saw their stepgrandparent several times per year during this time. The second most frequent contact occurred in person, at the present time. Most respondents had contact between several times per year and once per year (mean = 3.57; mode = 3.0). Forty-two percent did not have a stepgrandparent during grade school and 7 percent did not have a stepgrandparent during high school.

Currently, 2 percent of the steggrandchildren had personal contact with the stepgrandparent daily, 6 percent had weekly contact, and 9 percent monthly. In addition, 32 percent saw the stepgrandparent several times per year, 32 percent once per year, 6 percent less than once per year, and 13 percent almost never saw the stepgrandparent.

Table 1. Stepgrandchildren's Contact with Stepgrandparents Currently, during High School, and during Grade School

Type	Time	Response	Mean	SD	Median	Mode
In Person	NOW	53	3.56	1.39	4.0	3
By Letter	NOW	54	5.17	1.28	6.0	6
By Telephone	NOW	54	4.87	1.68	6.0	6
In Person	HS	54	3.37	1.81	3.0	3
By Letter	HS	54	5.40	1.25	6.0	6
By Telephone	HS	54	4.68	17.6	6.0	6
In Person	GS	54	4.74	2.29	5.0	7
By Letter	GS	54	5.75	.216	6.0	7
By Telephone	GS	54	5.64	1.67	6.0	7

0 = Daily; 1 = Once/Week; 2 = Once/Month; 3 = Several/Year; 4 = Once/Year; 5 = Less Than Once/Year; 6 = Almost Never; 7 = Not Applicable.

Using Pearson correlational analyses, it was found that the occupational prestige of the father was significantly related to the amount of contact ($r = .386$; $p < .01$). The higher the occupational prestige score of the father, the less contact was reported between the stepgrandparent and the stepgrandchild. Health status of the stepgrandparent was also related to the frequency of contact ($r = .264$; $p < .05$). The lower the student rated the health of the stepgrandparent, the less contact was reported. There were no other significant correlations.

In the t-test analyses, only one significant relation was discovered. It was found that students who selected the stepgrandparent from the stepmother's side, saw their stepgrandparent less often than those who selected from the stepfather's side ($t = 2.42$; $p < .05$). No significant differences were found in frequency of contact for those of different marital status.

Satisfaction with Amount of Contact

A total of 63 percent of the stepgrandchildren perceived the amount of contact at the *present time* to be much less or somewhat less than they would have wished. Thirty-one percent said that the amount of contact was about right; 6 percent perceived the amount of contact as somewhat more or much more than they would have wished.

The occupational prestige of the stepfather ($r = .310$; $p < .05$) and stepgrandparent ($r = .371$; $p < .01$) was related to satisfaction with contact. The higher the occupational prestige the less satisfied the students were with the amount of contact with their stepgrandparent. No other variables were related.

Importance of the Relationship

The respondent's relationship to the selected stepgrandparent was rated as follows: extremely important (6%); important (42%); neither important nor unimportant (35%); unimportant (15%); and extremely unimportant (4%).

The age of the student was related to the importance of the relationship ($r = .232$; $p < .05$).The older the respondents were the less important the relationship was to them. Also, the respondents who acquired the stepgrandparent at a later age rated the relationship as less important ($r = .276$, $p < .05$). Satisfaction with the parent's remarriage was also related to the importance of contact ($r = .335$; $p < .01$). The more dissatisfied the respondents were with the remarriage of their parent, the lower they rated the importance of the relationship with the stepgrandparent. Importance of the relationship to the stepparent was significantly related to importance of the relationship to the stepgrandparent ($r = .377$; $p < .05$). Respondents who classified the relationship with their stepparent as important, also rated the relationship with their stepgrandparents as important. The frequency of contact was significantly related to the importance of the relationship ($r = .412$; $p < .001$). Students who had more current contact with their stepgrandparent rated the relationship as more important. In addition, the more satisfied the respondents were with the amount of contact at the present time, the more important was the relationship with their stepgrandparent ($r = .478, p = .01$).

A significant difference was found in the acquisition of the stepgrandparent and the importance of the relationship ($t = 2.01$; $p < .05$). Respondents who acquired their stepgrandparent following the divorce of their parent saw the relationship with the stepgrandparent as being less important than the respondents who acquired their stepgrandparent following a parent's death.

Personal and Social Roles

The items shown in Table 2 are listed according to whether they represent a *social* or *personal* role. Item scores for each of these roles were summarized. On the Social Role scale the respondents strongly agreed or agreed with the following items: 55 percent of the respondents said that the stepgrandparent should be involved in family activities; 57 percent thought that it was important to spend part of their holiday visiting the stepgrandparent; 89 percent believed that the stepgrandparent deserved respect; 33 percent felt an obligation toward the stepgrandparent; and 76 percent believed that they should do what is proper so the stepgrandparent would not think less of them.

The responses to the items of the Personal Role scale were as follows: 35 percent of the respondents thought that the stepgrandparent had brought an important sense of perspective to their life; 87 percent said that they would be sad if their

Table 2. The Perception of Stepgrandchildren Regarding the Personal and Social Roles of their Stepgrandparent

Items	SA (%)	A (%)	U (%)	D (%)	SD (%)
Social Roles					
Family activities	14.8	40.7	20.4	18.5	5.6
Spend holidays	13.0	44.4	14.8	22.2	5.6
Give respect	40.7	48.1	5.6	0.0	5.6
Special obligations	11.1	22.2	40.7	20.4	5.6
Proper behavior	22.2	53.7	7.4	14.8	1.9
Personal Roles					
Sense of perspective	13.0	22.2	25.9	25.9	13.0
Sad when dead	37.0	42.6	11.1	5.6	3.7
Personal relationship	14.8	35.2	33.3	11.1	5.6
Emotional attachment	11.1	35.2	31.5	14.8	7.4
Learn from	24.1	42.6	16.7	13.0	3.7

SA = Strongly Agree, A = Agree, U = Undecided, D = Disagree, SD = Strongly Disagree stepgrandparent died; 50 percent related that having a personal relationship with their stepgrandparent was very important; 46 percent found the emotional attachment with their stepgrandparent as pleasurable; and 67 percent believed that they could learn a lot from their stepgrandparent.

The item scores representing social role were summed, as were scores on personal role items. The scores on the social scale ranged from zero to twenty, the mean was 7.14. These scores indicate that more than half the respondents either strongly agreed or agreed with the items on the Social Role scale. Findings for the personal role scale were similar (Mean = 7.6).

The child's age on becoming a stepchild was positively related ($r = .258$; $p < .05$) to the social role, but not the personal role. The older the students were when they became stepchildren the higher they rated the relationship with the stepgrandparent as a social role. Significant relations were also obtained comparing the satisfaction with the remarriage of the parents and both the social and personal roles ($r = .241$; $p < .05$ and $r = .241$; $p < .05$ respectively). Only personal role was related to the importance of the relationship to the stepparent ($r = .282$; $p < .05$). As importance of the relationship to the stepparent decreased, the perceived personal role of the stepgrandparent decreased. There was a relation between both social role ($r = .500$; $p < .01$) and personal role ($r = .410$; $p < .01$) and satisfaction with the amount of contact. The respondents who wanted less contact with their stepgrandparent disagreed with the items on the social and personal roles. Additionally, as the scores on the social and personal role scale decreased, the importance of the relationship decreased. (SR $r = .755$; $p < .01$ and PR $r = .809$; $p < .001$).

Expected Behaviors

These stepgrandchildren had few expectations of their stepgrandparents. Fifty-nine percent expected that a stepgrandparent is someone who gives them gifts of money. The behaviors most stepgrandchildren did not expect of their stepgrandparents included: takes the respondent places (74%), can go to for advice (85%), informs of family heritage (52%), can rely on for emotional comfort (72%), acts as liaison between respondent and parents (76%), can turn to for personal advice (56%), gives respondent financial support (81%), aids in rearing the respondent's children (81%), or one whose occupation they can imitate (75%). A total score was tabulated from the "no" responses for this scale. The range was from one to ten, with a mean of 6.85.

The results of the Pearson correlation analyses showed that students who had older stepgrandparents expected fewer behaviors ($r = .278$; $p < .001$). Also, the older the student was the fewer behaviors were expected of the stepgrandparent ($r = .215$; $p < .05$). Fewer behaviors were expected when health status was poorer ($r = -.347$; $p < .01$). A significant correlation was found between the frequency of contact with the stepgrandparent and the expected behaviors. As the number of expected behaviors decreased the contact decreased ($r = .429$; $p < .001$). There was also a significant relation between the behaviors expected and importance of the relationship ($r = .634$; $p < .001$). As the number of expected behaviors decreased, the importance of the relationship decreased. In addition, the fewer behaviors expected, the lower the role of expectations were for both the social and personal roles (SR $r = .622$; $p < .001$; PR $r = .623$; $p < .001$).

Relationship Strengths

The overall relationship strengths score ranged from one to fifty, with a potential range from one to sixty. The mean score was 28. This strength score mean represents a relatively neutral relationship; i.e., neither high nor low strengths. The majority of respondents stated that the stepgrandparent seldom or never did the following: try to control their behavior (91%), bring up past problems (87%), using sarcasm when talking to the stepgrandchild (91%), which demonstrates a lack of negative behavior (see Table 3).

Table 3. Strengths in the Stepgrandchild/Stepgrandparents Relationship

Items	N (%)	S (%)	O (%)	F (%)	VF (%)
Shows affection	8.5	23.4	29.8	25.5	12.8
Stands behind	23.4	17.0	34.0	14.9	10.6
Controls behavior	66.0	25.5	6.4	2.1	
Brings up past	70.2	17.0	4.3	8.5	
Respect disagreements	23.9	8.7	19.6	39.1	8.7
Uses sarcasm	80.9	10.6	4.3	2.1	2.1
Feel comfortable	4.3	6.5	17.4	36.1	32.6
Expresses appreciation	8.3	12.8	28.8	29.8	19.1
Feel needed	14.9	17.0	27.7	27.7	12.8
Feel important	8.5	12.8	28.8	29.8	19.1
Good listener	17.0	17.0	23.4	25.5	17.0
Available to talk	23.4	21.3	19.1	23.4	12.8
Interested in activities	19.1	23.4	12.8	27.7	17.0
Treats like an adult	8.5	4.3	17.0	38.3	31.9
Trusts decisions	6.4	8.5	25.5	40.4	19.1

N = Never, S = Seldom, O = Occasionally, F = Frequently, VF = Very Frequently

The respondents rated the following responses frequently or very frequently; shows affection toward me (38%), stands behind me when times are tough (26%), is respectful of my right to disagree (48%), feel comfortable with stepgrandparent (72%), expresses appreciation toward me (49%), makes me feel needed (40%), helps me feel important (49%), is a good listener (42%), is interested in my activities (45%), treats me like an adult (70%), and trusts my decisions (60%).

Several variables were related to the strengths score. The students who lived farther from their stepgrandparents scored lower on the relationship strengths scale ($r = .298$; $p < .05$). A significant relation was also found between the strengths and the age of the student at the time he/she obtained a stepgrandparent ($r = -.294$; $p < .05$). The respondents who obtained their stepgrandparent at a later age scored lower on the relationship score. Also, the stepgrandchildren who were more dissatisfied with the remarriage of their parents scored lower on family strengths ($r = -.304$; $p < .05$). The importance of the relationship with the stepparent was related to strengths ($r = -.444$; $p < .01$). As importance of the relationship to the stepparent decreased, relationship strengths with the stepgrandparent decreased.

A significant correlation ($r = -.377$; $p < .05$) was found between the amount of contact and strengths score. This negative correlation indicates that as amount of contact decreased the strengths score also decreased. In addition, the higher the strengths score, the more the respondents desired an increase in the amount of contact ($r = -.454$; $p < .001$). Importance of the relationship was correlated with relationship strengths ($r = -.822$; $p < .001$). The stepgrandchildren who rated the relationship with their stepgrandparent as more important scored higher on strengths. Relationship strengths was related to social role ($r = -.831$; $p < .001$) and personal role ($r = -.753$; $p < .001$). The greater the agreement with social role and personal role behaviors the stronger the relationship. Another comparison was made between behaviors expected and strengths. A significant correlation was found ($r = -.701$; $p = .001$) indicating that the fewer behaviors expected, the lower the family strengths.

DISCUSSION

The results of this study should be considered within the methodological limitations. This sample was a convenience sample of young adult, mostly white college students from the upper midwest. Generalizability to even young adult stepgrandchildren is questionable, and stepgrandchildren in different age groups may vary considerably from young adults in their relationship with the stepgrandparent. In addition, the validity and reliability of the scales used should be assessed more thoroughly with the stepgrandchildren sample.

The current research does provide a descriptive base for further study in this area and allows for clarification of some previous speculations about the stepgrandchild-stepgrandparent relationship. Perhaps the most relevant overall finding of the study is that the stepgrandchild-stepgrandparent relationship is active even in young adulthood. The stepgrandchildren reported that they see their stepgrandparents between several times per year and once per year on the average and would like more contact. Although not a majority, many saw the relationship as important or extremely important. These findings indicate that the relationship goes beyond a formal tie and involves actual interaction and meaning to the family system.

Stepgrandchildren perceive this relationship as both moderately social and personal. It might be concluded that the results regarding the personal and social roles indicated neither a strong personal nor a strong social relationship. However, it appears that most of the stepgrandchildren in this study viewed their stepgrandparent not only as someone whom they cared for as an individual, but also as someone whom they respected. Regarding behavior, stepgrandchildren expected very little from their stepgrandparents, apart from gift-giving. These results confirmed a previous hypothesis by Cherlin and Furstenberg that the exchange of services between the stepgrandparent and the stepgrandchild would be modest [7].

The strength of the stepgrandchild-stepgrandparent relationship was most often rated as neutral. The stepgrandchildren in this study did not view their stepgrandparents as infringing upon their lifestyle, nor did they establish a strong relationship bond with them. The respondents' indication that the stepgrandparents were not controlling supports Cherlin and Furstenberg's speculation that few stepgrandparents would have a high degree of parent-like authority over their stepgrandchildren.

Individual and Family Variables

Research on grandparenting and suggestions about stepgrandparenting indicated some variables which may influence the stepgrandchild's relationship with the stepgrandparent. Of the variables used in this study, gender of the respondent or stepgrandparent and marital status of the stepgrandparent were not related to any of the relationship measures.

Three factors of age were examined in this investigation: a) respondent's current age; b) age of the stepgrandparent; and c) age of the respondent on becoming a stepchild. Older stepgrandchildren saw the relationship as less important perhaps because they had been more involved in other interests away from their extended stepfamily. Current age of the stepgrandchild was also related to the social role but not the personal role. Older stepgrandchildren may desire more social interactions and chose their relationship with their stepgrandparent as a social outlet.

The stepgrandchildren in this study expected fewer behaviors from older stepgrandparents. These findings might be explained in an examination of health status of the stepgrandparents. The stepgrandchildren who rated the health of the stepgrandparent lower also expected fewer behaviors from them. In this study, health and age were significantly related ($r = .288; p < .05$).

Over half of the young adults in this sample became stepchildren after the age of ten. Cherlin and Furstenberg suggested that the older the child is on becoming a stepgrandchild, the less important the relationship will be. The present study confirmed this. Furthermore, relationship strengths were lower for the stepgrandchildren who acquired their stepgrandparent at a later age. McGoldrick and Carter found that older children (adolescents) experience the most difficulty in stepfamilies [15]. These difficulties probably also influence the relationship with the extended stepfamily. The addition of a stepgrandparent for the older child may be not only affected by such dynamics, but also plagued by both a lack of a history in the relationship and a life stage at which the child is more involved with peers.

The higher occupational prestige of the *father,* the less contact there was between the respondent and the stepgrandparent. In addition, higher occupational prestige of the *stepfather* was related to higher satisfaction with the amount of contact but not actual amount of contact. Potentially, higher occupational prestige of the stepfather could infer more job mobility for the stepfamily, creating distance from the stepgrandparent. However, no significant relation was found between distance and the amount of contact. Finally, the respondents wanted more contact with stepgrandparents who had a higher occupational prestige. College students may have more in common with stepgrandparents from a higher occupational status.

Relationship strengths between the stepgrandchild and the stepgrandparent were related to distance. Particularly in relationships with a short history, distance could dictate a more formal tie with less opportunity or expectation for a strong relationship.

The stepgrandparents from the remarriage following the divorce of a parent were evaluated lower on importance of the relationship than stepgrandparents from the remarriage following the death of the biological parent. Stepchildren may find it easier to accept the remarriage of their parent if the relationship was brought on by the death of the biological parent rather than through the divorce of the parent; consequently, they may be more accepting of their stepparent's kin. Some children of divorce refuse to give up their image of the ideal first family and accept a new model [16]. Stepgrandchildren who were more dissatisfied with the remarriage of their parents rated the relationship with their stepgrandparents as less important. Some family therapists have observed in case studies that the stepgrandparents who did not approve of the remarriage of their adult child could not accept their stepgrandchildren [3, 4]. The same situation appears true for stepgrandchildren.

In addition, respondents who rated the importance of the relationship with the stepparent as lower also rated the perceived personal role, relationship strengths, and the importance of the stepgrandparent lower. When the stepchildren did not get along with the stepparents they apparently did not want to establish a relationship with the stepgrandparent. This mediation process was consistent with research by Robertson who found that the grandchildren's relationship with grandparents was influenced by the adult child's relationship with their parent [13]. It appears that mediation within families may have a profound effect on the relationship between stepgrandparents and stepgrandchildren even into young adulthood. The rewards for acceptance of stepgrandparents after the child has left home may be considerably less. Therefore, if a relationship has not already developed by young adulthood, it may never evolve.

In this study, it was found that respondents had more contact with stepgrandparents from the stepfather's side than from the stepmother's side. However, whether the relationship was on the custodial or the noncustodial side was not significantly related to any of the variables. Contrary to previous suggestions, the stepgrandparents connection to the family made little difference in the relationship between stepgrandparent and stepgrandchild [7, 8].

Other factors

Each of the family variables were correlated to one another in order to determine if there was any relation between these variables. Present amount of contact was related to importance of the relationship to the stepgrandparent, the social and personal role, the expected behaviors, and relationship strengths. As the contact between the stepgrandchild and the stepgrandparent increased, importance of the relationship increased. Greater interaction between stepgrandparents and stepgrandchildren may help build a bond and a friendship between the two. More contact may help the stepgrandparent and the stepgrandchild get to know one another better which would explain the increase in social and personal roles and the increase in relationship strengths.

Implications of the Study

The stepgrandparent relationship does seem to have a place in the lives of many young adult stepgrandchildren. Information on this relationship would be helpful to individuals who plan on entering into a reconstituted family. New stepfamilies might begin to understand the importance of establishing relationships with stepgrandparents, especially when the children are young. The relationship with their stepgrandparent has potential for becoming an additional resource to their family. The present research should be used to educate families about the potential role stepgrandparents can play in their child's life. Children who have stepgrandparents may have an extra set of relatives they can turn to for support. Based on the results of this study, certain issues regarding stepgrandchild stepgrandparent relations may need to be dealt with in counseling or educational settings. These include role clarity, relationship quality, behavioral expectations, and contact. Because the relationship appears to be mediated by the parent/stepparent, these individuals need to be included in any effort to deal with the stepgrandparent role. In other words, a systems approach should be used to explore the relationship of the stepgrandparent to the stepgrandchild.

The Need for Further Research

This study was meant as groundwork for further research on the stepgrandparent-stepgrandchild relationship. More in-depth research is needed to support these findings and to substantiate the conclusions made here. Research which examines the relationship from the stepgrandparent's perspective would seem beneficial. Further research might also include the view of the stepparent and the parent. In addition, a younger sample of children may be closer to the situation than the young adults in this sample. Information from stepgrandchildren who had stepgrandparents as a result of their *grandparents* remarriage was not included in this study. It would be interesting to study possible differences in these types of stepgrandparents. Finally, more research is needed to address the issue of the mediation process between the stepgrandparent, the stepparent, and the stepgrandchild.

REFERENCES

1. U. S. Department of Commerce, Bureau of the Census, *Statistical Abstract of the U.S. 1986* (106th Edition), United States Government Printing Office,Washington, D.C., p. 79, 1985.
2. P. Glick, Remarriage: Some Recent Changes and Variation, *Journal of Family Issues, 4*, pp. 455-478, 1979.
3. E. B. Visher and J. S. Visher, *Stepfamilies: A Guide to Working With Stepparents and Stepchildren,* Brunner/Mazel Inc., New York, 1979.
4. C. S. Chilman, Remarriage and Stepfamilies: Research and Implications, in *Contemporary Families and Alternative Life Styles,* E. D. Macklin and R. H. Rubin (eds.), Sage, Beverly Hills, pp. 147-164, 1981.
5. F. F. Furstenberg, Remarriage and Intergenerational Relations, in *Aging: Stability and Change in the Family,* J. March (ed.), Academic Press, Inc., New York, 1981.
6. R. Saltz, Evaluation of a Foster Grandparent Program, in *Child Welfare Services: A Sourcebook,* A. Kalushin (ed.), Macmillan, Inc., New York, 1970.
7. A. J. Cherlin and F. F. Furstenberg, *The New American Grandparent: A Place in the Family a Life Apart,* Basic Books, Inc., New York, 1986.
8. R. Kalish and E. Visher, Grandparents of Divorce and Remarriage, *Journal of Divorce, 5*, pp. 127-140, 1981.
9. F. F. Furstenberg and G. B. Spanier, *Recycling the Family: Remarriage after Divorce,* Sage, Inc., Beverly Hills, 1984.
10. National Data Program for the Social Sciences Codebook for the Spring 1976, *General Social Survey, July, 1976 National Opinion Research Center,* University of Chicago, Chicago, 1976.

11. T. S. Hartshorne and G. J. Manaster, The Relationship with Grandparents: Contact, Importance, Role Conception, *International Journal of Aging and Human Development, 15,* pp. 233-245, 1982.
12. J. F. Robertson, Grandmotherhood: A Study of Role Conceptions, *Journal of Marriage and the Family, 39,* pp. 165-174, 1977.
13. J. F. Robertson, The Significance of Grandparents, *Gerontologist, 16,* pp. 137-140, 1976.
14. G. F. Sanders and J. Walters, Life Satisfaction and Family Strengths of Older Couples, *Lifestyles: A Journal of Changing Patterns, 4,* pp. 194-206, 1985.
15. M. McGoldrick and E. A. Carter, Forming a Remarried Family, in *The Family Life Cycle: A Framework for Family Therapy,* M. Carter and E. A. McGoldrick (eds.), Gardner Press, New York, 1980.
16. V. Wood and J. Robertson, The Significance of Grandparenthood, in *Roles and Self in Old Age,* J. Gubrium (ed.), Human Sciences Press, Inc., New York, 1975.

Contributors

PAT COLLINSWORTH received her Ph.D. at Arizona State University. She is Research Associate in the Office of Parent Development International at Arizona State University. Her experience as a counseling psychologist has included leadership of support groups serving culturally diverse populations of parents and grandparents. She has developed strategies for use with intergenerational therapy and methods for assessing programs of intervention.

MICHAEL A. GODKIN is Associate Professor of Family and Community Medicine at the University of Massachusetts Medical School, where he trains students in communication skills, Community Medicine, care of the medically underserved, and clinical research. His research focuses on maladaptive families and he has published extensively on elder abuse and maladaptive parenting behavior.

DOLORES PUSHKAR GOLD studied Clinical and Experimental Psychology at the University of Manitoba, obtaining her Masters degree in 1961, and Social Psychology at the University of Saskatchewan, obtaining her Doctorate in 1966. She is a Professor in the Psychology Department at Concordia University. Dr. Gold was one of the five founding members of the Centre for Research in Human Development at Concordia University and has been the Director of the Centre for Research in Human Development since 1991. She is presently directing a longitudinal study examining the personality, intellectual and social variables that predict maintenance and change in active and competent functioning in elderly people and in elderly couples.

ALAIN GRAND, M.D., has a Ph.D. in Sociology and is Professor of Public Health and Director of the Laboratory: "Aging, Community Health and Socialization" in Toulouse, France.

ARLETTE GRAND-FILAIRE is a Health Sociologist in the Regional Comity for Health Education of Toulouse, Midi-Pyrénées, France.

DIANNE GRISWOLD received her Ph.D. from Arizona State University and is Professor of Education at Auburn University in Montgomery, Alabama. She trains teachers, parents and grandparents to work together in support of child development. Her multicultural research involves assessment of parent behavior and evaluation of intervention programs serving young children. She is an author of numerous articles regarding curriculum and instruction.

PHILIP A. HALL teaches at the Worden School of Social Service, Our Lady of the Lake University, San Antonio, Texas. His practice and research interests center on community-based program development and evaluation. He received the Ph.D. from the University of Chicago, MSW at Washington University, and BA from Cornell University.

JON HENDRICKS, PH.D., is Professor and Chair, Department of Sociology, Oregon State University. He is President, Association for Gerontology in Higher Education and has previously served as an officer of The Gerontological Society of America and The American Sociological Association. Hendricks is Associate Editor for the *International Journal of Aging and Human Development*, Series Editor for *Perspectives on Aging and Human Development Series*, and Consulting Editor for Gerontology, Baywood Publishing Company, Inc., NY. Hendricks is a member of Worldwide Umbrella Exchange and is widely published in the field of social gerontology.

LYNNE GERSHENSON HODGSON is Professor of Sociology and Chair of the Department of Sociology and Gerontology at Quinnipiac College in Hamden, Connecticut. She received her Ph.D. in Sociology from Cornell University in 1980. Her research interests include grandparent/adult grandchild relationships and family issues surrounding Alzheimer's disease. Currently she is working with Stephen J. Cutler on an Alzheimer's Association funded study on "Anticipatory Dementia."

PAT M. KEITH is Professor of Sociology at Iowa State University. Current research interests include gender roles in later life and guardianship of older people. Recent work includes *Older Wards and their Guardians* (with Robbyn Wacker).

DR. SARAH T. KERR, a graduate of the University of Michigan, received her Ph.D. from the United States International University in San Diego. She completed her internship at Metropolitan State Hospital in Norwalk. Subsequently she was a staff psychologist for the Senior Health Assessment program and received an appointment as Assistant Clinical Professor in Pulmonary and Critical Care Medical Division at the University of California, Irvine. Dr. Kerr currently resides in Newport Beach with her husband, where she maintains a private practice in individual and group psychotherapy, clinical hypnosis and marriage, family counseling.

Dr. Kerr is known for expertise concerning personal interrelations, stress reduction and communication skills. She teaches older adults for Coastline Community College and presents on-going talks for community organizations, "Personal Enhancement Programs" for women, and programs for mothers and daughters, "Differing Personality Styles." Her lectures for the Women's Opportunity Center at U.C.I. "Change, Challenge and Opportunity" emphasize the unparalleled technological and demographic changes of the twentieth century bringing heretofore unknown opportunities for individuals of all ages. Dr. Kerr's dissertation and studies on long-lasting marriages as do her commentaries, "Word to the Whys," point toward many of these new opportunities for long productive lives.

Although a founding member of the Board of Directors for establishing Adult Day Care Centers in the Newport Beach area, being among the first to recognize the need for adult day-care centers for the frail and ailing elderly, she understands and promotes the recognition and needs of the healthy aging adult. Dr. Kerr is a member of the Board of Directors for the Emeritus Institute for Coastline Community College, helping establish life-long learning curriculum for Older Adults.

NIELI LANGER, DSW, is Director of the Incarnate Word Social Gerontology Program and Aging Institute which offers both a Masters and certificate program in Gerontology. Her expertise is in ethnogerontological social work and curriculum development. She is a co-author of the book *Elder Practices: A Multidisciplinary Approach to Serving the Elderly in the Community* (University of South Carolina Press, 1995).

JEANNETTE C. LAUER is Dean of the School of Arts and Sciences, U.S. International University, San Diego. She received her Ph.D. in Social History from Washington University, St. Louis. She is author or co-author of numerous journal articles and eight books, including *'Til Death Do Us Part: How Couples Stay Together* (Harrington Park, 1986) and *Marriage and Family: The Quest for Intimacy,* 2nd Edition (Brown & Benchmark, 1994).

ROBERT H. LAUER is Adjunct Professor of Human Behavior, U.S. International University, San Diego. He received his Ph.D. in Sociology from Washington University, St. Louis. He is author or co-author of numerous journal articles and sixteen books, including *Social Problems,* 6th Edition (Brown & Benchmark, 1995), *'Til Death Do Us Part: How Couples Stay Together* (Harrington Park, 1986), and *Marriage and Family: The Quest for Intimacy,* 2nd Edition (Brown & Benchmark, 1994).

JULIE PELLMAN received her Ph.D. from the University of Missouri— Kansas City in 1988. Since graduation, she has held a Lecturer appointment at the Columbia University School of Public Health, Division of Geriatrics and Gerontology. She also served as an Evaluation Consultant for the New York City Board of Education, Office of Research, Evaluation, and Assessment. In addition, she has been a consultant for the Hunter Brookdale Center on Aging, Catholic Charities Diocese at Brooklyn, and the Senior Citizens League of Flatbush. She has been an Adjunct Professor at the New School for Social Research and at New York University. Dr. Pellman is a member of the American Psychological Association, APA divisions 20 and 27, American Public Health Association, American Public Health Association of New York City, Gerontological Society of America, Eastern Psychological Association, Midwestern Psychological Association, and the Brooklyn Coalition for the Homeless.

CANDIDA C. PETERSON is Associate Professor of Psychology at the University of Queensland, Australia, with research interests in life-span developmental psychology and family relationships. She has a B.A. degree from University of Adelaide and a Ph.D. from University of California, Santa Barbara, and has previously taught at Northern Illinois University and Murdoch University, Western Australia. She is the author of over sixty journal articles and six books on topics in life-span developmental psychology.

KARL A. PILLEMER, Ph.D., is Associate Professor of Human Development and Family Studies at Cornell University. He is also Co-Director of The Cornell Applied Gerontology Research Institute, one of six Edward Roybal Centers funded by the National Institute on Aging. His major research interests lie in the family relationships of the elderly. His research projects include a longitudinal study of the social relationships of family caregivers to persons with Alzheimer's disease. He currently is conducting a federally-funded evaluation study of social support interventions for family caregivers to dementia patients. Pillemer has also worked extensively in the areas of conflict and abuse in the family relations of elderly people. He has published over two dozen articles on this topic, and with Rosalie S. Wolf he is co-author of *Helping Elderly Victims: The Reality of Elder Abuse*, and co-editor of *Elder Abuse: Conflict in the Family*. His interests also include developing interventions to improve the quality of nursing home care, and aging and long-term care policy.

JACQUES POUS, M.D., is Professor of Public Health and Director of the Department of Public Health, University of Toulouse, France.

CÉCILE QUIROUETTE obtained her Master's degree in Clinical Psychology in 1989 and is completing her Ph.D. at Concordia University in Montreal, Canada. Her doctoral research is on middle-aged women's expectations and preparations for old age. She is presently working with a psychogeriatric team as a clinical psychologist and her current interests include the assessment of cognitive impairment in older adults, as well as psychosocial interventions with older couples.

KAREN A. ROBERTO, PH.D., is Professor and Coordinator of the Gerontology Program at the University of Northern Colorado. Her research focuses on family and friend relationships in later life and the influence of chronic illness on the psychosocial functioning and quality of life of older women. Among her recent publications are two edited books: *The Elderly Caregiver: Caring of Adults with Developmental Disabilities* (1993) and *Older Women with Chronic Pain* (in press). She is a fellow of the Gerontological Society of America and has served on the Executive Committee of the Association for Gerontology in Higher Education.

CHRISTOPHER H. ROSIK received his Ph.D. in clinical psychology from the Fuller Graduate School of Psychology. He is currently employed as a psychologist at the Link Care Center in Fresno, California. Dr. Rosik's areas of specialization include bereavement and grief, dissociation, and religious issues in psychotherapy.

GREGORY F. SANDERS, PH.D., is an Associate Professor of Child Development and Family Science at North Dakota State University. His specialty areas include later life families and family strengths. He has published research on life after 100, attitudes toward the elderly, caregiving, the quality of family relationships in later life families, and intergenerational equity. He is the past chair of the Child Development and Family Science Department and is the Coordinator of the Gerontology Minor Program at North Dakota State University.

ROBERT B. SCHAFER is a Professor in the Department of Sociology at Iowa State University, Ames, Iowa. He received his Ph.D. from The Pennsylvania State University. He has conducted research and published in the areas of the family and social psychology. Current research includes a study of family food behavior supported by the Center for Designing Foods to Improve Nutrition, Iowa State University.

JOHANNA STROES, M.A., current works as a Recreation Coordinator of Older Adult Programs for the City of Fort Collins in Colorado. She completed her under-graduate degree in Human Development and Aging at the University of California at Davis. Johanna received her masters degree while working as a graduate assistant to Karen A. Robert, Ph.D. in the Gerontology Program at the University of Northern Colorado in Greeley.

ROBERT D. STROM received his Ph.D. from the University of Michigan. He is Professor of Lifespan Developmental Psychology and Director of the Office of Parent Development International at Arizona State University. He has served as a Danforth Scholar, Commonwealth Scholar, and Research Fellow of the Japan Society for the Promotion of Science. His studies involve assessment of educational needs and curriculum development for children and adults.

SHIRLEY STROM is a graduate of Western Michigan University. She is a Research Coordinator for the Office of Parent Development International, an experimental and applied studies center at Arizona State University. Her projects to improve parent and grandparent influence have been supported by the Danforth and Rockefeller Foundations. She is the author of several books and articles on building better intergenerational relationships.

JEANNE L. THOMAS, PH.D., is Professor of Psychology and Chair of the Psychology Department at the University of Wisconsin–Parkside. Her research interests include parent-child relationships in later life, grandparenthood, and issues of sexual orientation in old age. Articles reporting her work have appeared in the *Journal of Gerontology: Social Sciences,* the *International Journal of Aging and Human Development,* the *Journal of Applied Gerontology,* and *Research on Aging.* She is the author of *Adulthood and Aging.*

DEBRA W. TRYGSTAD, M.S., is an independent Intergenerational Consultant and a Community Education Coordinator for older adults at Moorhead Community Education. She received her M.S. degree in Child Development and Family Science at North Dakota State University and published research on grandparenting and stepgrandparenting. She currently works in adult education and has a special interest in validation therapy.

ROBBYN R. WACKER is Associate Professor in the Gerontology Program at the University of Northern Colorado. She has been involved in a number of projects on the social and legal concerns of older persons. Most recent work includes a nationwide study of services provided to older adults by municipal recreation departments and senior centers. A current project is "Improving Quality of Care for Nursing Home Residents: An Innovative Community Program to Enhance Certified Nurses Aide Training" sponsored by the Retirement Research Foundation.

ROSALIE S. WOLF is Executive Director of the Institute on Aging at The Medical Center of Central Massachusetts and an Assistant Professor in the Departments of Medicine and Family and Community Medicine at the University of Massachusetts Medical Center. She is a co-editor of *Elder Abuse: Conflict in the Family* and co-author of *Helping Elderly Victims: The Reality of Elder Abuse.* Her activities in the field of elder abuse include organizing the National Committee for the Prevention of Elder Abuse and serving as its president and co-editing its publication, the *Journal of Elder Abuse & Neglect.*